IRELAND IN OLD PHOTOGRAPHS

COUNTY WICKLOW

DEREK STANLEY

The History Press Ireland

First published 2016

The History Press Ireland
50 City Quay
Dublin 2
Ireland
www.thehistorypress.ie

The History Press Ireland is a member of Publishing Ireland,
the Irish book publishers' association.

British Library Cataloguing in Publication Data.
A catalogue record for this book is available from the British Library.

ISBN 978 1 84588 905 0

Typesetting and origination by The History Press
Printed and bound by TJ International

CONTENTS

ACKNOWLEDGEMENTS

I am grateful to my friends and family who have helped me by providing photographs, inspiration and information for this book. In particular, I should like to thank Mike Cremin, Fergal MacAlister, the late Pat O'Brien, Seamus O'Connor, Peter O'Hara, Julie Power, John Ryan and my wife Theresa who, as always, has provided me with so much support and encouragement.

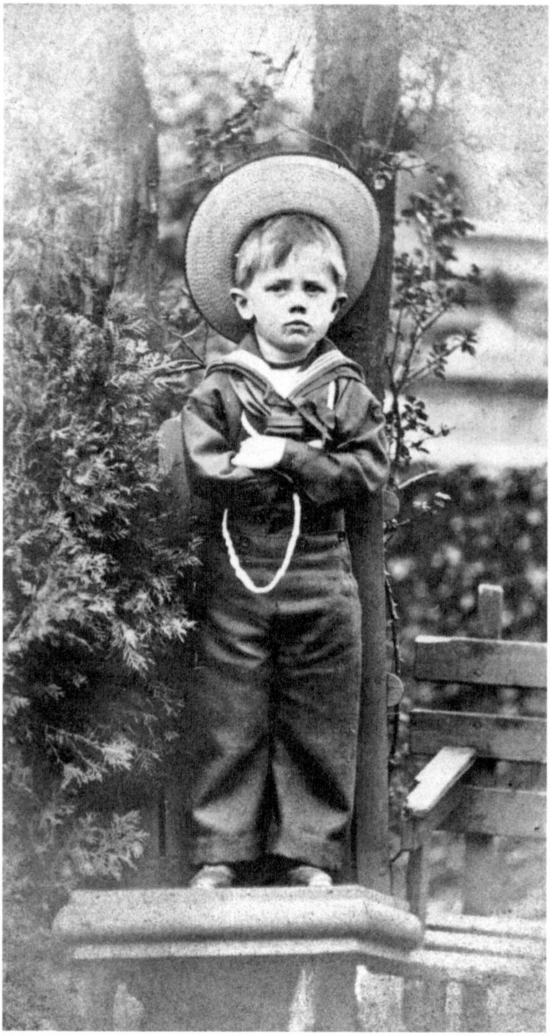

An early photograph of a young Ralph Howard, seventh Earl of Wicklow (1877-1946), in a fancy sailor suit, which features a wide striped collar, a satin kerchief and a rope lanyard. The look on the boy's face and his attitude with arms folded suggests he would rather be somewhere else! He was educated at Eton and Sandhurst and pursued a career in the army, becoming a major in the special reserve of South Irish Horse. He was elected to the Irish Senate in June 1921 and served for six years until he was defeated in the Seanad election in 1928. He died in 1946 and his only son succeeded him as the eighth Earl of Wicklow.

INTRODUCTION

County Wicklow, with its golden beaches, wooded valleys, majestic mountains and stunning lakes, rivers and waterfalls, is truly an area of great natural beauty. It is easy to see why the county is known as the 'Garden of Ireland'. It is difficult to give a full appreciation of the area in a book of this size. However, the images have been chosen to give a flavour of Wicklow and some of its history.

Wicklow has a wealth of archeological sites and monuments. Its heritage includes many ancient standing stones and prehistoric mounds from the Neolithic Stone Age of over 3,500 years BC. There are historic hillforts and ringforts throughout the county. Visitors from all over the world come to experience the beauty of the Christian monastic settlement at Glendalough, founded by St Kevin in the sixth century.

The county has a rich and varied history and in particular an independent people, who were always willing to fight heroically to protect their territory and country against invaders. There is much in their history to make them proud. This book only touches upon some of the activities of the clansmen, rebels and patriots, but perhaps some of the images and narrative will inspire readers to do further research.

It is fortunate that so many photographs and postcards from the early 1900s are still available today. Although some areas have remained much the same, there are other views in this book that show streets or buildings now completely altered or, in some cases, demolished. The images should give some fresh insights into local history and heritage and also evoke memories of times past.

My previous books on Dublin in the 'Images of Ireland' series have been well received; I have been contacted by readers in Ireland, France, America and Australia commenting on how they have enjoyed the images and relating their memories of past events and places. I do hope that this book will bring similar pleasure to all who turn its pages, as County Wicklow is certainly a unique and special place.

Wicklow is a county with natural physical barriers and many books divide the county into regional areas. In the past, when travel and communication was difficult, coastal and inland areas were separated. However, today, there are good road links and excellent communications. This book describes some of the towns and villages around the county using old photographs and postcards from my own collection. The narrative starts on the west of County Wicklow with images of Baltinglass and then heads south to Tinahely before going towards the east coast through Aughrim and Avoca to Arklow. After this the road takes us via Rathdrum and Glendalough to Wicklow town. From there the book includes views of Rathnew and Delgany, before showing some images of Greystones and Bray on the east coast. Finally there are views of Enniskerry and a return to the western side of the county including Blessington, Glenalmure and the Glen of Imaal.

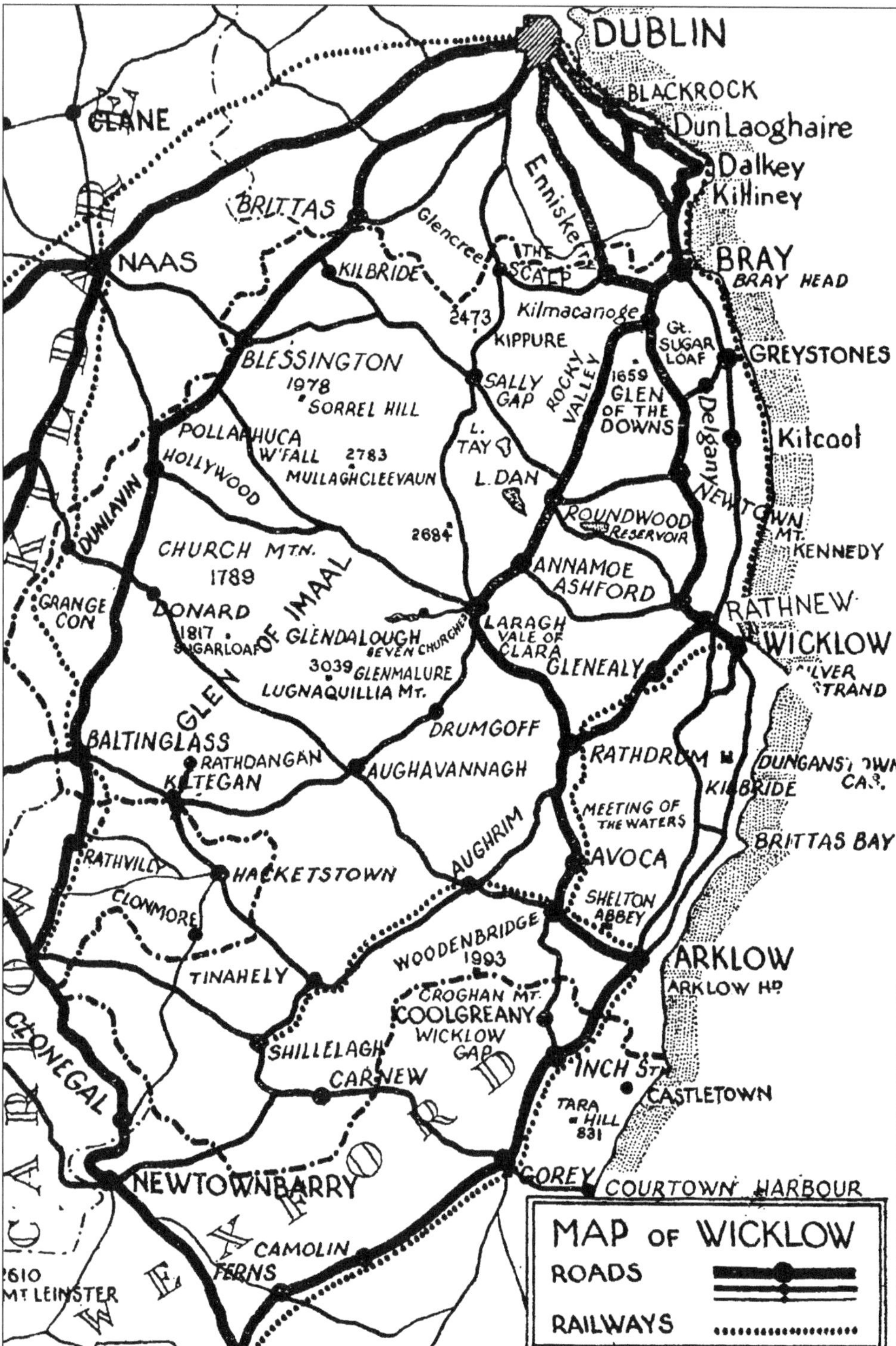

Map of Wicklow taken from an early guide published by the Irish Tourist Association, *c.* 1920.

1

BALTINGLASS, SHILLELAGH, COOLATIN, TINAHELY & AUGHRIM

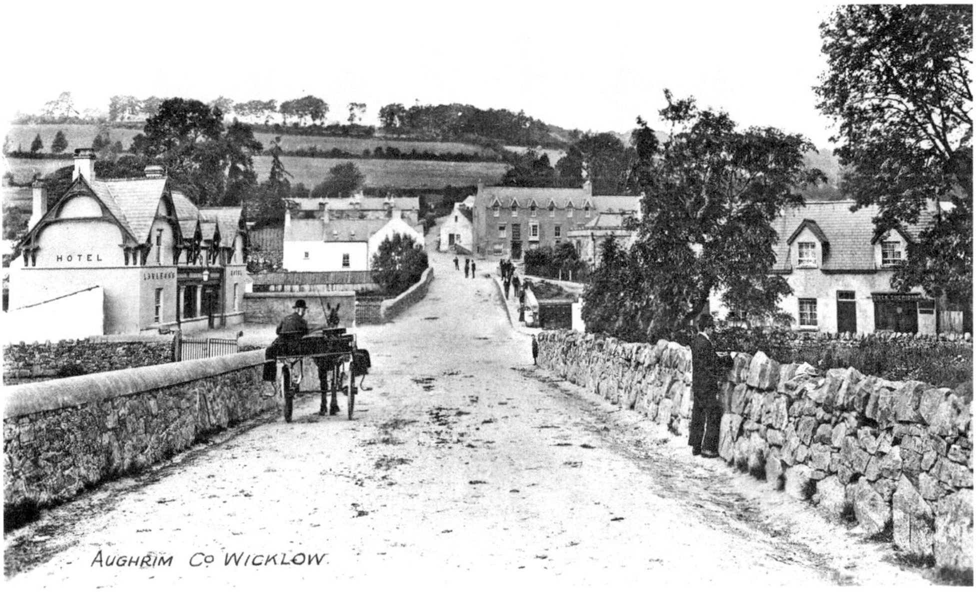

View of Aughrim from the bridge on a postcard dated 7 July 1939. Lawless's Hotel, established in 1787, is shown on the left. Aughrim is known as the 'granite village' due to the many local buildings constructed using this stone. The granite was quarried in the Tinakilly area and was of very good quality due to its low porosity. It was used extensively in the local area and in many Dublin churches. The granite was also exported to England. However, by 1952, quarrying in the Tinakilly area was discontinued as exports had slowly declined and the quarry was no longer commercially viable.

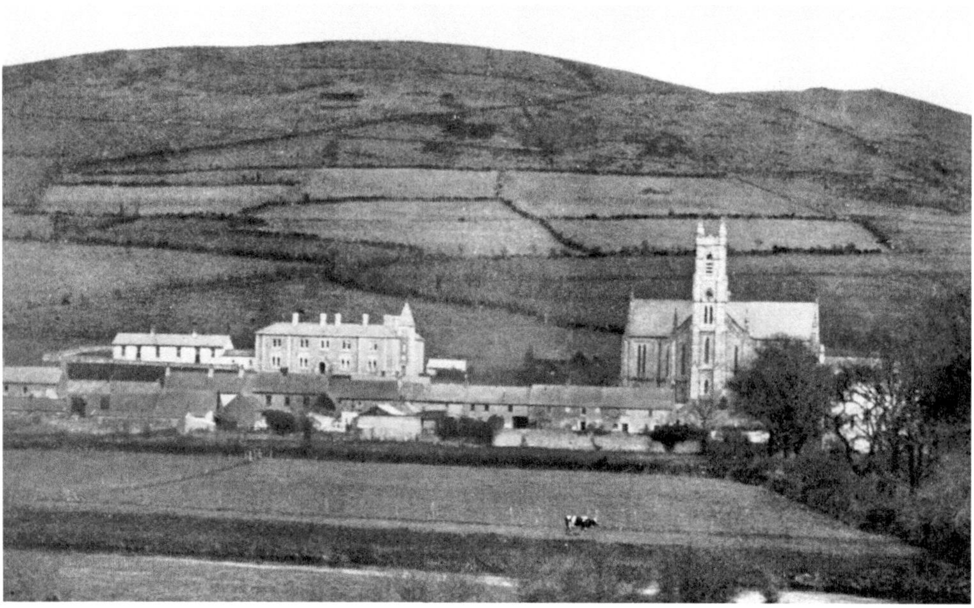

Baltinglass Hill, which rises steeply above the town, depicted on a postcard dated 10 October 1907. At the top of Baltinglass Hill lies a Stone Age passage grave. The outer walls of the grave are made of chalk, which makes the tomb visible from many miles away. Baltinglass Abbey and St Mary's church are on the banks of the River Slaney. The abbey was founded in the twelfth century by Dermot McMurrough (King of Leinster), who is said to be buried in the abbey. The Cistercians ran the abbey until the sixteenth century. It is now in a state of ruin.

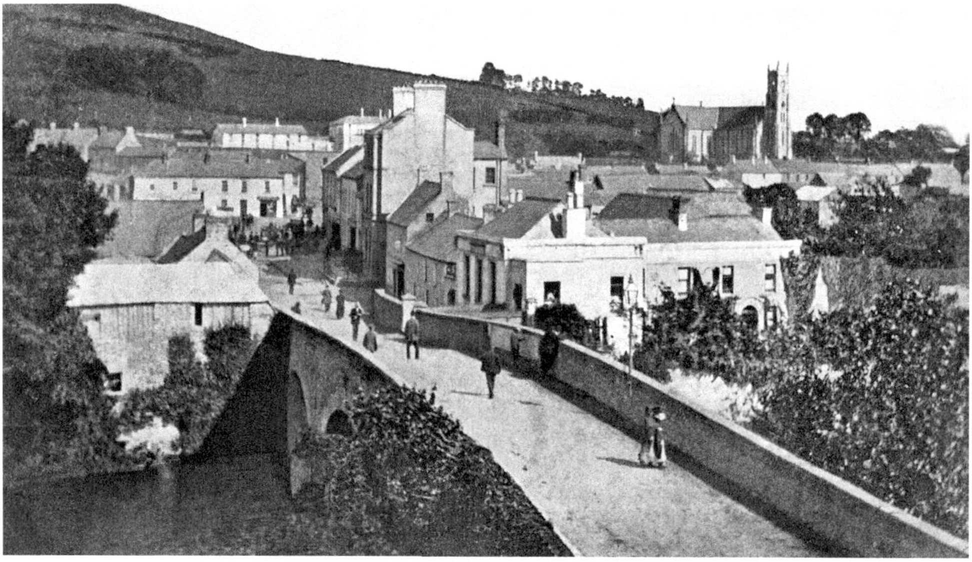

The bridge over the River Slaney at Baltinglass, on a postcard dated 22 October 1909. The road is busy with pedestrians and the abbey church, with its impressive Romanesque architecture, can be seen at a distance on the right. Both postcards on this page were published by McCann of Mill Street, Baltinglass.

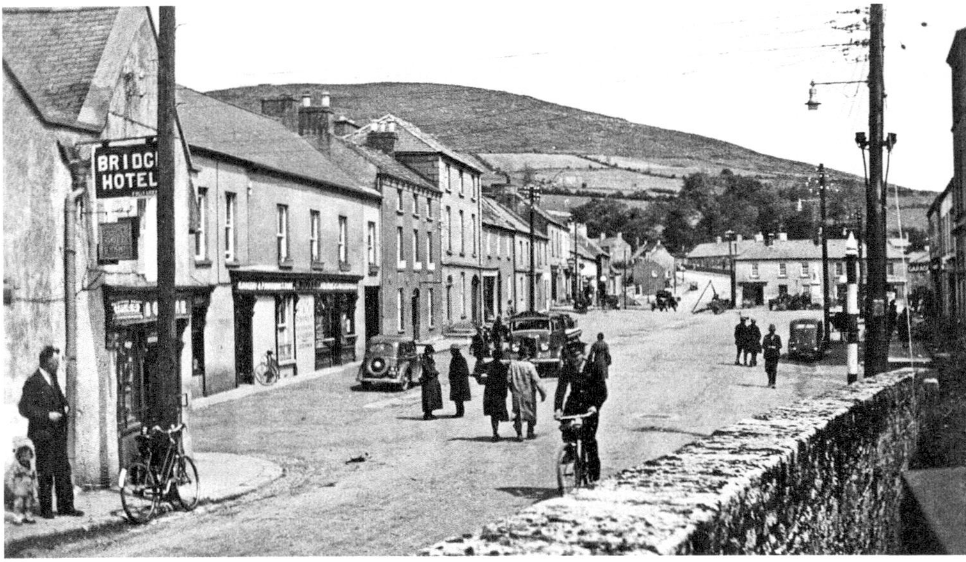

The main street, Baltinglass, *c.* 1950. The Bridge Hotel is on the left. This is a heritage town with a fascinating history and has held markets and fairs since 1617. Baltinglass had a courthouse, a bridewell, an infirmary and an infantry barracks. Men from the town took part in the 1798 rebellion under the leadership of Michael Dwyer. After the siege of Derrynamuck in 1799, a group of eight men, including John Ashe and Watt McDonald from Baltinglass, were captured and taken to the main square in Baltinglass, where they were all hanged.

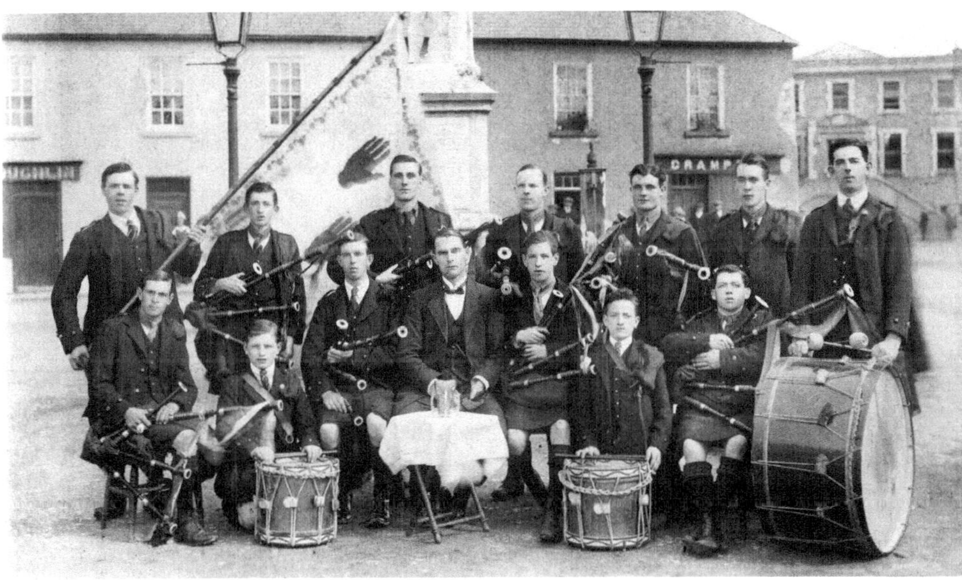

The O'Byrne Pipers Band from Baltinglass in the Market Square in 1918. They were the winners of the Championship Cup of Wicklow and Wexford of that year. They are photographed in front of a statue of a United Irishman, which was erected in 1904 to commemorate the heroism of Michael Dwyer, his comrade Sam McAlister (see page 126) and all those who took part in insurrections in 1798, 1803, 1848 and 1867.

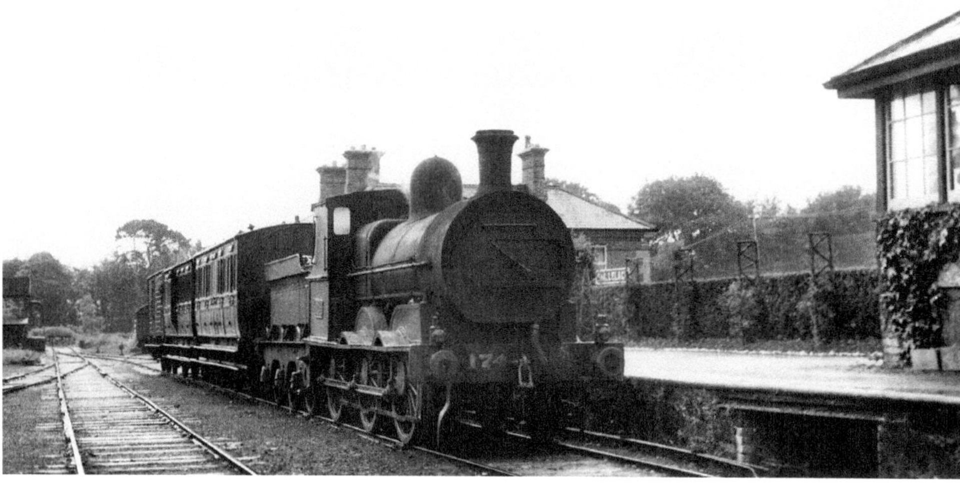

A train steams into Shillelagh Railway Station. The station opened on 22 May 1865, as the terminal of a branch line from Woodenbridge. The railway carried more visitors and brought increased trade and prosperity to the village. However, due to declining numbers of passengers and coal shortages during the Emergency (Second World War), the station closed for passenger and goods traffic on 24 April 1944.

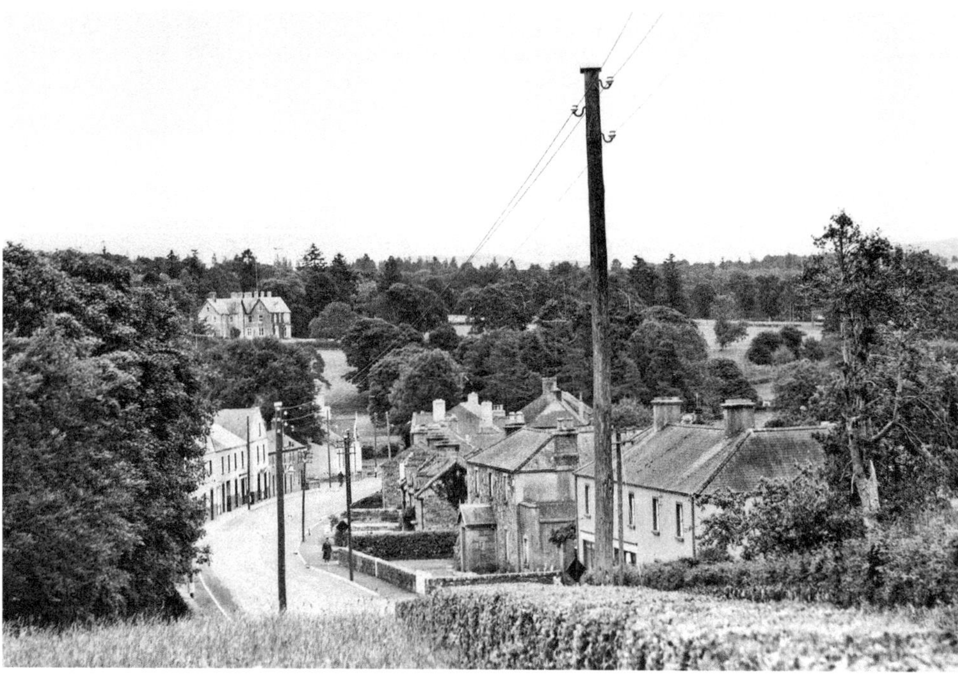

Main Street, Shillelagh. The village is situated on the banks of the Shillelagh River below the southern foothills of the Wicklow Mountains. The area is well known for its extensive oak woods and the Shillelagh forests have supplied timber for buildings and ship construction to England and Europe for many years.

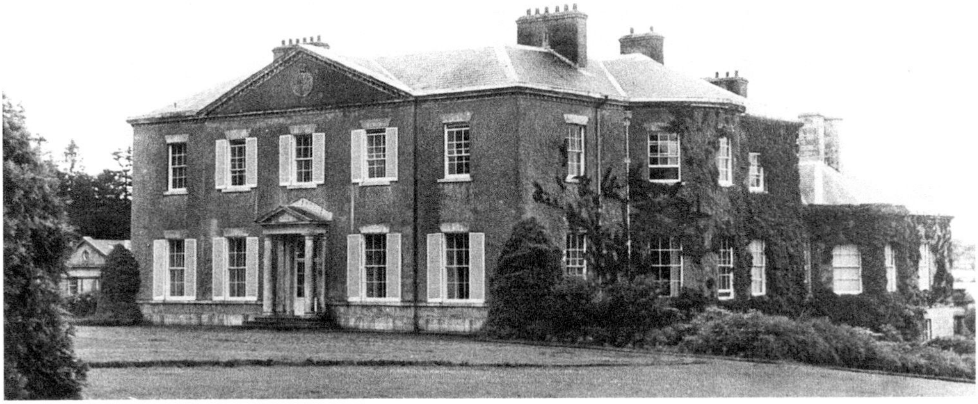

Coolattin House, Shillelagh, designed by John Carr of York and built around 1800 for the fourth Earl Fitzwilliam. It replaced a house that was burnt down in the 1798 Rebellion along with some Catholic churches and 160 houses in the nearby village of Carnew. The earl became Lord Lieutenant of Ireland in 1795, but on account of his support for Catholic Emancipation and his sacking of many Protestant Dublin officials, he was forced to resign the post after three months. He was a popular landlord and the Fitzwilliam Estate, which covered 36,000 hectares, was developed and cultivated using the latest agricultural methods of the time.

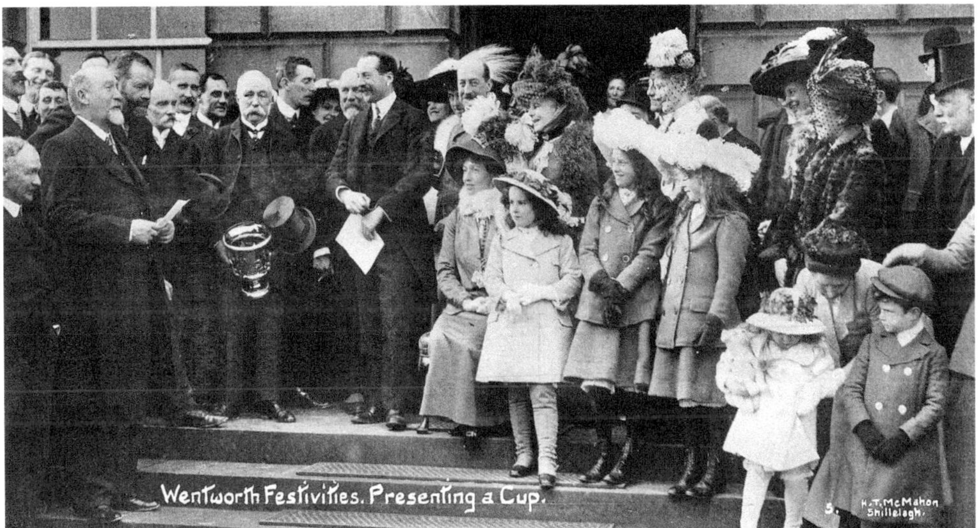

The Wentworth Festivities at Shillelagh showing the presentation of a Silver Cup on behalf of the Fitzwilliam tenants to celebrate the christening of Peter Wentworth Fitzwilliam, the fifth child and only son of the seventh Earl Fitzwilliam. Peter became the eighth Earl Fitzwilliam, but together with Kathleen Kennedy, sister of J.F. Kennedy, with whom he was said to be having an affair, he was tragically killed in a plane crash in France in 1948. Lady Fitzwilliam is shown seated with her children on her left. Earl Fitzwilliam, waiting to receive the cup, stands beside her on the right. The card, posted on 9 March 1911, was published by H.T. McMahon of Shillelagh.

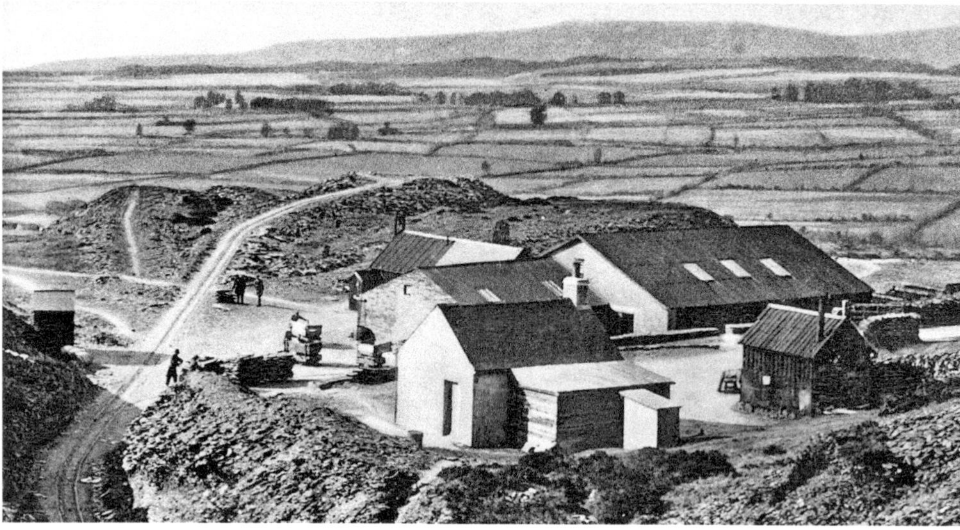

Kilcavan Slate Quarries, near Carnew, produced a dark grey slate, which had low water absorption and was resistant to frost. The slate was mainly used for roofing in Ireland and also exported to Europe. The quarry also had a by-product called 'Inner Tight', a fine grey powdered rock, which was ideal as a base for battleship paint. The quarries were worked between 1800 and 1940 and were a major source of employment in this area, particularly in the years of famine. The quarry closed finally in 1941.

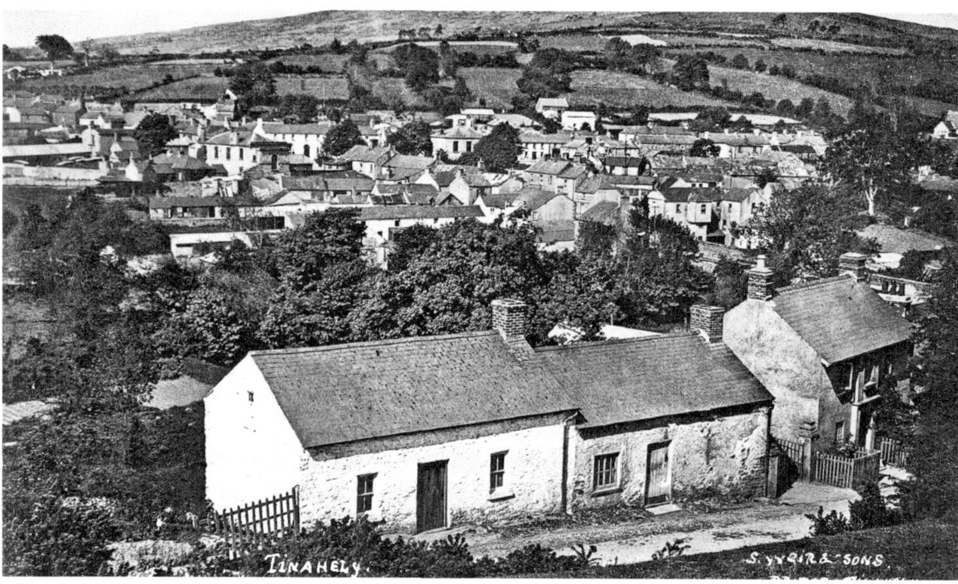

View of Tinahely on a card published by S. Weir & Sons in the 1950s. The town is on the banks of the River Derry, which is a tributary of the River Slaney. It was destroyed in the 1798 Rebellion, but was later rebuilt in the early 1800s by the fourth Earl Fitzwilliam, who lived in Coolattin House. Important district horse fairs were held there four times a year. The town is known for its triangular market square, which has the imposing Market House facing the courthouse, which is now an arts centre.

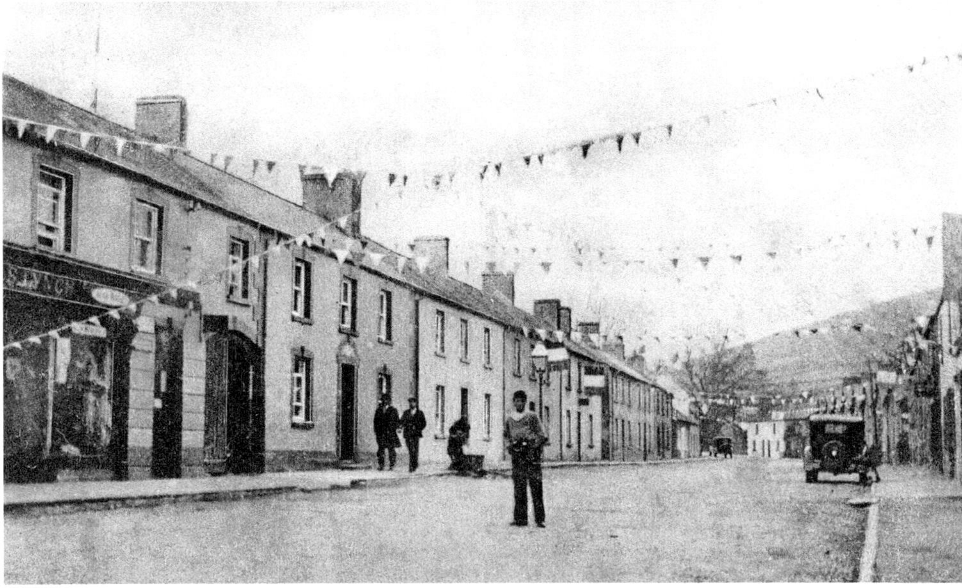

The Eucharistic Congress decorations in Kevin Street, Tinahely. The thirty-first Eucharistic Congress was held in Dublin in 1932 from 22-26 June and was celebrated in towns and villages throughout Ireland. The postcard was published locally by M. Lynch, draper, Tinahely, whose shop is shown on the left side of the street.

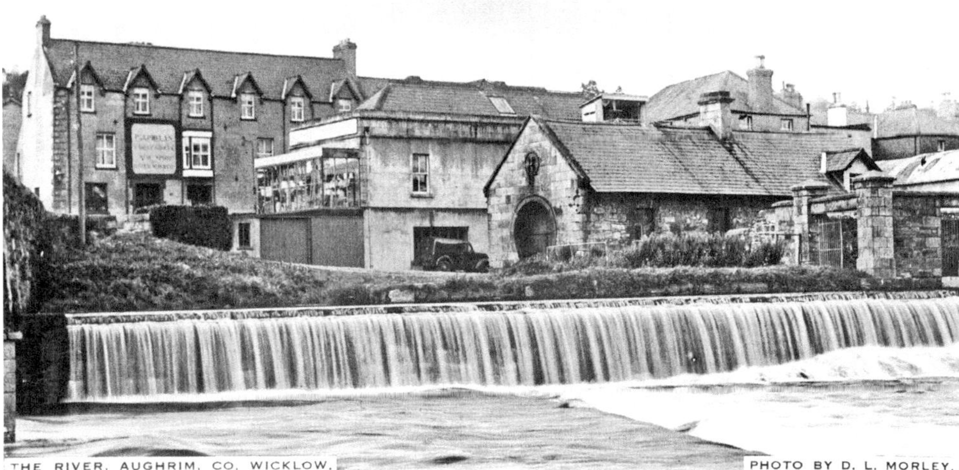

The cascading weir on the River Aughrim pictured on a postcard dated 9 June 1962. The river is known for its excellent fly-fishing. Trout and salmon can be found in the fast-flowing oxygenated water below the weir. The old forge built from local granite in 1873 for Lord Meath, has a horseshoe shaped entrance and is seen on the right.

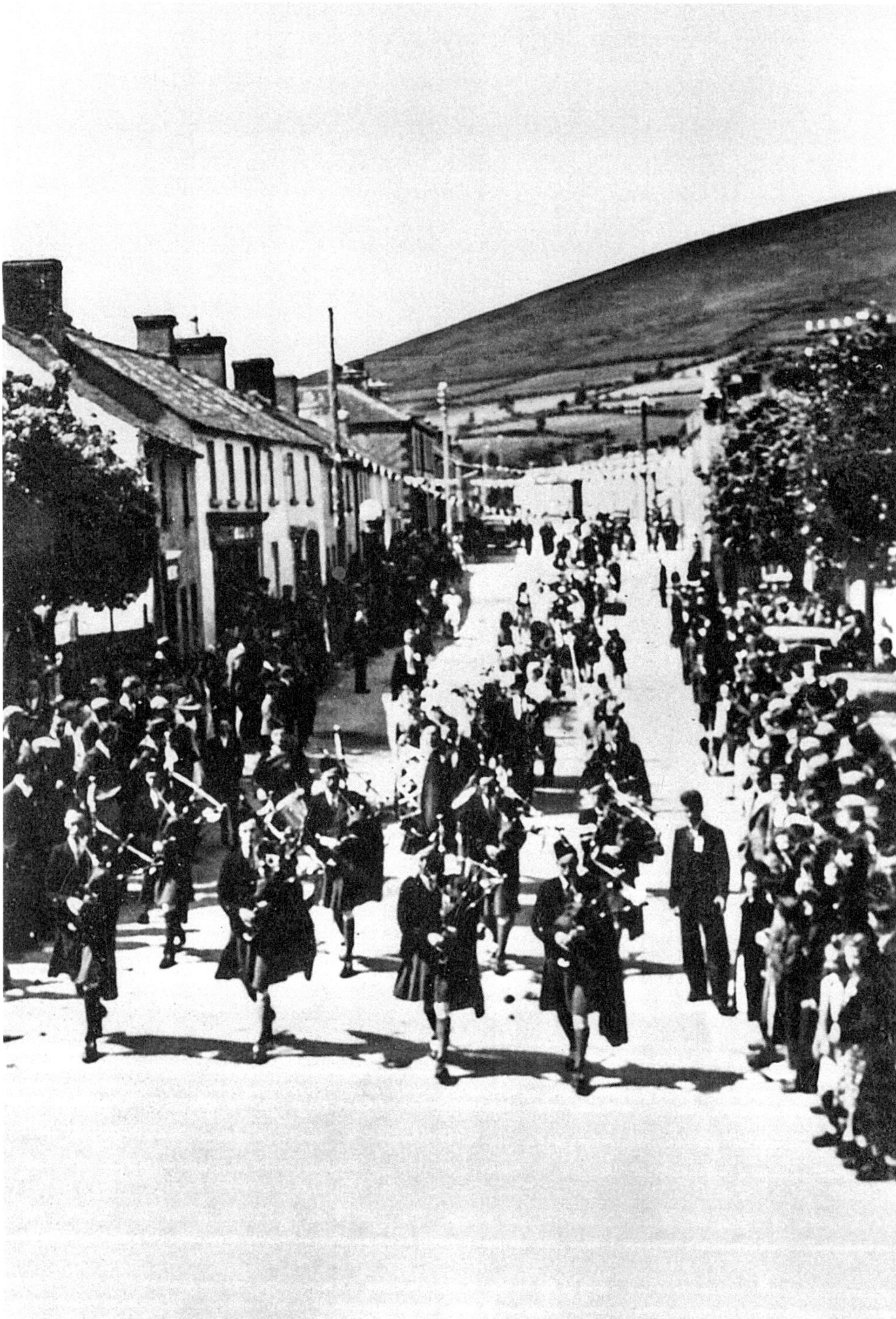

Crowds line the main street as a local Irish pipe band leads a procession of decorated floats and marching groups through Tinahely at summer carnival time.

2

WOODENBRIDGE, AVOCA & ARKLOW TOWN

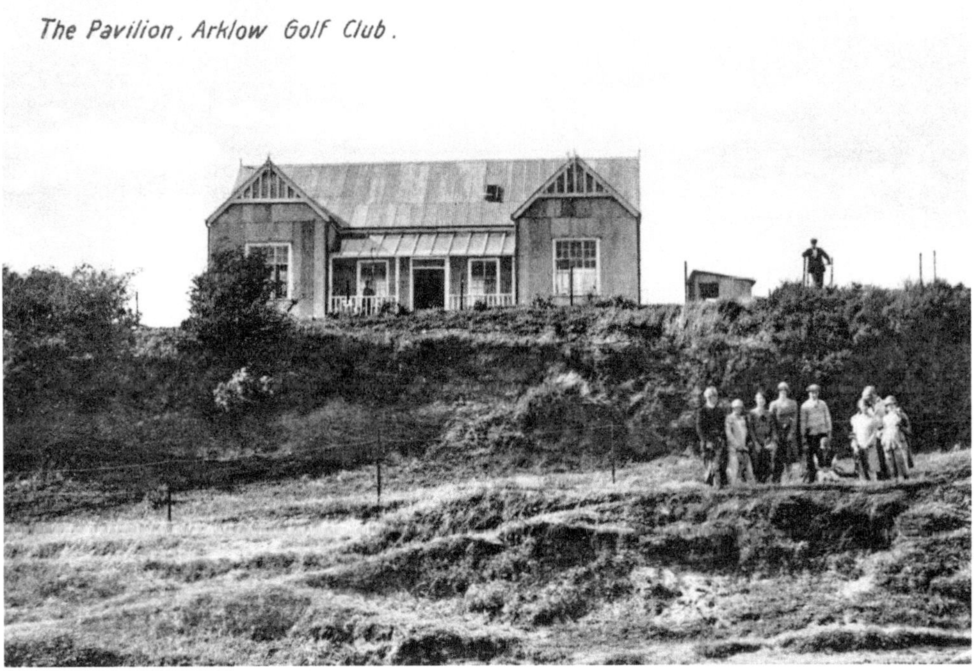

Arklow Golf Club was founded in 1927. Here a group of golfers gather on the first tee, which is in front of the wooden pavilion with its corrugated-iron roof. The links course was situated besides the South Strand and was only a short walk from town.

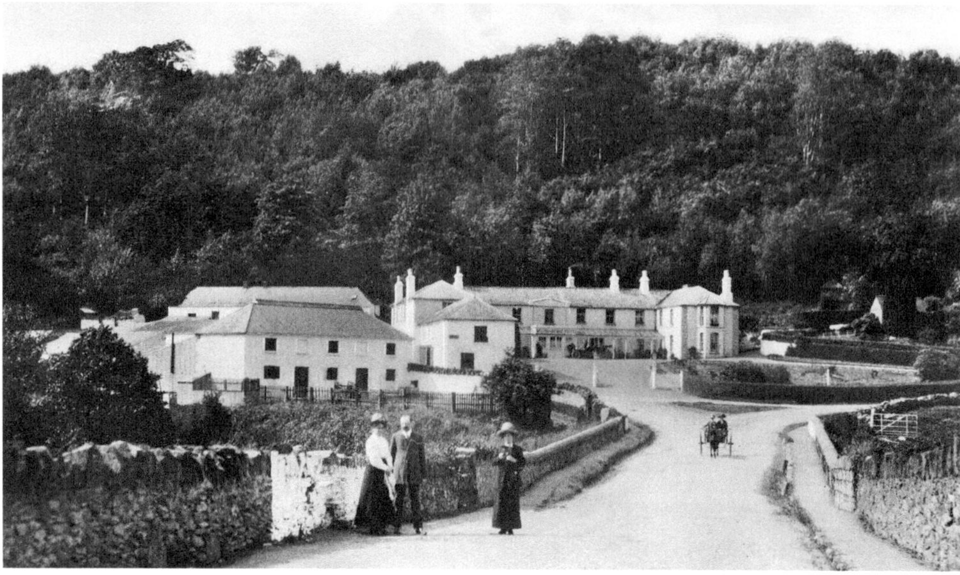

The Woodenbridge Hotel, established in 1608, claims to be the oldest hotel in Ireland. It was a coaching inn on the Dublin to Wexford Highway. An early visitor in the long history of famous patrons was Thomas Wentworth, the Earl of Strafford, who often stayed at Arklow Castle when he was Lord Lieutenant of Ireland in the 1630s. However, he came to a sad end when he was beheaded in London for being a Royalist and opposing parliament. This was just before the start of the English Civil War. Later notable visitors have included Daniel O'Connell, Sir Walter Scott, Charles Stewart Parnell, John Redmond and Michael Collins.

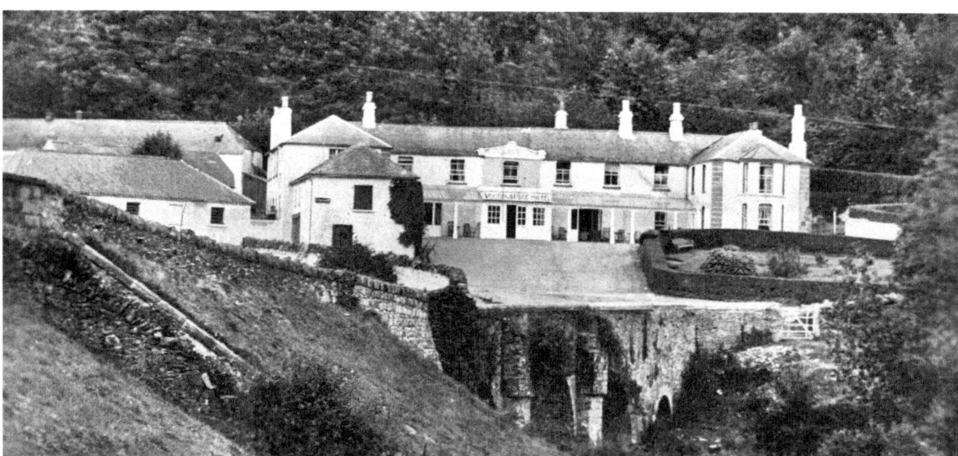

A peaceful scene outside the Woodenbridge Hotel on a card posted on 21 July 1909. The writer of the card to his mother in London says he is having a glorious time with the otter hounds and the hotel has dances every night. The Woodenbridge crossing was used by carriers taking mining shipments from the Avoca Valley to Arklow or Wicklow where the raw ore from copper, lead, zinc, iron and sulphur deposits at Avoca could be exported to Wales. In 1796, when gold was discovered on Croghan Mountain, the Woodenbridge Hotel became the centre point for the great Wicklow Gold Rush, when many visitors stayed there on the way to visit the gold works.

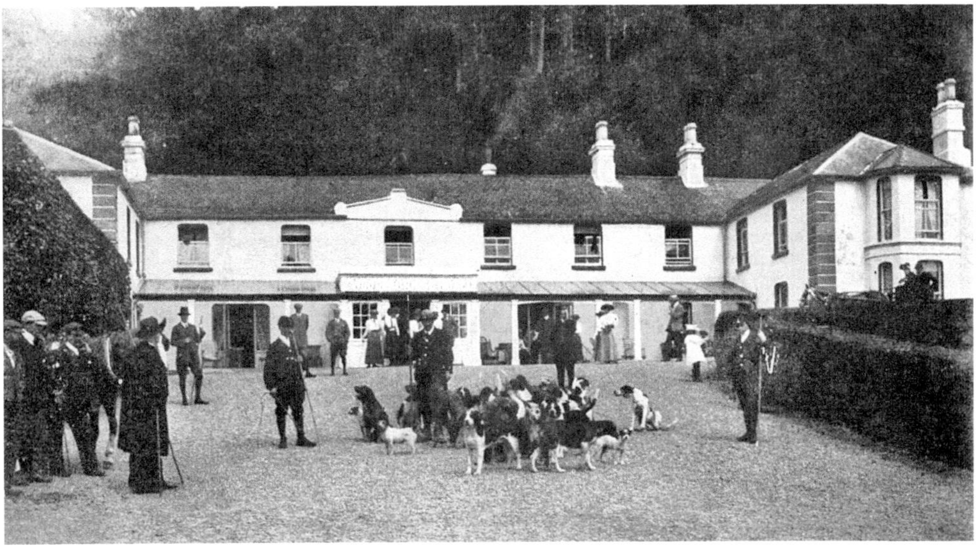

There was excellent fishing and hunting in the area and the hotel was the ideal location to stay. This postcard shows crowds gathering at the start of the meet outside the Woodenbridge Hotel, *c.* 1910. At that time, there were around twenty packs of otter hounds in the British Isles, including two packs in Ireland. The otter-hunting season was from April to September. The sport at Woodenbridge was enjoyed throughout the season and here the Border Counties pack of otter hounds have travelled from North Wales for the meet at Woodenbridge.

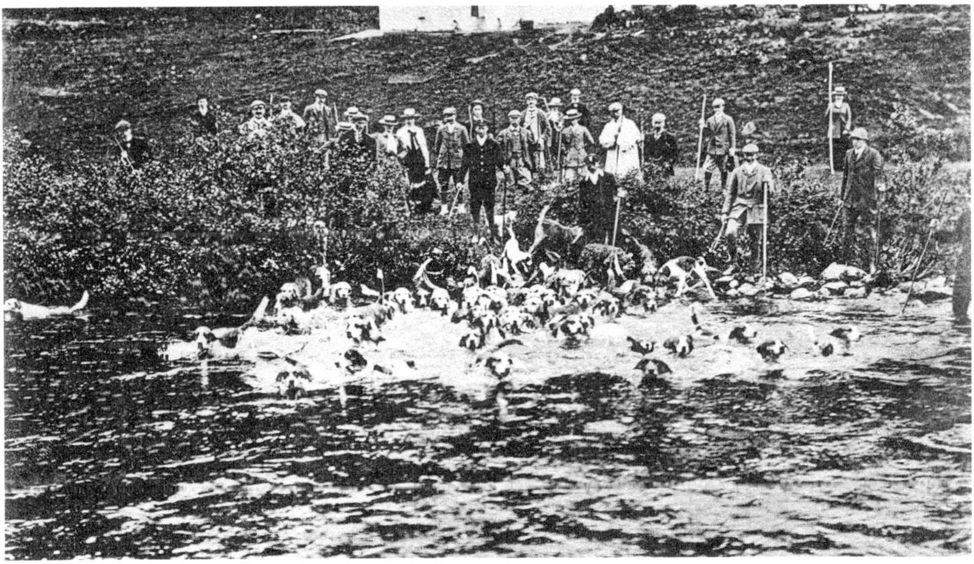

This postcard shows a hunt in progress with Captain Hastings and a pack of the 'King' otter hounds from the Curragh hunting at Woodenbridge on Saturday 7 June 1902. The men are on the riverbank with sticks and the dogs are in the river. It was reported in the press that the hunt was fortunate that day and an otter was put down and marked to ground, followed by a successful swimming hunt.

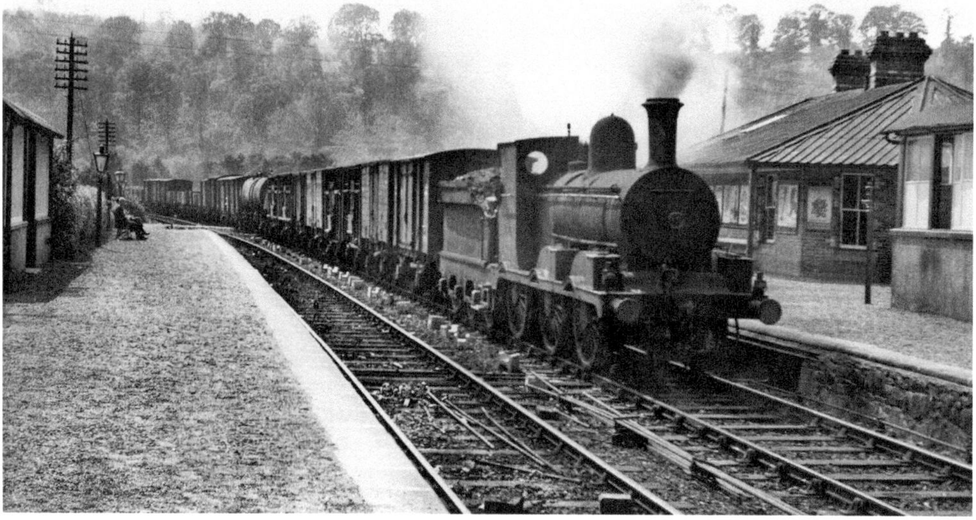

The arrival of the railway in 1863 brought an influx of new visitors to Woodenbridge and business at the Woodenbridge Hotel increased dramatically. The hotel offered weekend rail and hotel trips and special cheap rail and dinner tickets from Dublin during the week. The station was midway between Dublin and Wexford and was the junction for the Shillelagh branch, until it closed in 1944. Here a goods steam train (J18) is shown passing through Woodenbridge Station in August 1955. The station finally closed in March 1969.

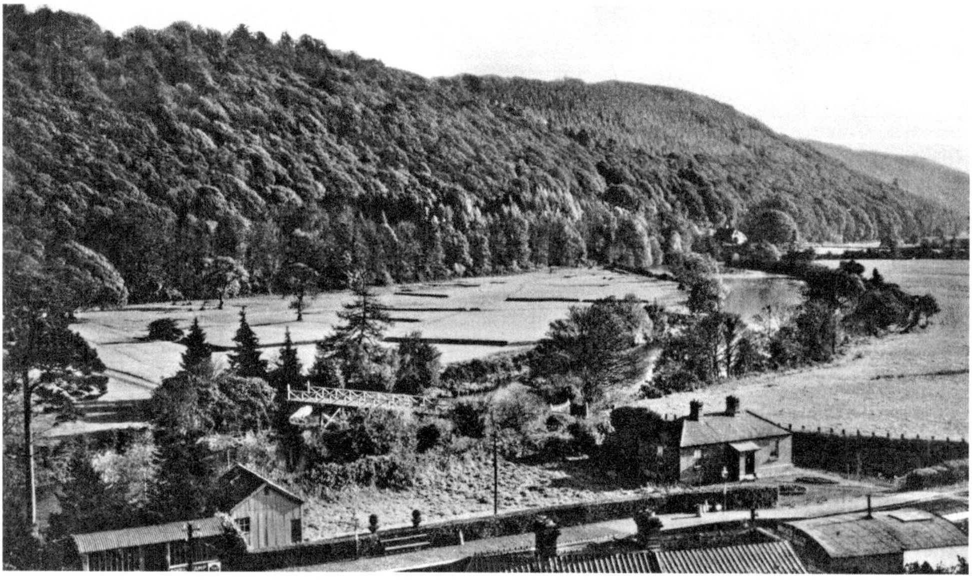

The Links at Woodenbridge Golf Club, which was founded in 1884 and is one of the oldest clubs in Ireland. It is a unique parkland course lying in the beautiful Vale of Avoca, overlooked by majestic tree-lined steep hillsides and crossed by two rivers. It is a paradise for golfers. The railway station can be seen in the foreground.

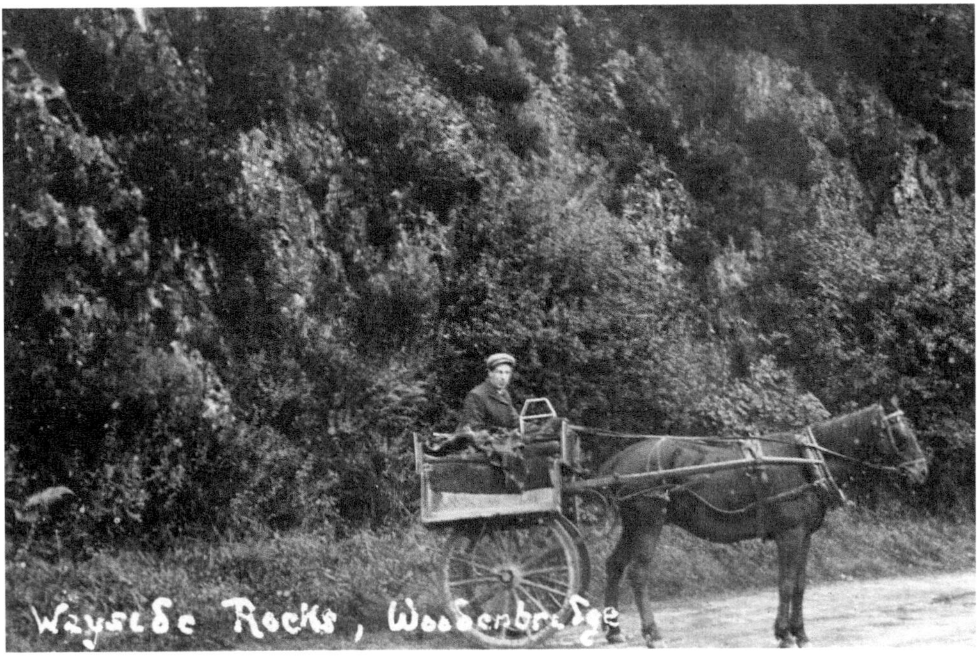

A farmer heading for market halts his horse to have a photograph taken at the Wayside Rocks at Woodenbridge, *c.* 1910.

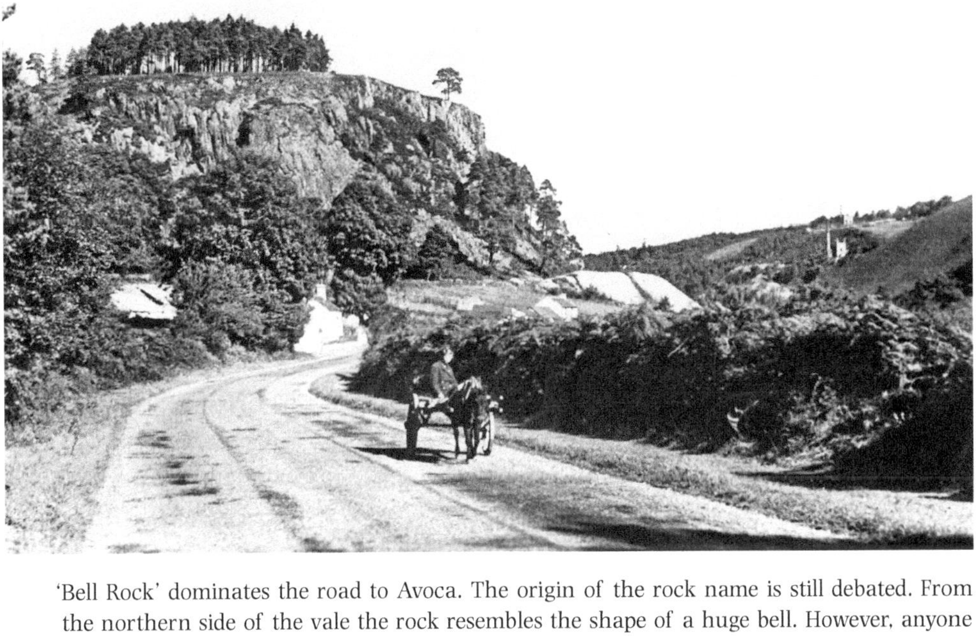

'Bell Rock' dominates the road to Avoca. The origin of the rock name is still debated. From the northern side of the vale the rock resembles the shape of a huge bell. However, anyone standing on the top of the rock could be seen from all the mines in the valley below. A large bell on the rock summit was rung each day to signal the starting and finishing times for the mining shifts and many claim this is this is the reason for the name 'Bell Rock'.

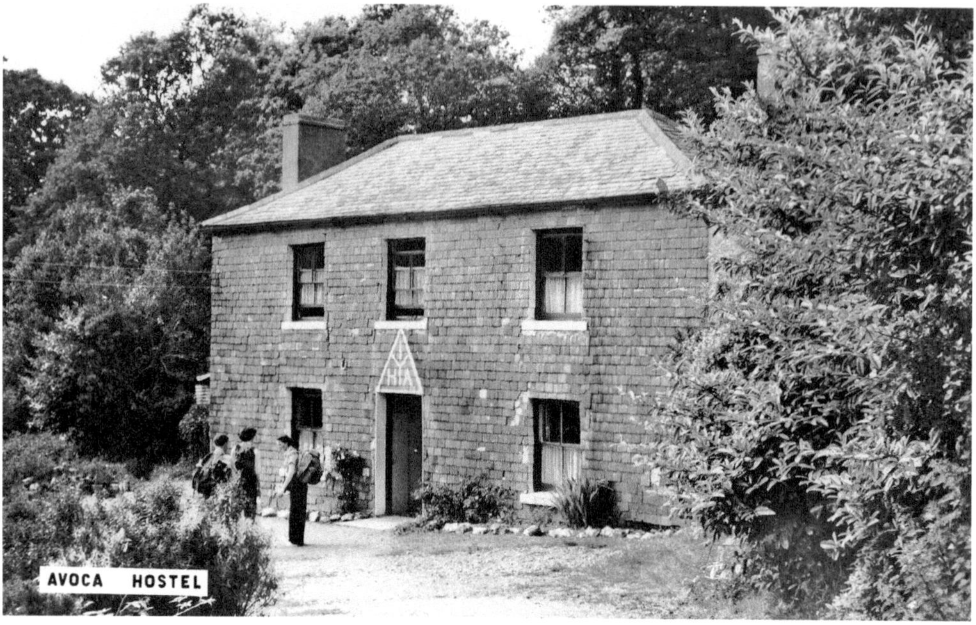

The Avoca Hostel was run by the An Óige Youth Hostel Association. The hostel was beside Avoca Town, near to the White Bridge. The house faced down the valley and was visible from the main Avoca road. It was a popular destination for walkers and cyclists. The young people could bathe in the River Avoca below the hostel. The 'Meeting of the Waters' was about one mile away.

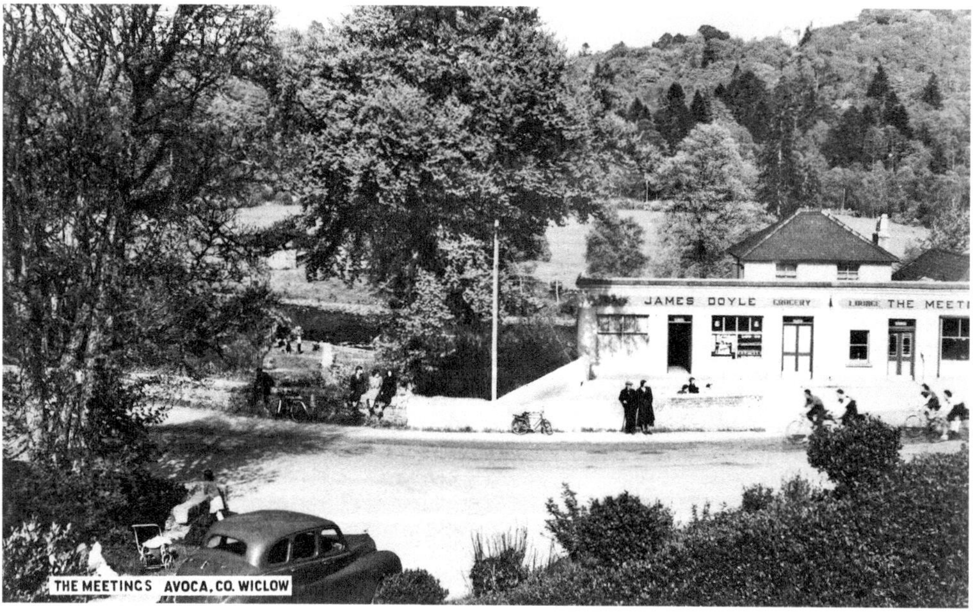

'The Meetings' Hostelry and shop at the 'Meeting of the Waters' in the Vale of Avoca. The pub dates from the 1800s and the gardens at the rear enjoy panoramic views of the converging waters of the Avonbeg and Avonmore rivers and the scenic countryside.

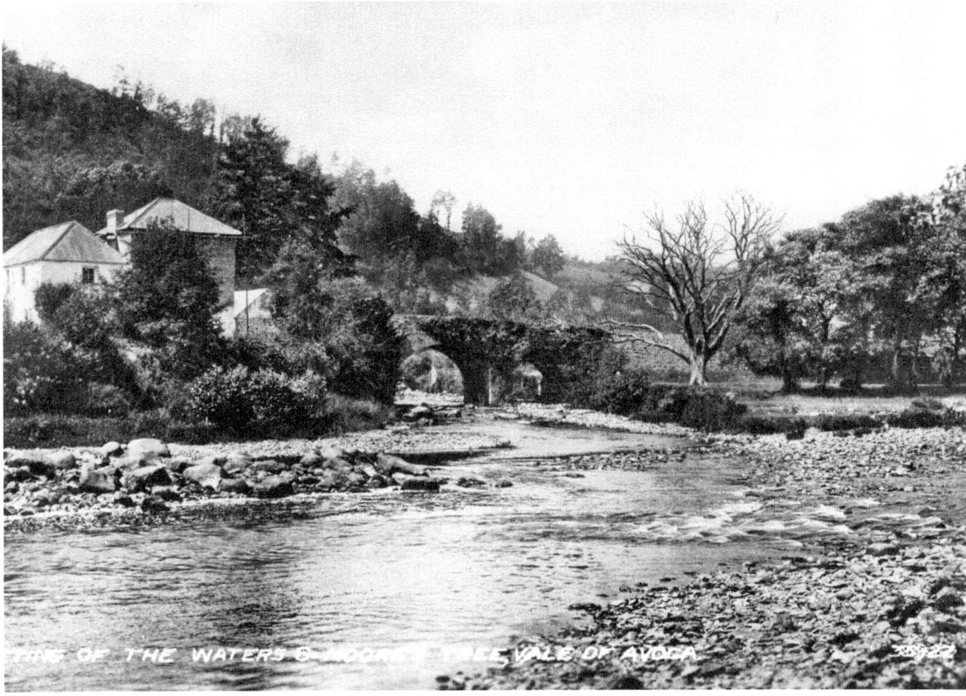

The 'Meeting of the Waters', Vale of Avoca. Three miles north of Avoca Village, the Avoca River is formed by the flowing together of the Avonmore and Avonbeg Rivers, which join in a setting of wooded beauty. The poet Thomas Moore enjoyed many days here, resting by the tree shown in the centre. In 'Summer 1807' he wrote: 'There is not in this wide world a valley so sweet/As that vale in whose bosom the bright waters meet;/Oh! The last rays of feeling and life must depart/Ere the bloom of that valley shall fade from my heart.'

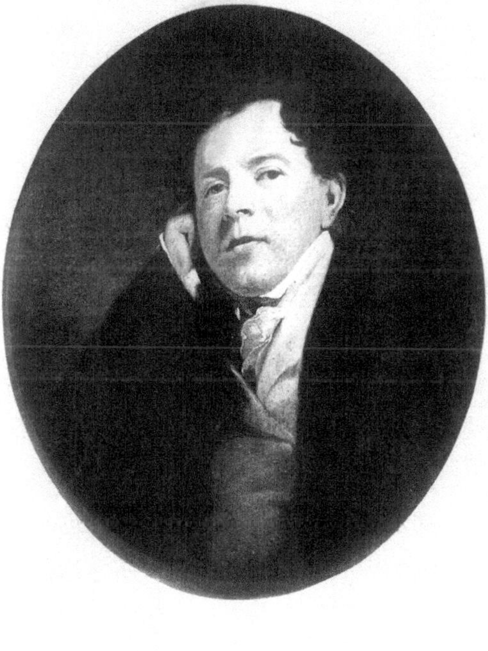

THOMAS MOORE.
BORN 28TH MAY 1779. DIED 26TH FEBY. 1852.
BY JOHN JACKSON, R.A.
NATIONAL PORTRAIT GALLERY, DUBLIN.

Thomas Moore was Ireland's greatest romantic poet and songwriter. He was born at 12 Aungier Street in Dublin on 28 May 1779. He was a law student at Trinity College Dublin; however, his talent was in music and poetry. He issued his first volume of *Irish Melodies* in 1808. He is remembered for the lyrics of 'The Minstrel Boy', 'The Last Rose of Summer', 'Believe Me if All Those Endearing Young Charms' and 'The Meeting of The Waters'.

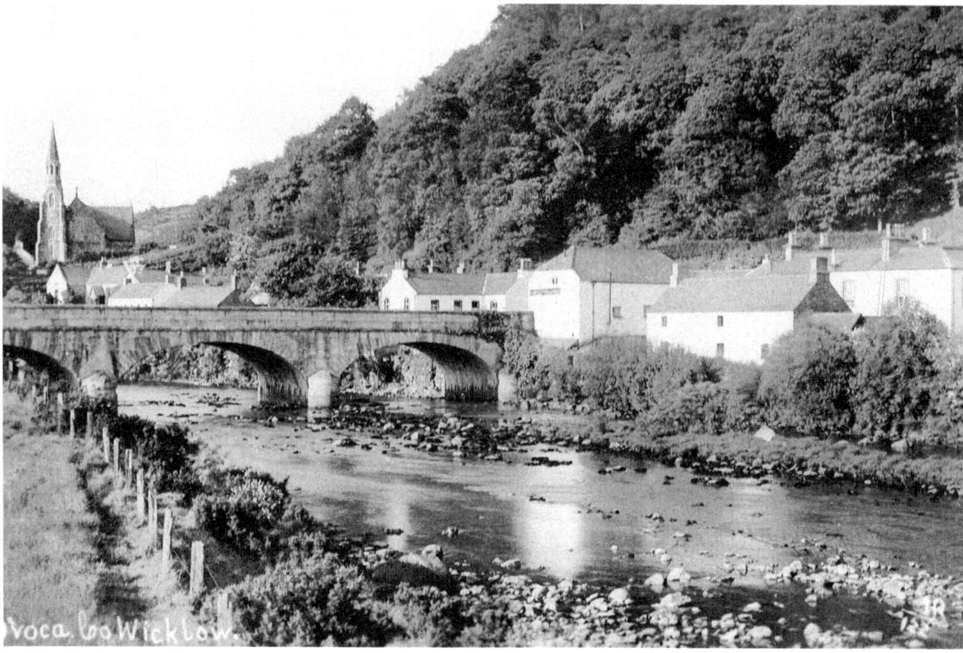

The bridge over the River Avoca that flows into the beautiful village of Avoca on the right. There has been copper mining in the valley since around 1720 and the miners and their families helped bring trade to the village. The tall steeple of the church of St Mary and St Patrick, built in 1862, can be seen in the distance.

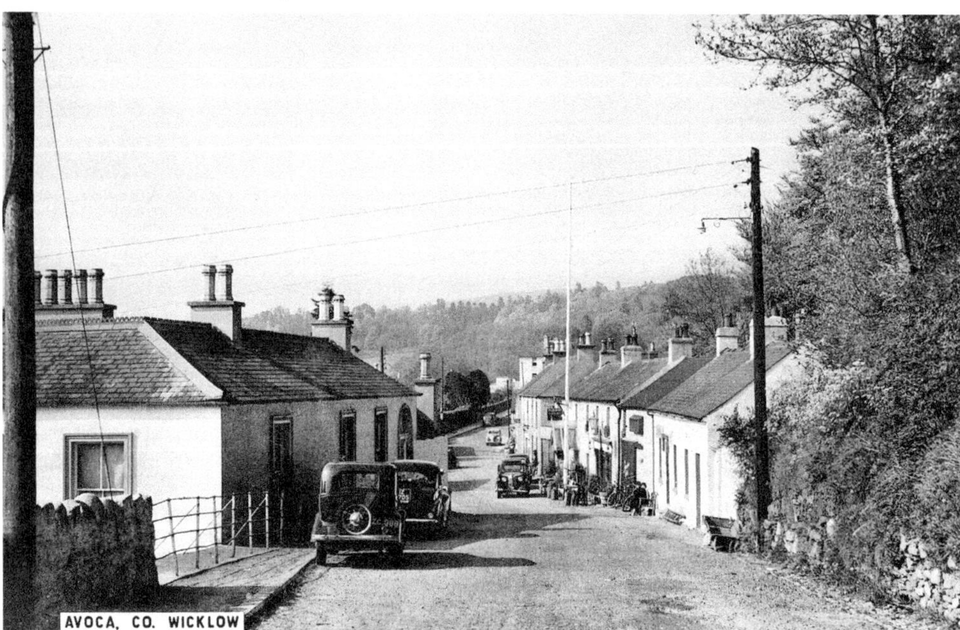

The main road through Avoca, *c.* 1950s. In the 1990s Avoca was the location of the fictional village in the popular BBC television series *Ballykissangel.*

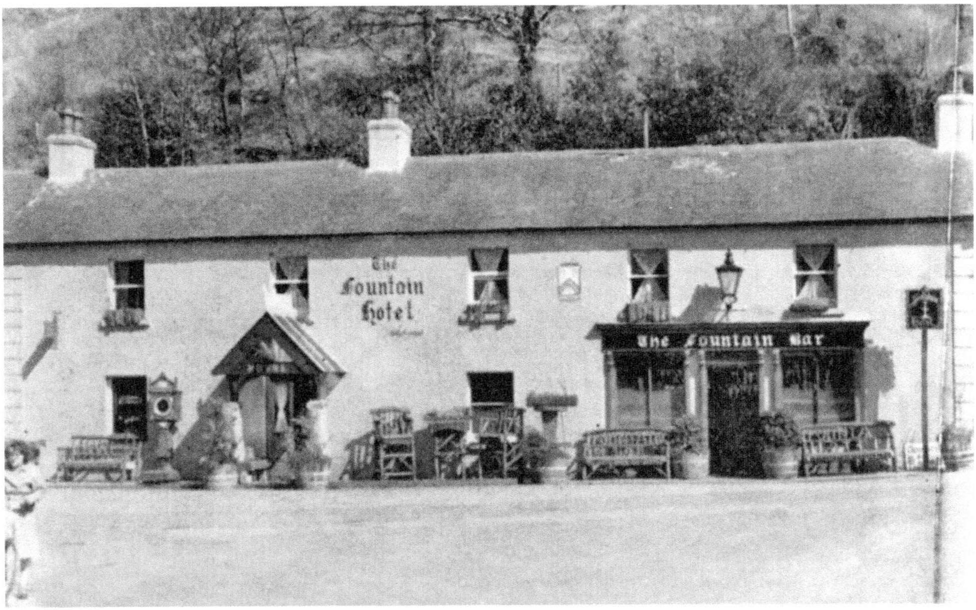

The Fountain Hotel and Bar, Main Street, Avoca, *c*. 1950. The hotel was used as a location for the BBC drama *Ballykissangel* in 1996 and renamed 'Fitzgeralds'. The hotel has kept the new name and is now a very popular destination for *Ballykissangel* fans. There has been a pub on this site used by local miners and visitors for over 200 years and many famous people have visited the pub, including Walt Disney and Mae West. Tourists often make a special journey to the village to visit the Avoca Handweavers Woollen Mill, which was founded in 1723 and is the oldest working mill in Ireland. It produces high-quality tweed garments.

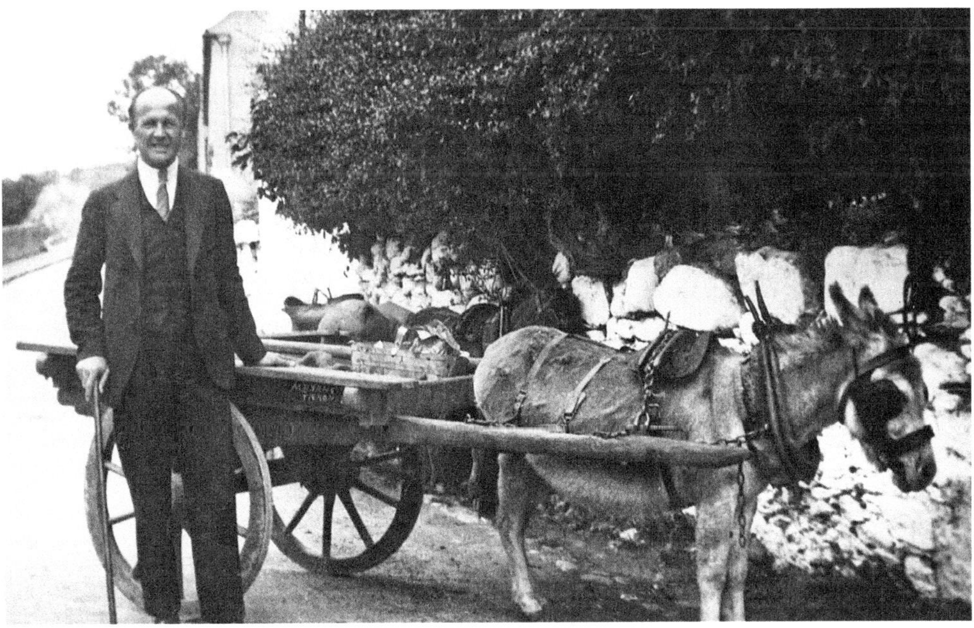

A farmer with his donkey and cart on deliveries in Avoca in June 1937.

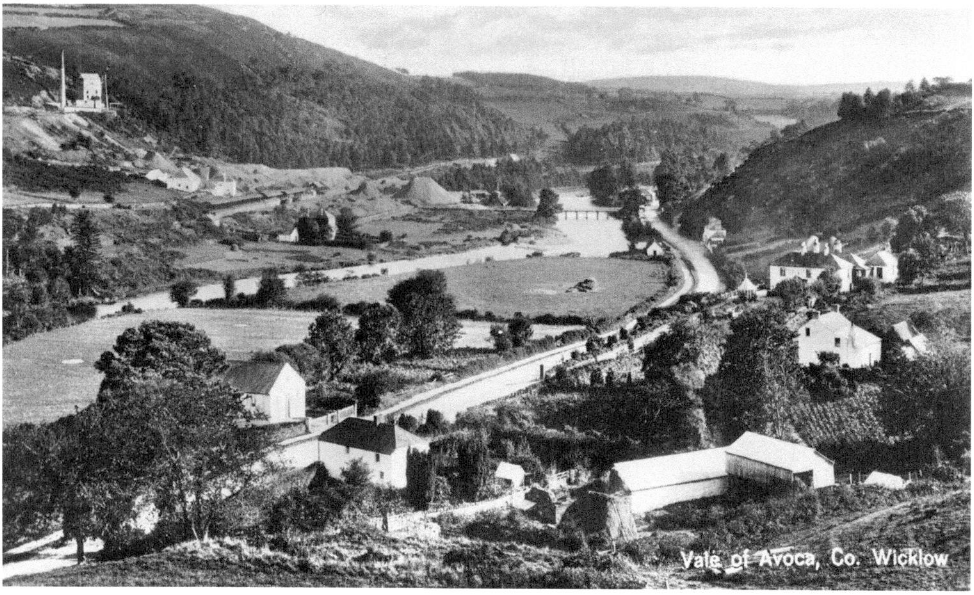

A postcard of the beautiful Vale of Avoca, showing the main road and the river with cottages dotted in the valley. Not all is perfection for on the left is the lofty chimney stack of a copper mine with huge mounds of mine waste on the slopes below.

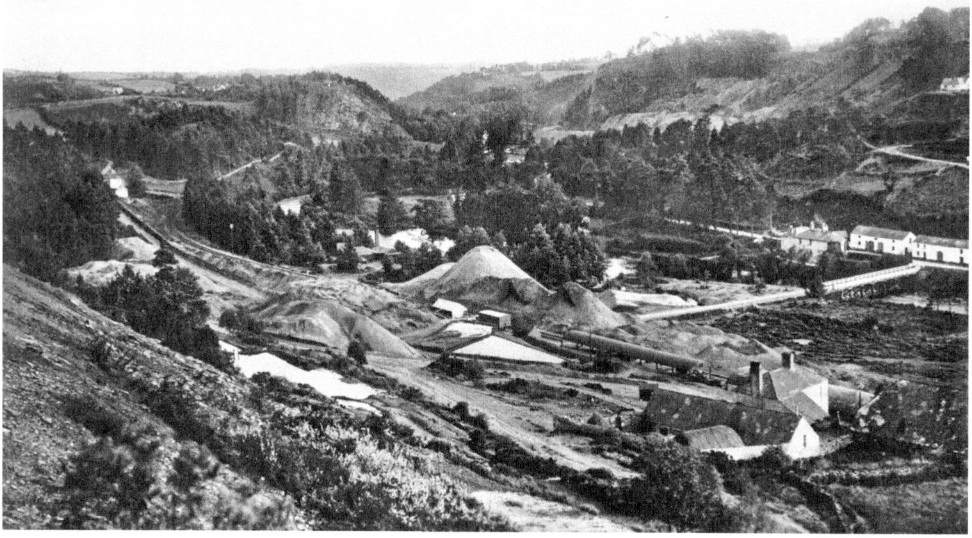

The mines in the Vale of Avoca with a number of rock waste spoil heaps. The mines were worked on both sides of the valley. There were three main sites – East Avoca, West Avoca and Cronebane. It is thought that copper was mined in the Bronze Age (around 1000 BC) and through medieval times. However, from the twelfth to the seventeenth century, the area mainly produced iron, followed by a period of lead mining up to 1750. After this, there was a return to mining copper, which lasted until large-scale mining was discontinued around 1915. However, there was some further mining between 1958-62 and 1970-82, when significant amounts of copper ore were produced.

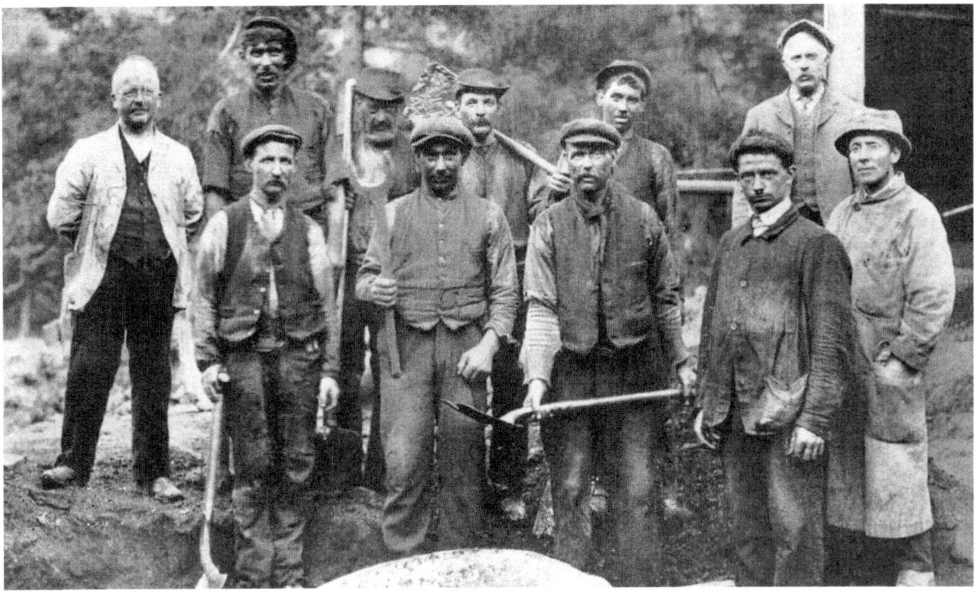

Ballygahan Ochre Workers, Avoca, *c.* early 1900s. Mining was an important source of employment for the area and in the 1840s around 2,500 people were employed in the Avoca mines. However, mining in the area started much earlier than this; the Greek cartographer, Ptolomy, who mapped Ireland in AD 150, showed Avoca on his map and it is likely that the Romans traded ore with the valley of Avoca at that time.

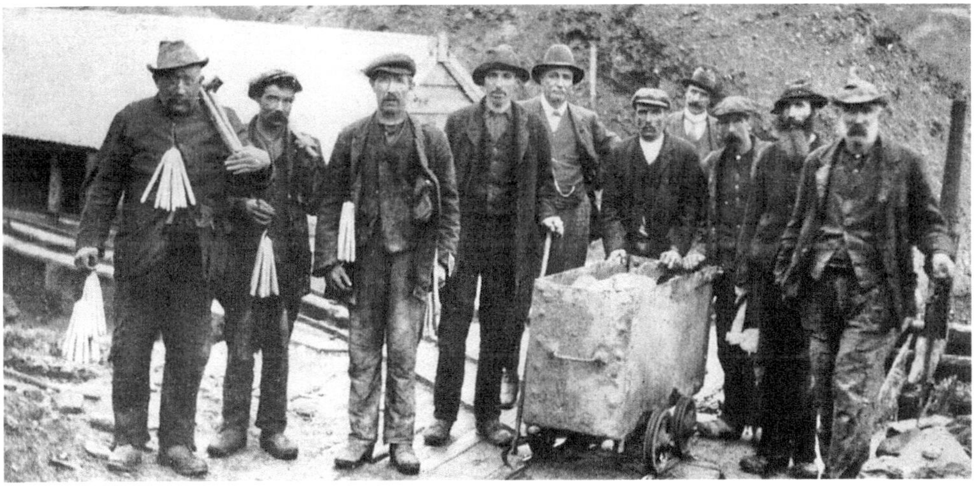

A group of Avoca miners, who worked long hours, often in difficult conditions. *Hall's Ireland*, published in 1841, stated that in May of that year 7,195 tons of ore was raised in Cronebane and probably an equal quantity in Ballymurtagh. This was shipped at Wicklow Harbour for the smelting houses at Swansea. The mining company got the equivalent of £1.25 a ton for it on the quay at Wicklow. The miners received 22.5p per ton for raising it, and the carriage to Wicklow was 25p per ton. The Avoca district had its own currency and from 1789 to 1852, the 'Cronebane Halfpenny', minted by the Associated Irish Mine Company, could be used to purchase goods.

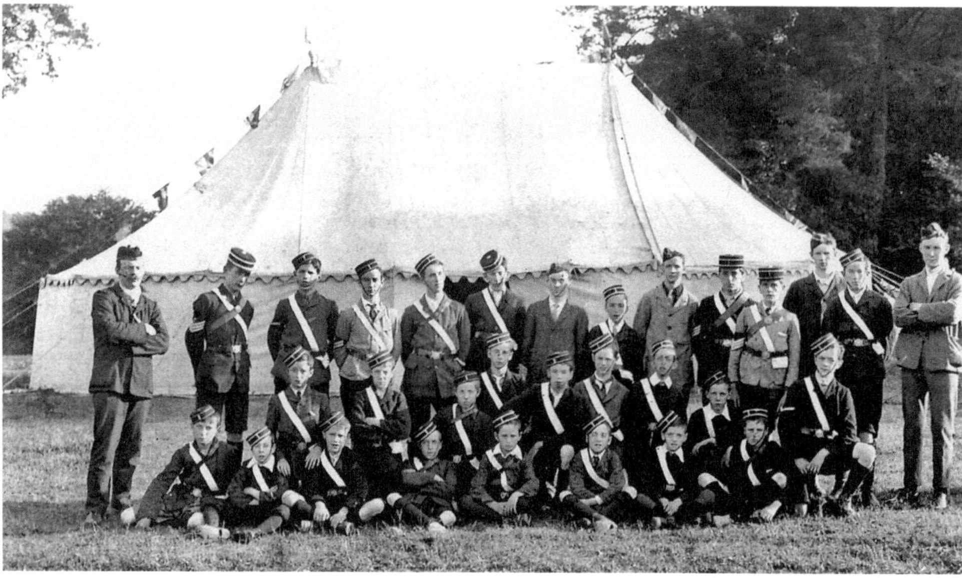

First Dublin Company Boys' Brigade camping at Avoca in 1906. The Boys' Brigade was an interdenominational Christian youth organisation founded in Glasgow in 1883 by Sir William Smith. It combined semi-military discipline, gymnastics, sports and religious services. Every year the group held summer camps with lots of activities. Their motto was 'Sure and Steadfast'. The movement was very popular and spread across the UK and Ireland. The First Dublin Company was founded in 1891.

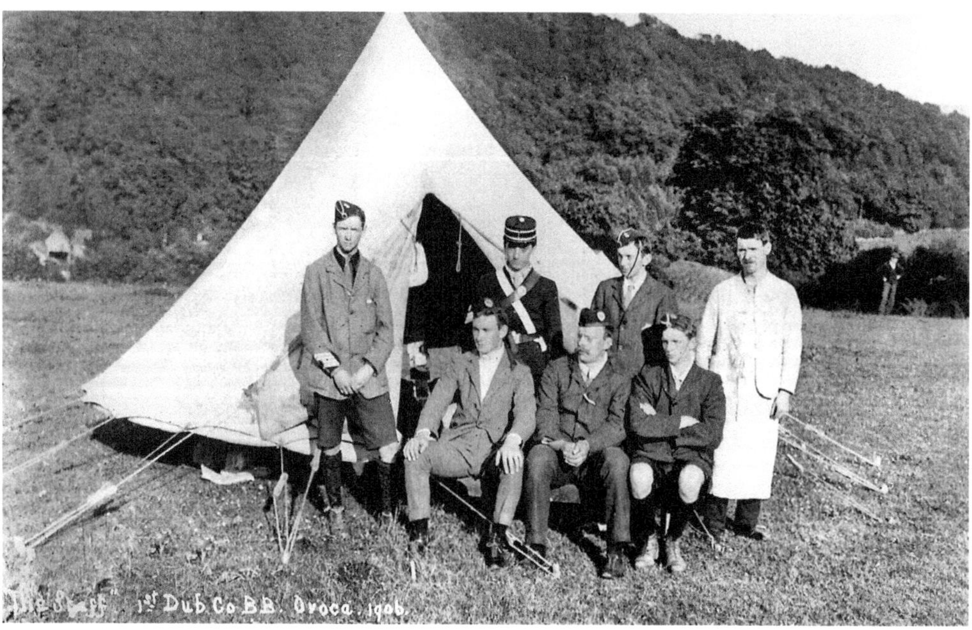

Some of the staff of the First Dublin Boys' Brigade in their uniforms outside their tent at Avoca in 1906. An important member of the staff in every camp was the cook, who needed to provide good, appetising food. Much of the routine in the camp revolved around mealtimes.

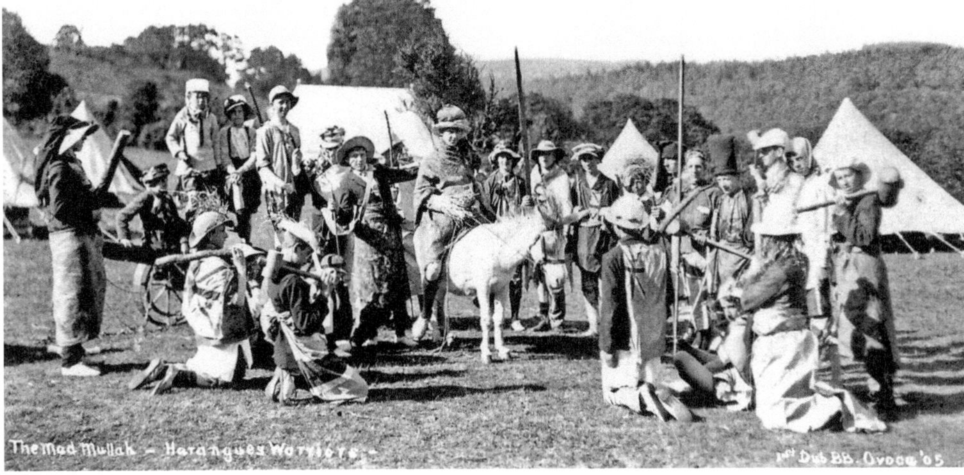

Games at the Dublin Boys' Brigade Camp in 1906. The boys must have enjoyed dressing up. The central figure on the donkey is surrounded by a motley crew, who carry various clubs and wooden poles. The postcard is entitled 'The Mad Mullah – Harangues Warriors'. This was a reference to Sayyid Mohammed Abdullah Hassan (known as the 'Mad Mullah') who, at that time in Somaliland, was leading the nomad tribes with some success in an anti-Christian and anti-colonial crusade against the British.

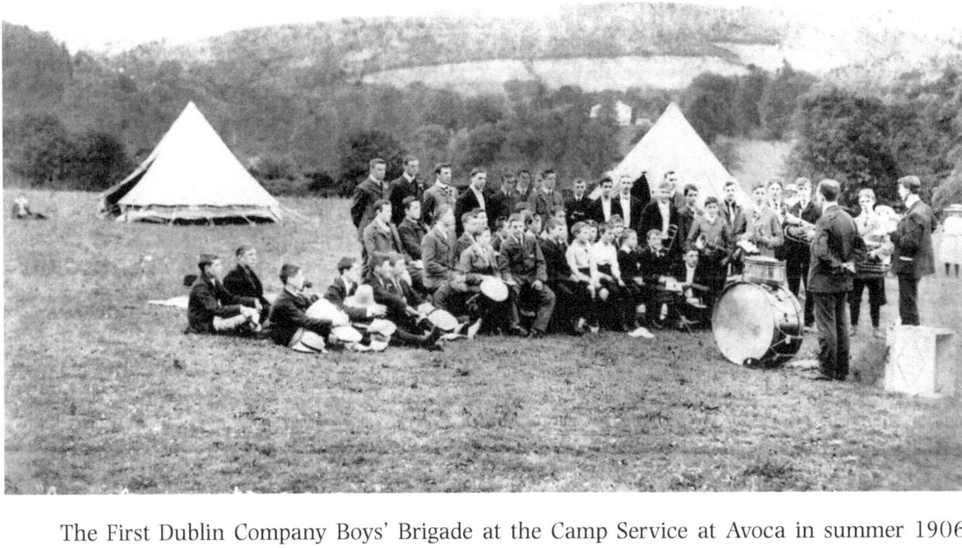

The First Dublin Company Boys' Brigade at the Camp Service at Avoca in summer 1906. There would be prayer meetings for the boys every day, but the Sunday service with music and hymns was one of the highlights of the week. The card shows the boys attentively listening to the camp leaders, who are standing by the big drum. Some of the boys have musical instruments and all are all dressed in their 'Sunday best'.

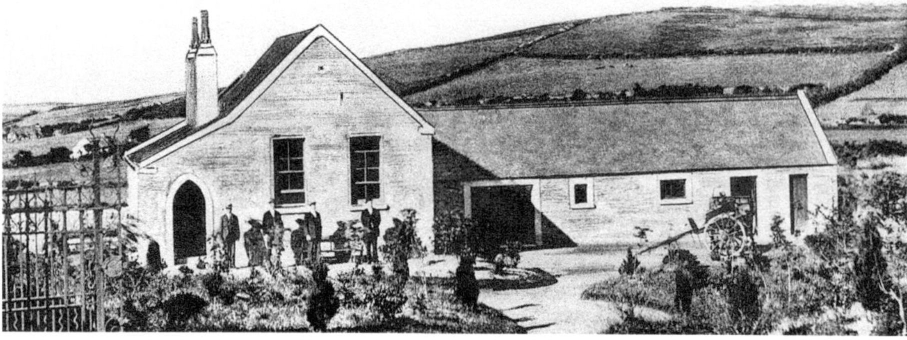

Near to Avoca is Conary and the Connoree Copper Mines. The mines employed many local people, but also had skilled miners from Wales and Cornwall. Large quantities of copper were produced between 1840 and 1850. The card shows parishioners of St Bartholomew's church standing outside the Conary Parochial Hall and stables. The hall was built as a schoolhouse in 1889 and the schoolteacher lived there in two rooms off the main hall. The walk known as the 'Pure Mile' in this area starts at the Community Hall, passes by St Bartholomew's church and ends at the Motte Stone.

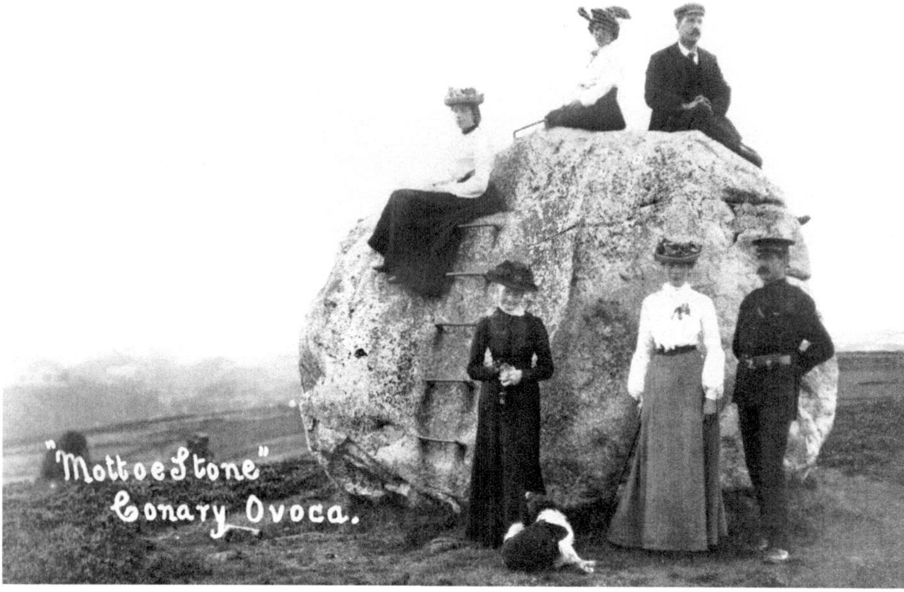

A group of visitors, including a guard in uniform, stand at the Motte Stone at Conary, Avoca. Three people have climbed the ladder of iron rungs on the west face of the stone to sit on the top and get an even better view of the magnificent scenery. They can see the valleys of the Avonmore, Avonbeg and Avoca with the valleys of Glenalmure and Glendalough in the mid-distance and the mountains of Lugnaquilla and Kippure in the background. This massive granite stone stands on the hilltop on Cronebane. It is 4 metres long, 3 metres broad and 3 metres high. The legend states that the stone was thrown there by Finn McCool from the summit of Lugnaquilla Mountain, which is the highest peak (925 metres) in Leinster. However, geologists consider the more likely explanation is that the boulder was carried in the great ice flows of the Ice Age and deposited when the ice melted.

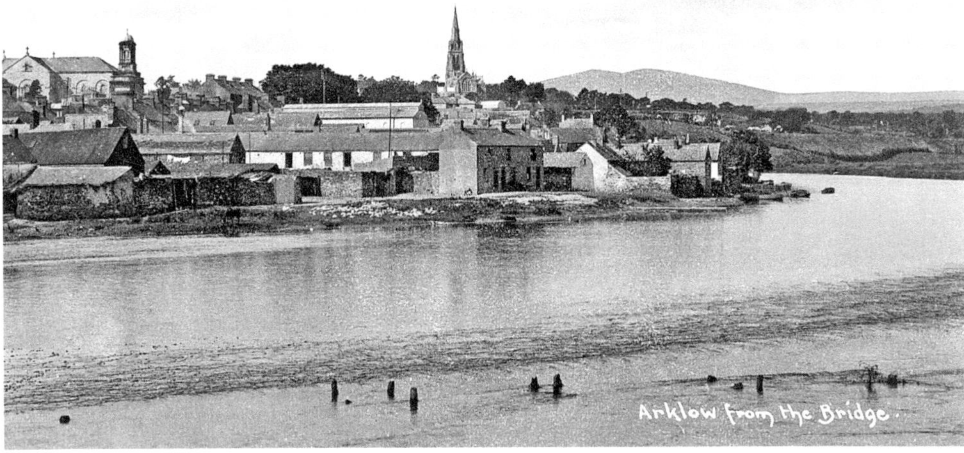

The historic town of Arklow from the stone arch bridge that spans the river at the centre of the town. Arklow stands on the south bank of the Avoca River. There has been a fishing and seafaring community here since the sixth century. The Vikings settled here in the ninth century and the Normans came during the eleventh century. The town developed from a small fishing centre to become one of the most important ports in Ireland.

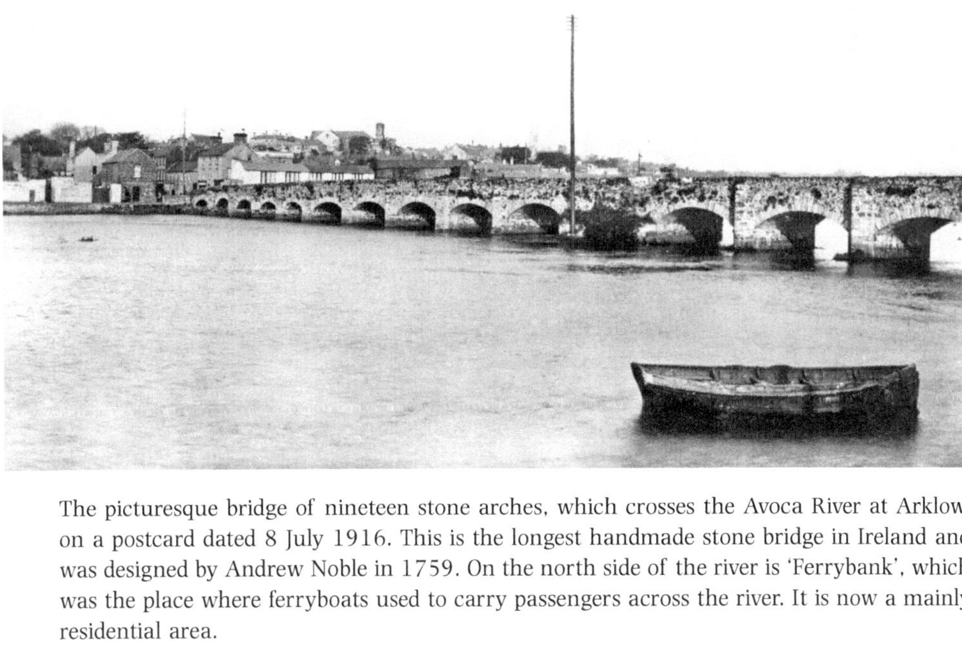

The picturesque bridge of nineteen stone arches, which crosses the Avoca River at Arklow, on a postcard dated 8 July 1916. This is the longest handmade stone bridge in Ireland and was designed by Andrew Noble in 1759. On the north side of the river is 'Ferrybank', which was the place where ferryboats used to carry passengers across the river. It is now a mainly residential area.

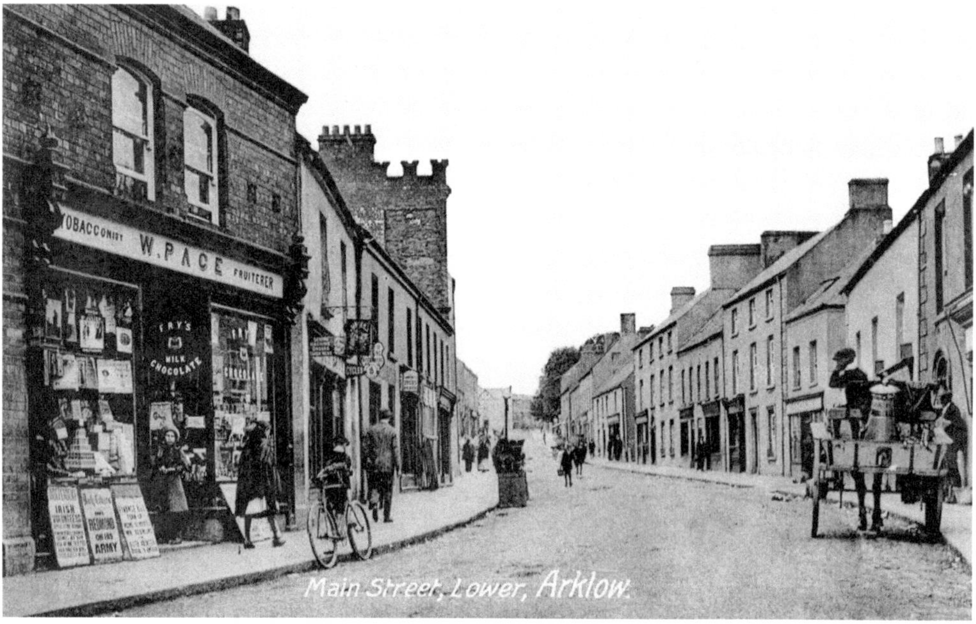

Arklow was always an important trading centre for the surrounding area. This view of the Lower Main Street, *c.* 1916, shows a good range of business premises. On the left, a young girl stands in the doorway of W. Pace, a tobacconist and fruiterer. It is notable that the bicycle outside the shop needed no lock!

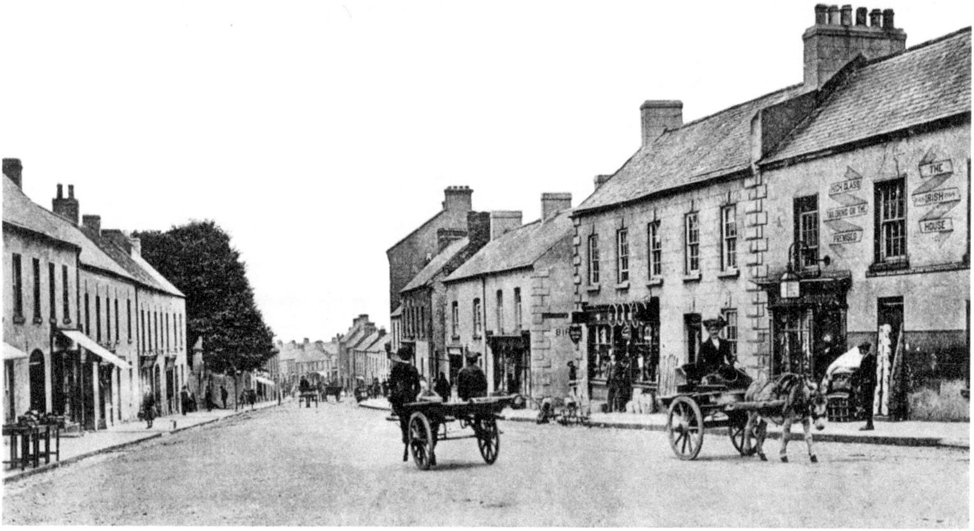

The Upper Main Street, Arklow, on a card posted from Arklow on 10 May 1916. The postcard has an interesting message from a soldier in C Company 2/5 SF, who writes, 'I have to take a loaded rifle with me wherever I go, as there are scores of rebels about here. I can't pick them out as they nearly all wear civilian clothes! Some of them sit at windows sniping and then walk out as cool as anybody. You can guess they take a lot of catching!' Arklow was evidently not a safe place for British soldiers after the Easter Rising.

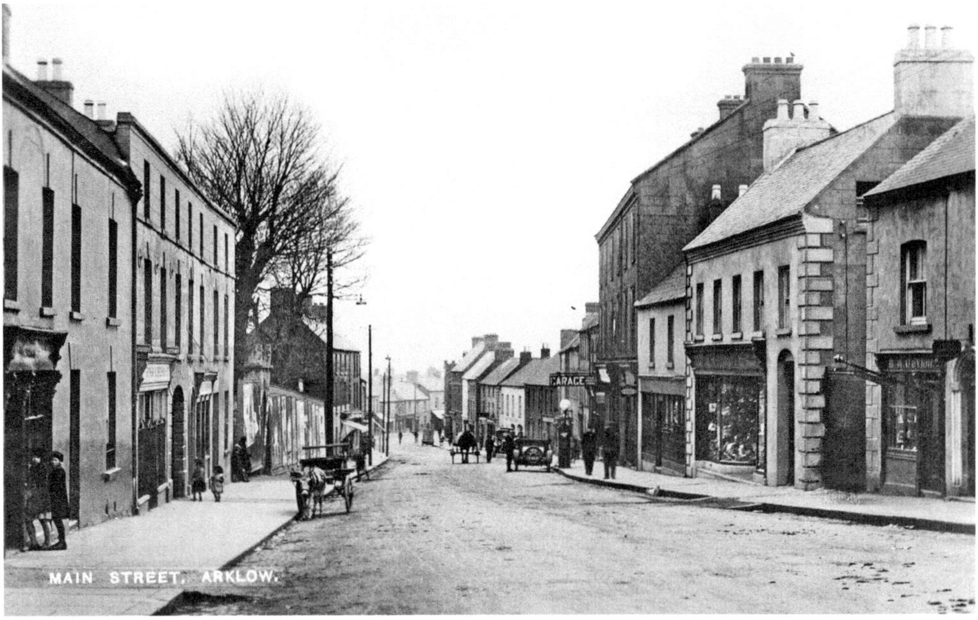

A later view of Upper Main Street on a card posted in 1932. On the right, a vintage car stands by the garage petrol pump. However, horse-drawn traffic is still the normal form of transport and a pony and trap wait outside a shop on the opposite pavement. Like the lower Main Street, there is a good range of small shops and business premises.

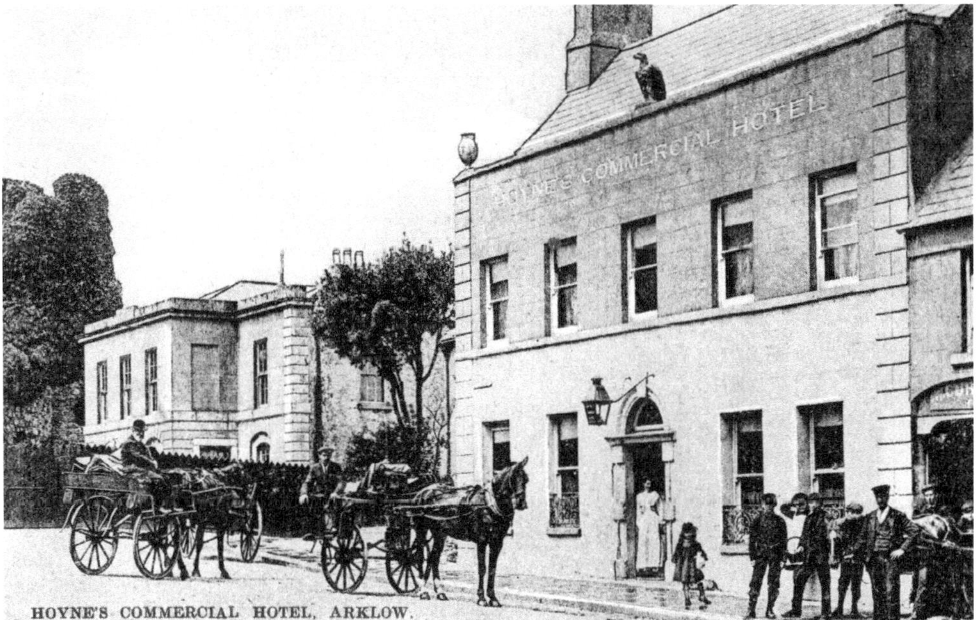

Jaunting cars wait outside William Hoyne's Tourist and Commercial Hotel at 62 Main Street, Arklow, *c.* 1910. The hotel was described as excellent in *Porter's Post Office Guide and Directory of the County of Wicklow, 1910*.

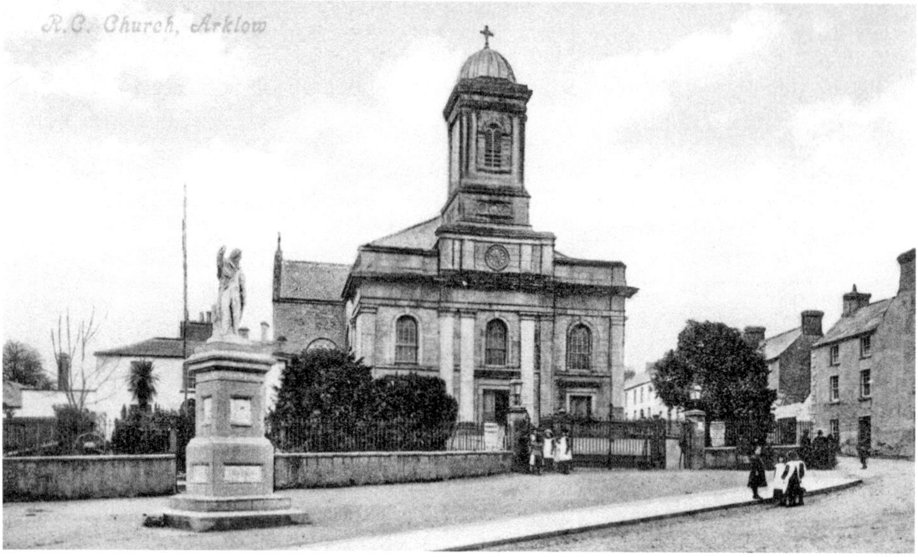

St Mary and St Peter's RC church, Arklow was built in the late 1850s and designed by Peter Byrne. It is shaped like a Latin cross and has a beautiful Italian ceiling with images of the four evangelists. There is also a fine Carrera marble altar with an impressive stained-glass window above the altar, showing the Passion.

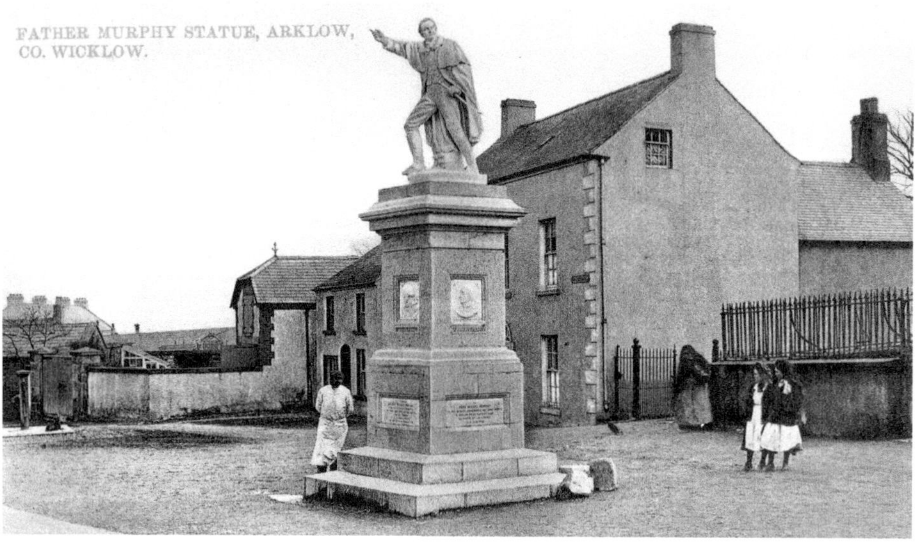

The Father Murphy Statue, Arklow, *c.* 1910. The Battle of Arklow took place on 9 June 1798. A large group of United Irishmen from Wexford attacked the town, which was defended by a strong force of Redcoats. The rebels were winning the battle against the entrenched British forces, when their leader, Father Michael Murphy, was killed. The Irish were disheartened and they withdrew with huge loss of life. This was probably the turning point of the 1798 Rebellion, as victory would have left the Wexford men with an open road to Dublin. The memorial statue, opposite the Catholic church, was erected to the memory of Father Murphy and the gallant Irishmen who fought in that battle.

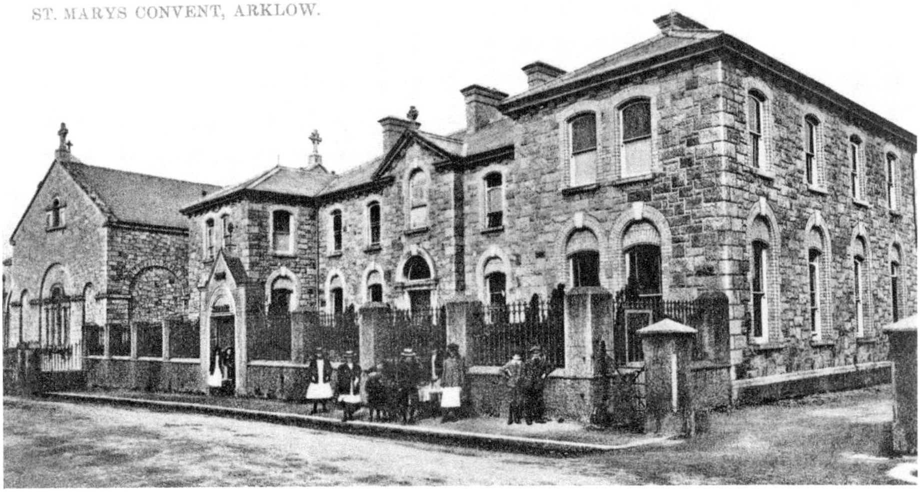

Pupils stand outside St Mary's Convent, Arklow, *c.* 1910. This school for girls was run by the Sisters of Mercy, who opened it as a boarding school in 1903. Some interior scenes from the film *Angela's Ashes*, directed by Alan Parker, were shot in the convent buildings in 1999.

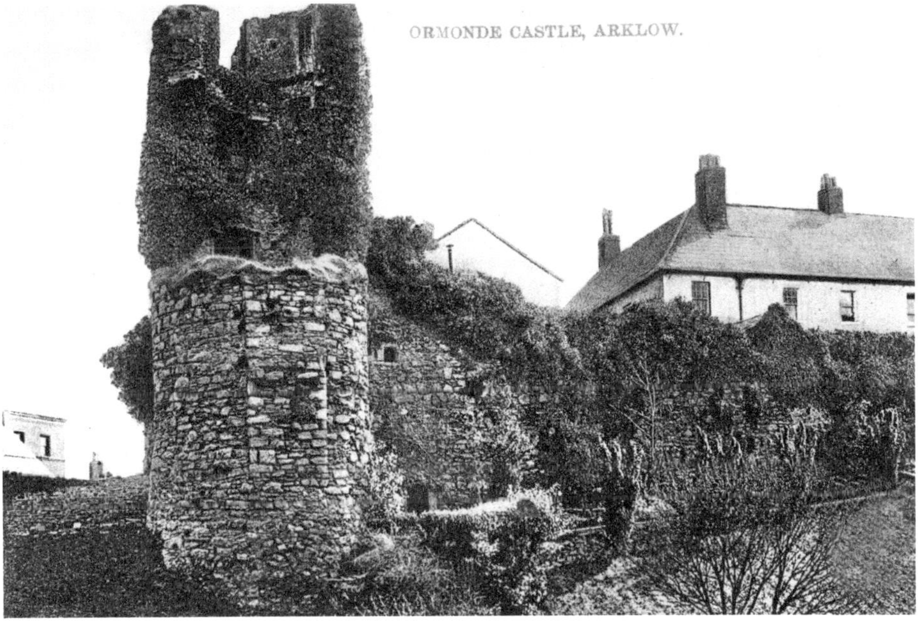

The ruins of Ormonde Castle on Upper Main Street, Arklow, said to have been built about 1210 by the Butlers of Ormonde. The castle was destroyed by Oliver Cromwell's forces in 1650. All that remains of the castle today is part of one of the six towers of the castle and a portion of a wall. The castle is said to be haunted by the ghost of a drummer boy who fell asleep at his post and failed to sound the alarm when the castle was attacked. For his punishment, he was locked in a small windowless room without food and water. However, his jailors failed to return until days later, when they found he had starved to death. To this day it is said his ghost will emerge if Arklow Town is attacked.

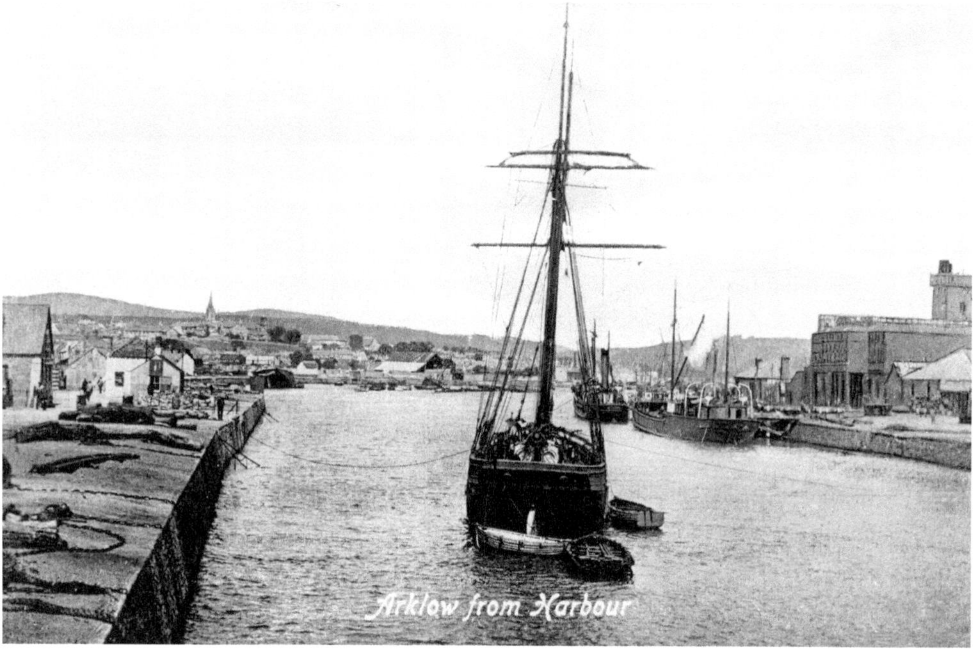

A tall-masted ship in the harbour at Arklow, which has for centuries thrived as a shipping centre, owning and operating smaller merchant vessels. It was once a very busy fishing port with the largest fleet in Ireland. In the 1890s, about 160 fishing vessels were based there. Arklow is also known for shipbuilding and John Tyrell & Son's boat-building yard had an international reputation.

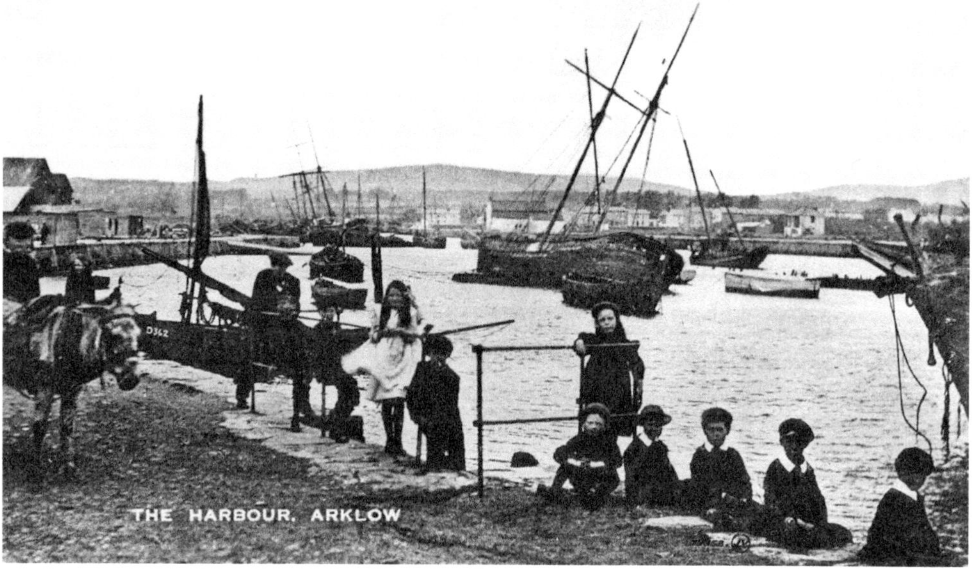

Children gather on the quayside in Arklow, which is busy with several ships in the harbour. In the late 1870s, Arklow was the largest schooner port in Ireland. The fleet of ships carried various cargoes for export, including large quantities of ore from the mines at West Avoca.

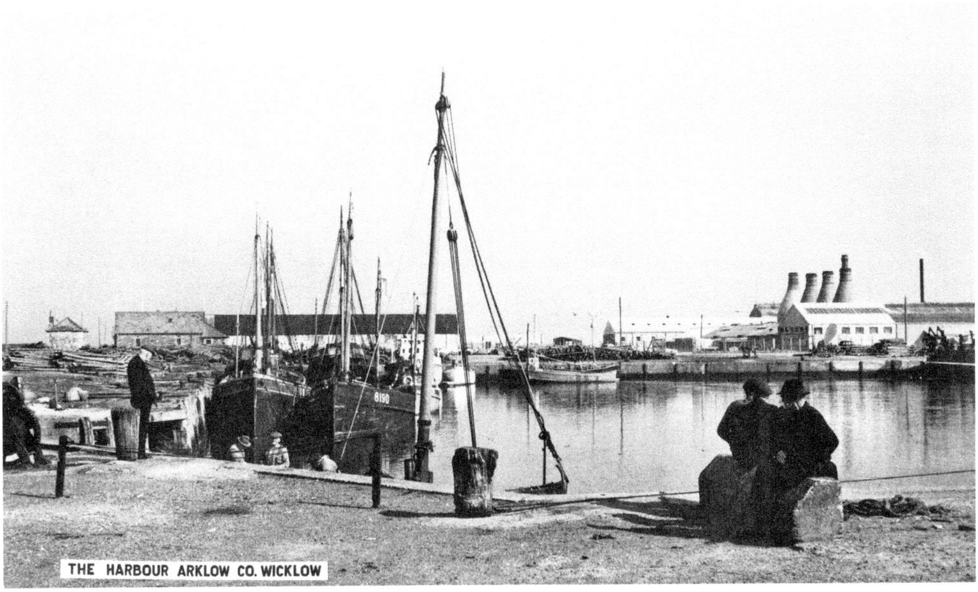

A busy Arklow harbour in the 1950s. The card shows part of the extensive dock buildings and a number of fishing vessels berthed in the harbour. Arklow was well known for copper exports, boat building and sea fishing. The town also had a reputation for producing fine pottery and knitwear. The inner harbour was built to reduce shipping congestion on the river.

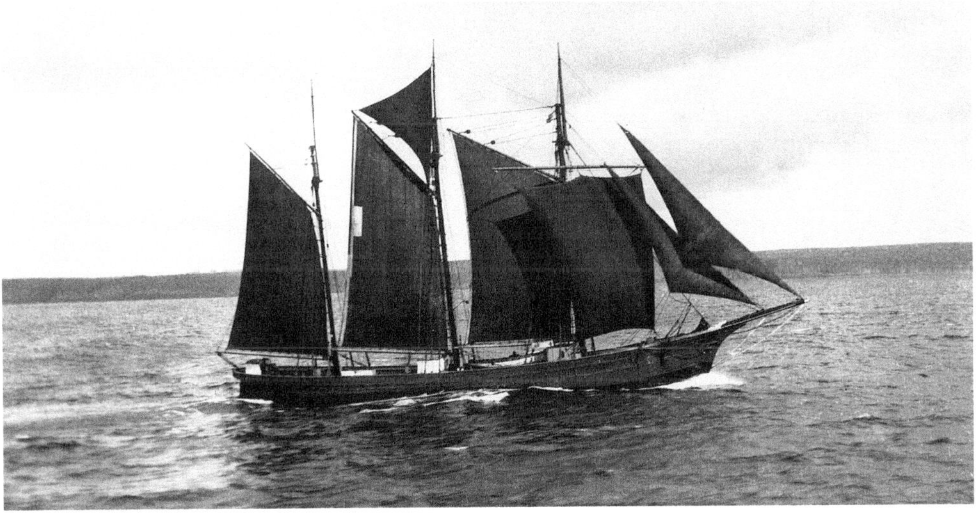

The *James Postlethwaite*, a three-masted wooden coastal schooner that sailed from Arklow after purchase in 1909. She was at Hamburg at the outbreak of the First World War and was commandeered by the German authorities. Her masts were cut down and she was used as a river barge during the war years. The crew was interned and they returned to Arklow with the ship in 1919. She had an auxiliary engine fitted in 1926 and continued to trade until she was laid up in Arklow in the early 1950s. The schooner was then used in John Huston's film *Moby Dick* and was renamed *Devil Dan* for the film. When the filming was complete, the schooner was taken to Youghal to be broken up.

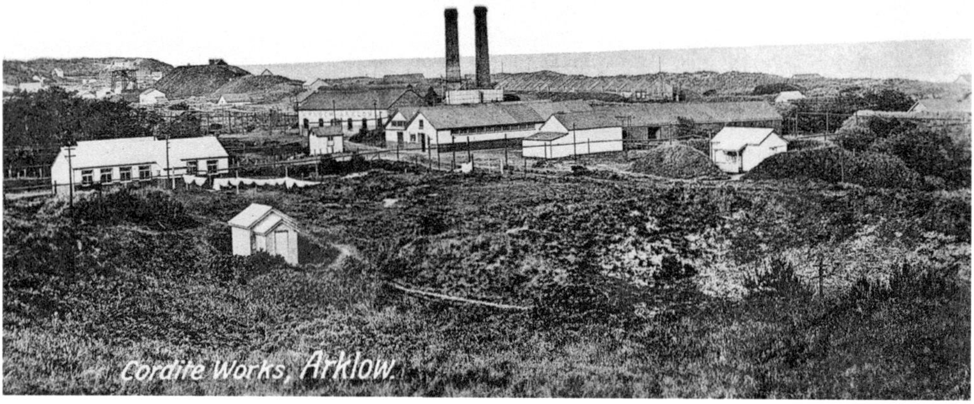

The Cordite Works, Arklow. Porter's Directory stated that the leading industry in Arklow in 1910 was the manufacture by Messrs. Kynoch, Ltd. of cordite, high explosives, guncotton and sulphuric acid. The Kynoch factory opened in 1895, initially producing cordite. It expanded and by 1910, around 500 people were employed at the works, which covered 120 hectares. Most of them lived near the works. The manufacture of these materials was hazardous and great care was taken to avoid accidents, although some did occur. The factory was very busy during the First World War, employing many more workers and producing large quantities of munitions for the troops. However, a big explosion occurred in 1917, causing the deaths of twenty-seven workers and extensive damage to the factory.

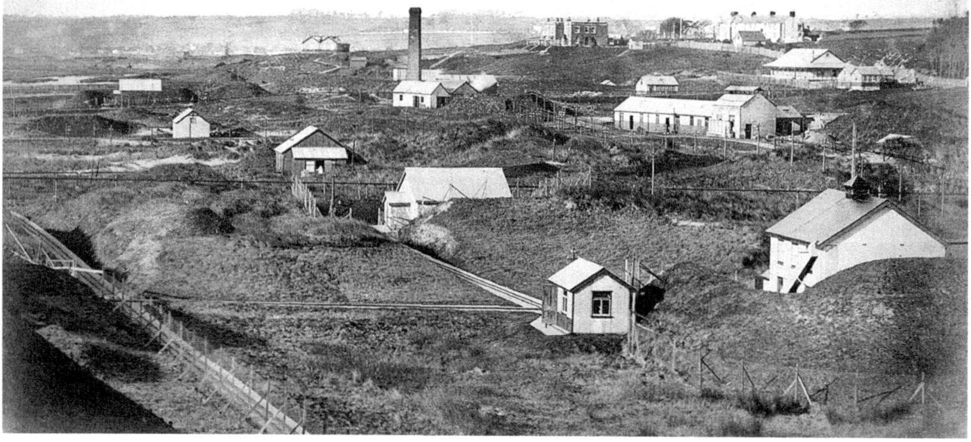

Postcard from Arklow dated 6 May 1907, showing the extensive industrial site with the sheds and chimneys of the various chemical factories, brick, tile and paving works.

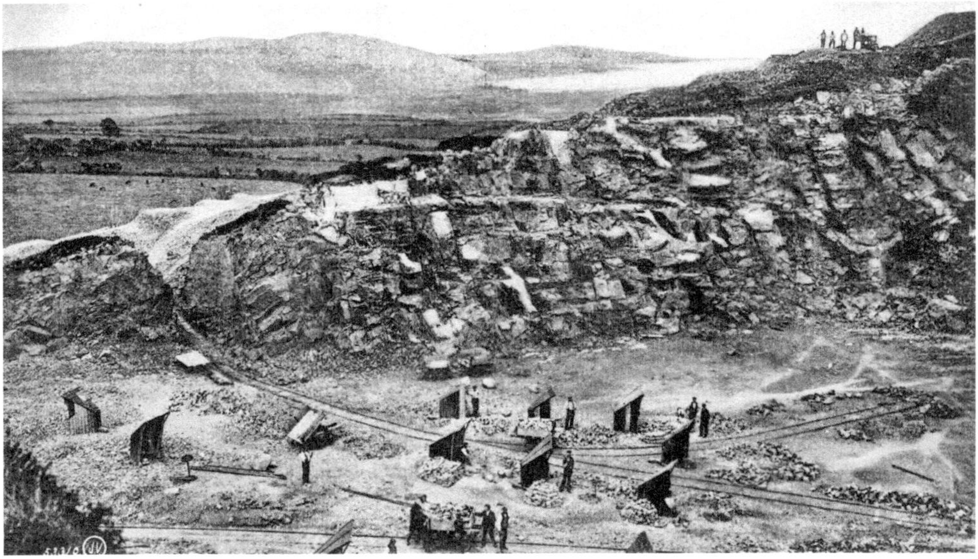

The Parnell Quarry, Arklow. In 1884, Charles Stewart Parnell, although a prominent politician, was also interested in industrial development. He rented Big Rock town land from his cousin William Proby, Earl of Carysfort, and began quarrying as there were rich deposits of granite and quartz. Parnell introduced new machinery and constructed an inclined railway from the quarry to Arklow harbour. Large amounts of granite were exported to Liverpool, Cardiff and Gibraltar from the port. The Parnell quarries continued until the 1920s, when commercial factors forced their closure. Apparently, while working at the quarry, Parnell crushed his hand in machinery and a servant dressed the injured fingers with cobwebs from the cellar walls, which stopped the bleeding. Galen is said to have used cobwebs in a similar way in Egypt around AD 200.

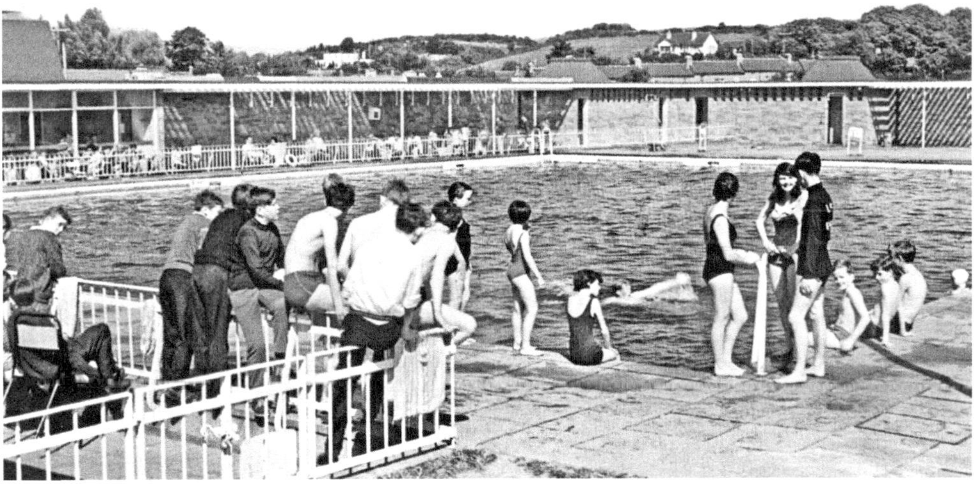

Youngsters gather at the Holiday Centre open-air swimming pool at Arklow in the early 1960s. At the time, this was said to be one of the finest amusement centres in Ireland. There was a games room, a large boating lake, a pitch and putt golf course, and facilities for tennis and croquet. There was dancing each night and regular concerts in the ballroom.

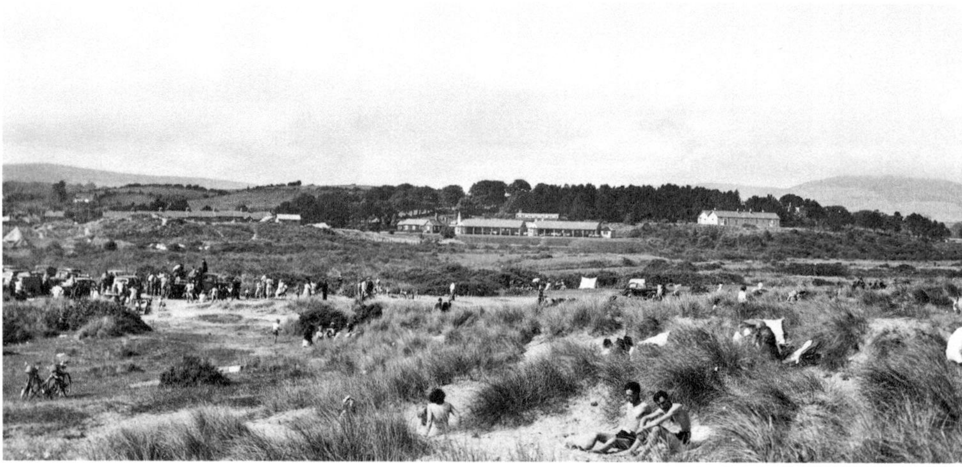

Holidaymakers enjoying the sunshine on the sand dunes, North Beach, Arklow, *c.* 1960. The sandy beach was very popular and was known for its safe bathing. The dunes are also a site of special interest for rare wildlife species and plants.

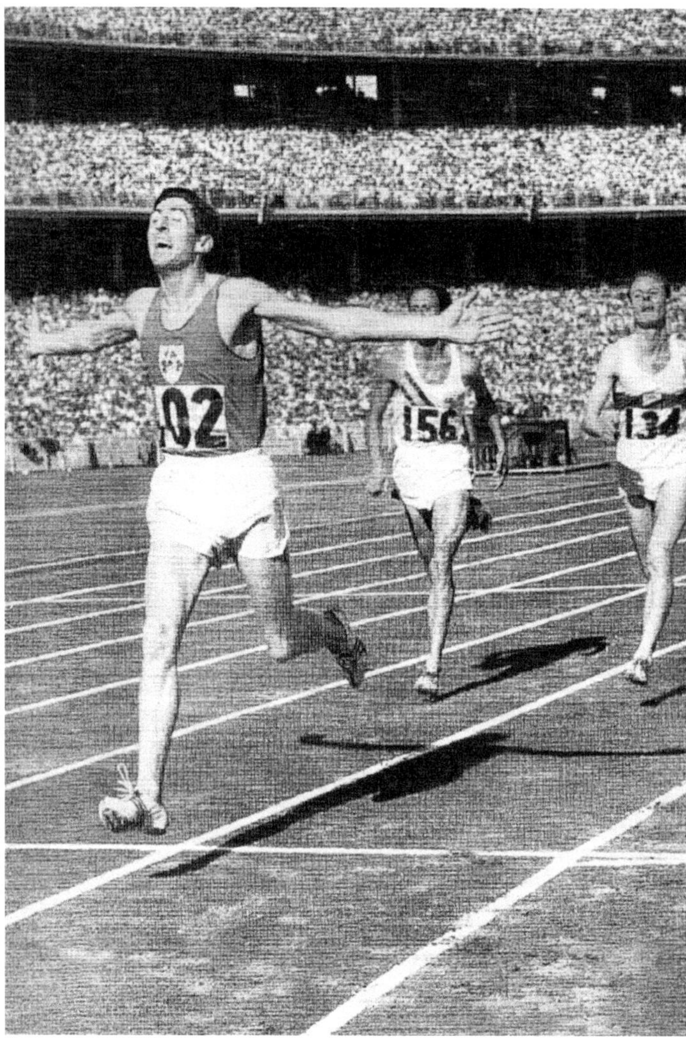

Ron Delaney, the great Irish athlete, was born in Arklow on 6 March 1935. Here he is shown winning the 1,500 metres final in the Summer Olympics held in Melbourne in 1956. He won the race in the new Olympic record time of 3 minutes 41.2 seconds. There was great celebration as no Irishman had won an Olympic gold medal in athletics since Bob Tisdall in the 400-metre hurdles race in Los Angeles in 1932.

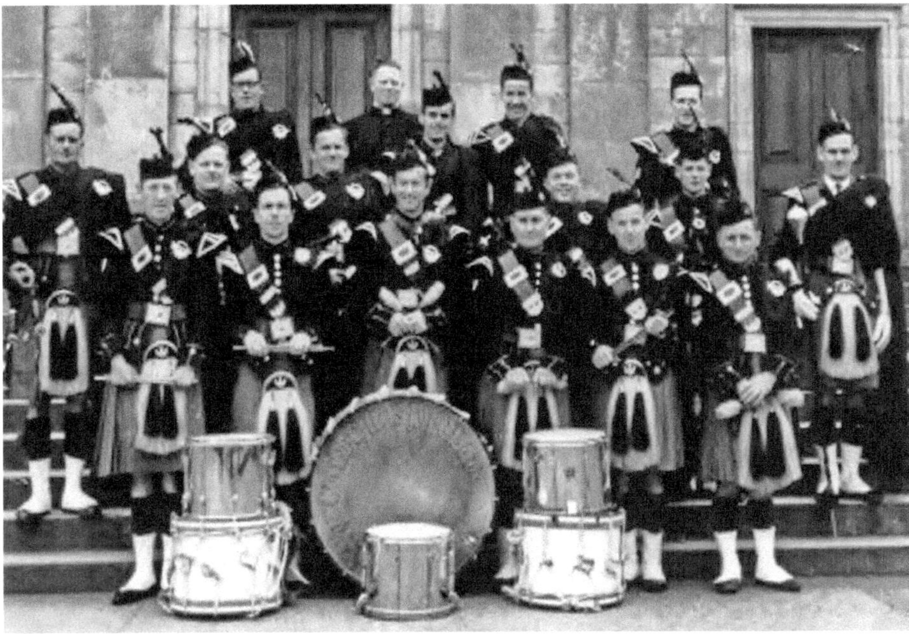

St Colmcilles Pipe Band, Arklow, 1964. From left to right, back row: Lar Cullen, Fr Battelle, Larry Kenny, Tommy Duffy; middle row: John O'Brien, George Brennan, Willie Walker, Pat O'Brien, Dinny Kavanagh, Olly Redmond, Nicky Brennan; front row: Charlie Gaule, Michael Morgan, Paddy Kavanagh, Jimmy Storey, Pat Byrne, John Byrne.

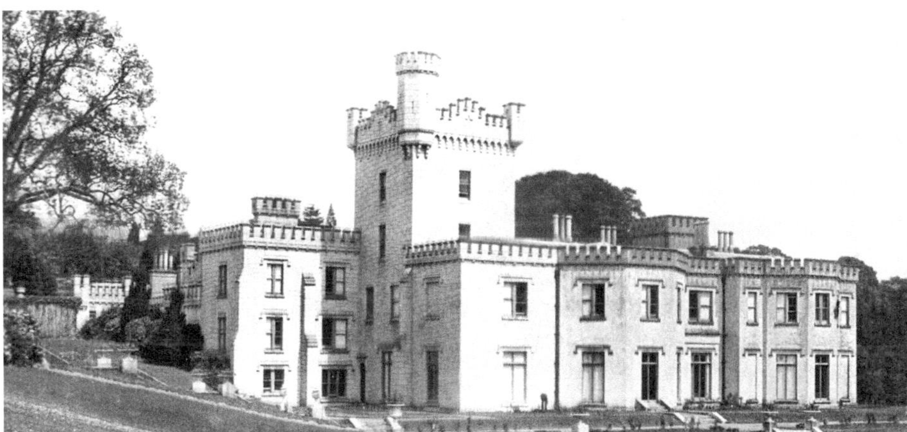

Glenart Castle, on the road from Woodenbridge to Arklow, was built around 1750 as a hunting lodge, but was enlarged to a castle in the early 1800s by John Joshua Proby, the first Earl of Carysfort. It was formerly known as Kilcarra Castle. The building is dominated by the square tower with battlements. William Proby, the fifth Earl of Carysfort, was born in 1836. He became High Sheriff in 1866 and Lord Lieutenant of County Wicklow in 1890. He married Charlotte, daughter of Revd Robert Booshy, in 1860, but the marriage was childless and the titles expired on his death in 1868. The castle later became the Retreat House of the Vincentian Fathers and was called 'St Kevins'.

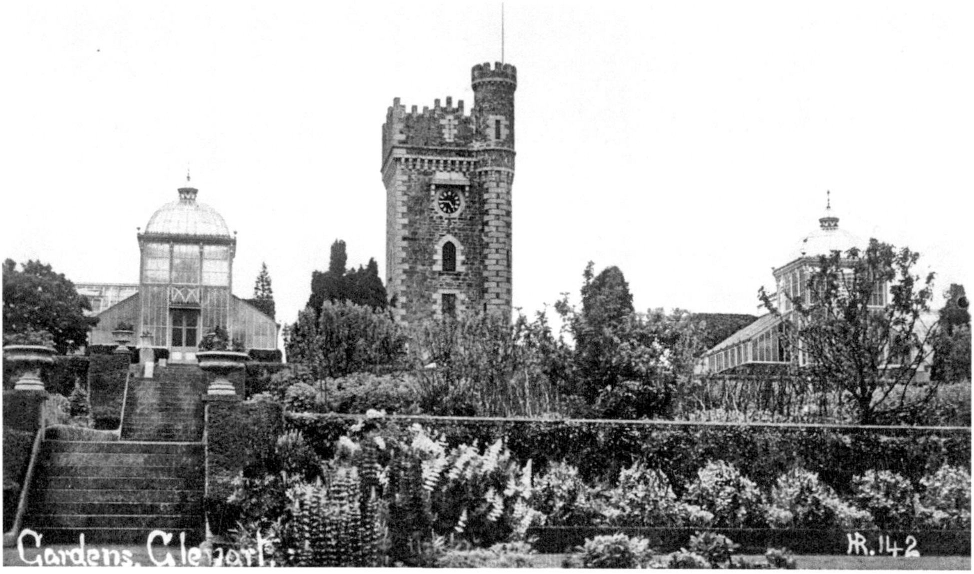

Glenart Castle had over 24 hectares of grounds and woodlands. William Shepherd was employed by William Proby, the fifth Earl of Carysfort, to make new gardens in 1872. The gardens were beautifully landscaped with picturesque rock gardens and superb terraces. There were specimen trees, ferns and alpine plants. The large glasshouses housed exotic plants.

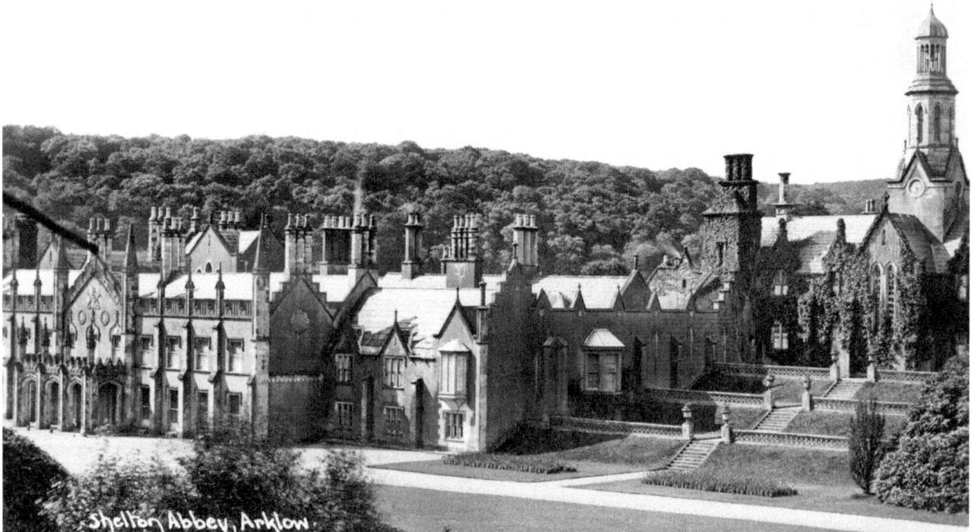

Shelton Abbey, Arklow. This was the ancestral home of the Howard family, Earls of Wicklow. The postcard message, dated 28 December 1910, gives a flavour of Christmas at the abbey as it describes a Christmas dinner with a big Christmas tree from which everyone got presents. The hunt was meeting there the following morning. The children on the estate were to have their Christmas tree and there was to be a fancy-dress ball held that night.

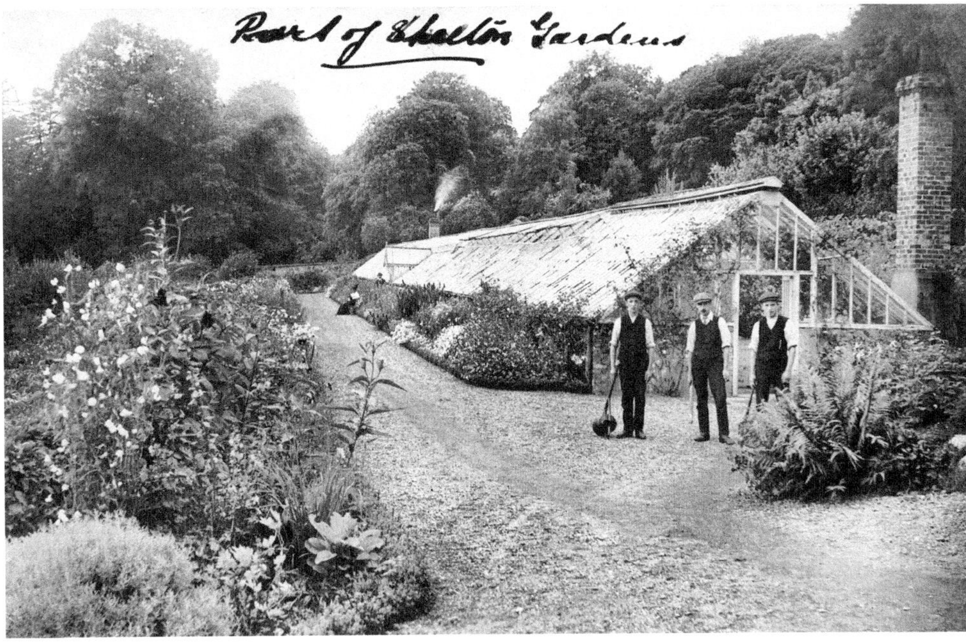

There were extensive landscaped gardens at Shelton Abbey. This card, posted in September 1910, shows one of the greenhouses with some of the gardeners from the estate. The Howard family last lived at the abbey in the early 1900s and later it was used by the Irish State as a detention centre. The last member of the Howard family, William Cecil Howard, eighth Earl of Wicklow (see page 4), who had no descendants, died in 1979 and his title, Earl of Wicklow, became extinct.

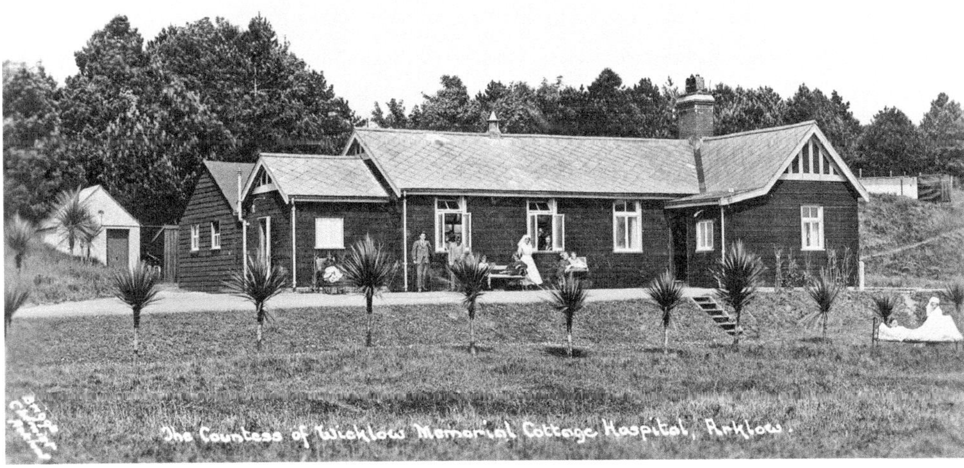

Nurses and patients in the grounds of the Countess of Wicklow Memorial Hospital, Arklow. The hospital opened in April 1921 after buildings belonging to Kynochs, who built the Cordite factory in Arklow, were adapted to make a much-needed hospital for the area. There were three wards and an operating theatre. The hospital was very busy and had to be further extended in 1931 and 1932.

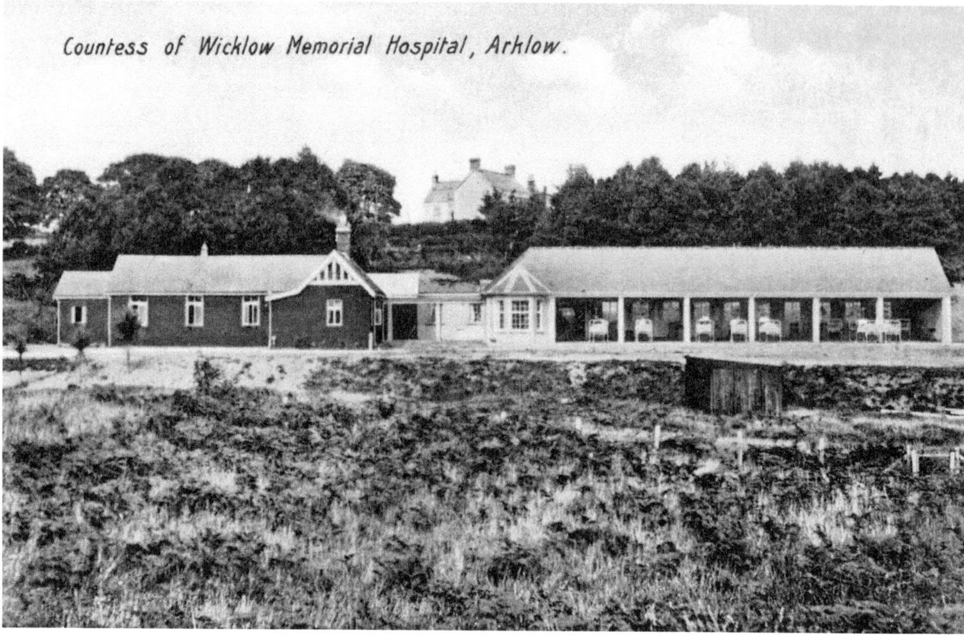

The open wards at the Countess of Wicklow Memorial Hospital, Arklow. In the pre-antibiotic era, therapy for tuberculosis (TB) included bed rest, fresh air and sunshine. The hospital had a good reputation and was recognised as a centre for the treatment of bone tuberculosis. On the open-air wards the patients were fully exposed to the outdoors at night, even in the winter. Despite the cold nights, many patients preferred to be on these wards. The treatment led to some successful outcomes, when the patient's own immune defences overcame the infection. However, in October 1943, Albert Schatz, a 23-year-old graduate at Rutger's University, New Jersey, discovered streptomycin, which was the first effective treatment for TB. Over the following years the drug saved many lives and many sanatoriums were closed. The Countess of Wicklow Memorial Hospital finally closed in July 1961.

3

RATHDRUM, GLENDALOUGH & WICKLOW TOWN

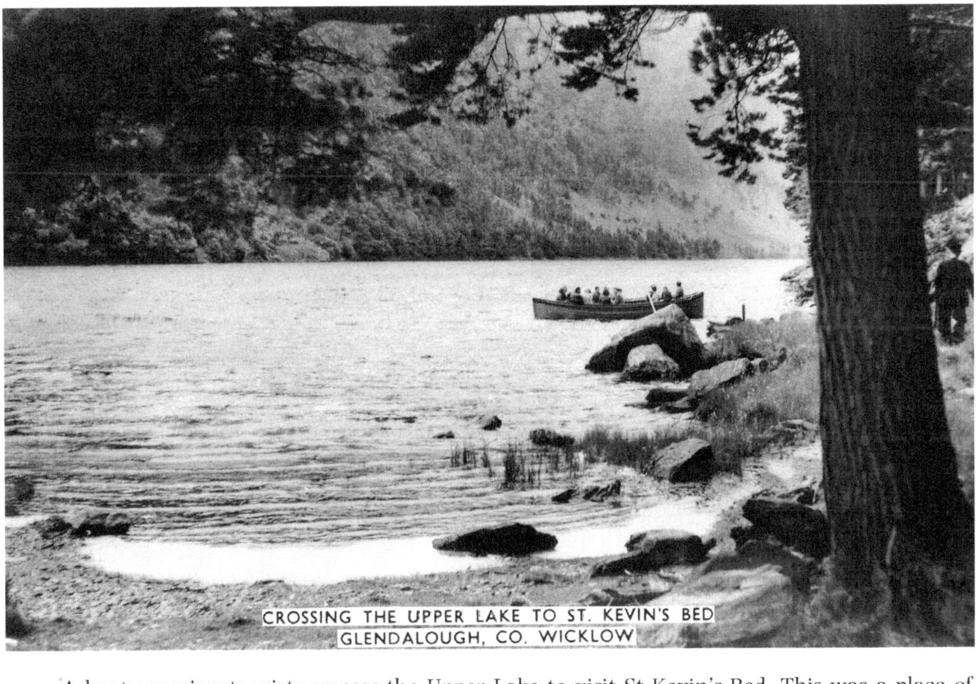

A boat carrying tourists crosses the Upper Lake to visit St Kevin's Bed. This was a place of retreat and solitude for St Kevin. Here he could pursue a life of prayer, fasting and penance. The bed was excavated in bare rock about 90 metres high on the cliff overhanging the Upper Lake. It is only 1.21 metres wide, 2.13 metres long and 1.06 metres high. Some archaeologists think that the bed was originally a prehistoric rock-cut tomb.

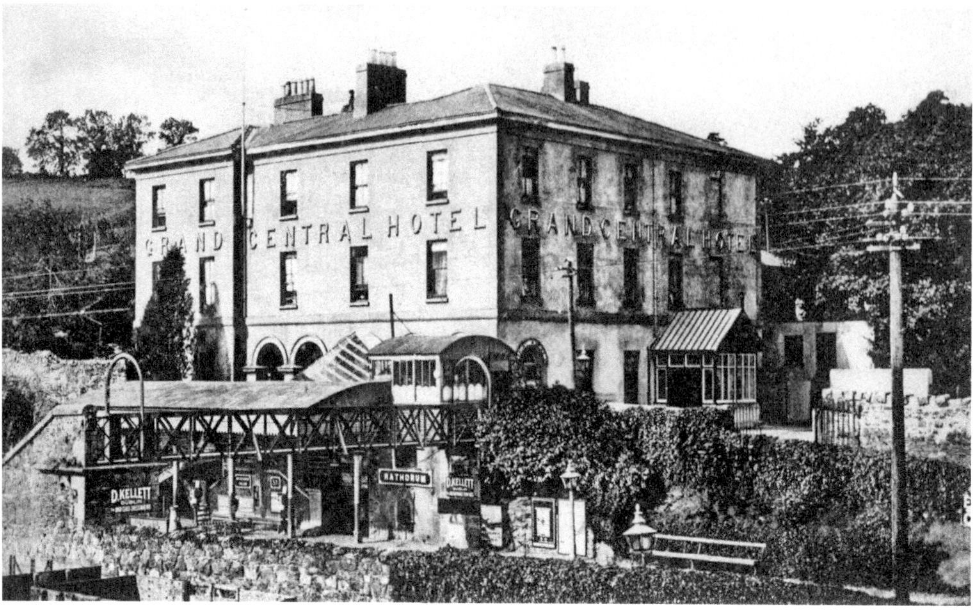

The Grand Central Hotel and railway station on a card dated 1905. The station opened on 18 July 1863. The hotel was built adjacent to the station by the Dublin and South Eastern Railway as 'The Royal Fitzwilliam Hotel' and opened on 26 October 1863. It was run by the Breslin sisters. The railways brought an increase in visitors to Rathdrum and many stayed at the hotel. However, over the years business declined and while the station is still open on the Dublin-Rosslare line, the hotel closed in 1931.

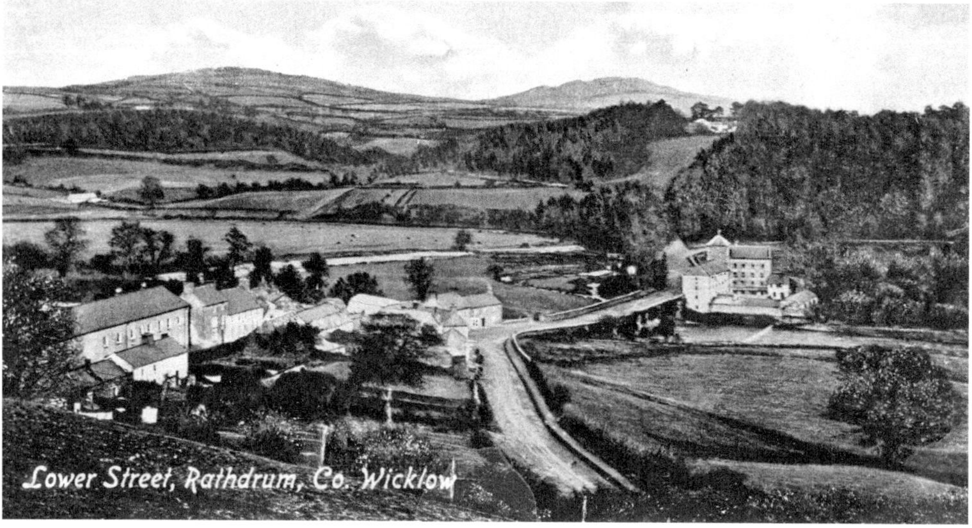

A distant view of Rathdrum on a card posted in July 1917, published by J. Wedick, stationer of Rathdrum. The village is built on a hill on the western side of the beautiful Avonmore Valley. The view shows the valley and hills in the distance and the street curving down to the bridge over the River Avonmore. The bridge has four arches and it leads to the mill on the far bank of the river.

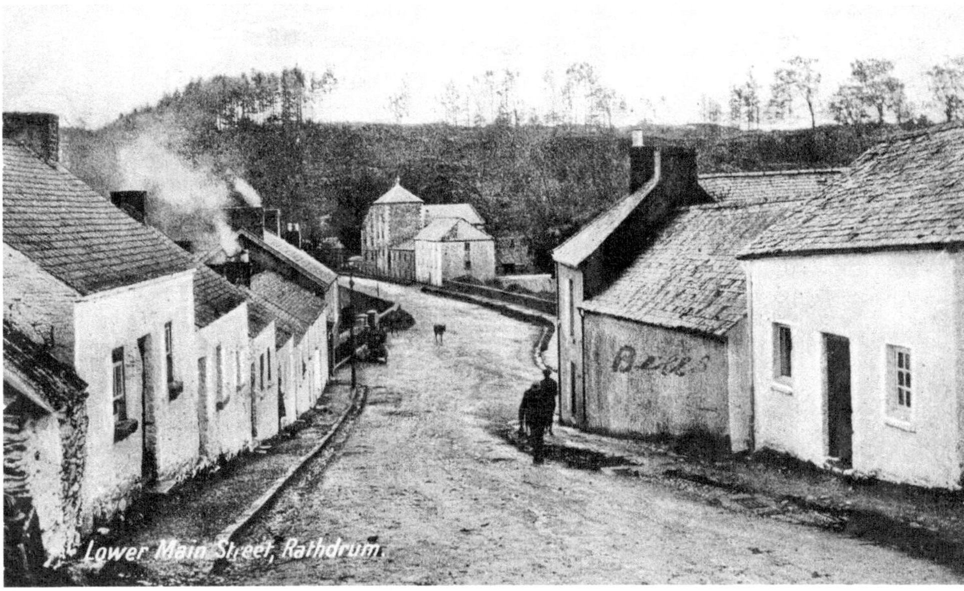

Lower Main Street, Rathdrum, looking down the street towards the bridge, *c*. 1920. The single-storey cottages, which have slate roofs, slope down the fairly steep gradient. At the bottom of the street, over the bridge on the right, is Rathdrum Mill. The flour mill was taken over by James Comerford around 1850. He expanded the business and in 1880 he built an additional waterwheel, running four pairs of millstones.

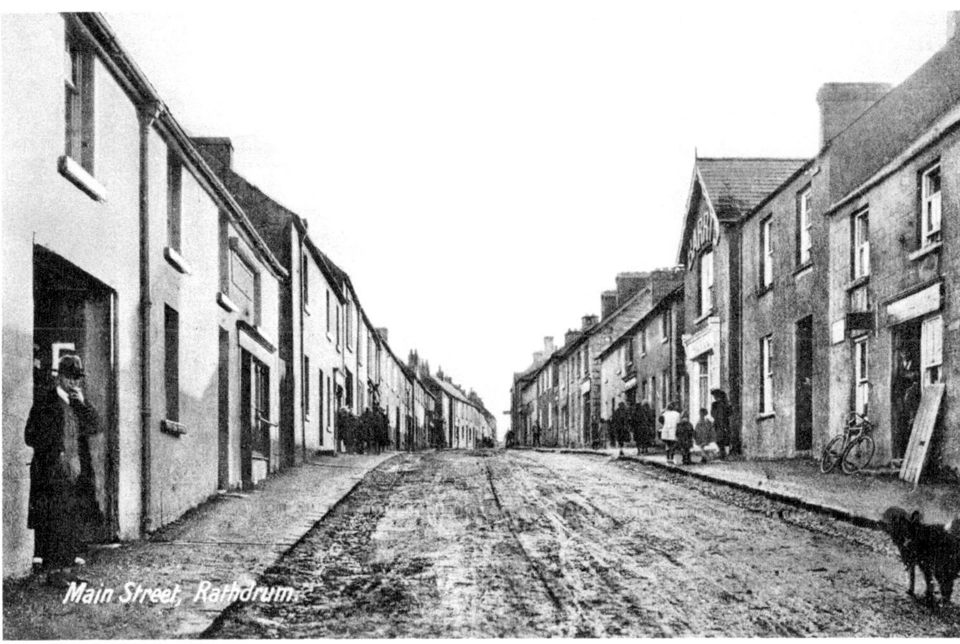

Upper Main Street, Rathdrum, *c*. 1920. The road is quiet with a few pedestrians. A man stands in the doorway of the post office on the right. There is a mixture of housing and traditional shop fronts with rendered and painted finishes. All open directly on to the street.

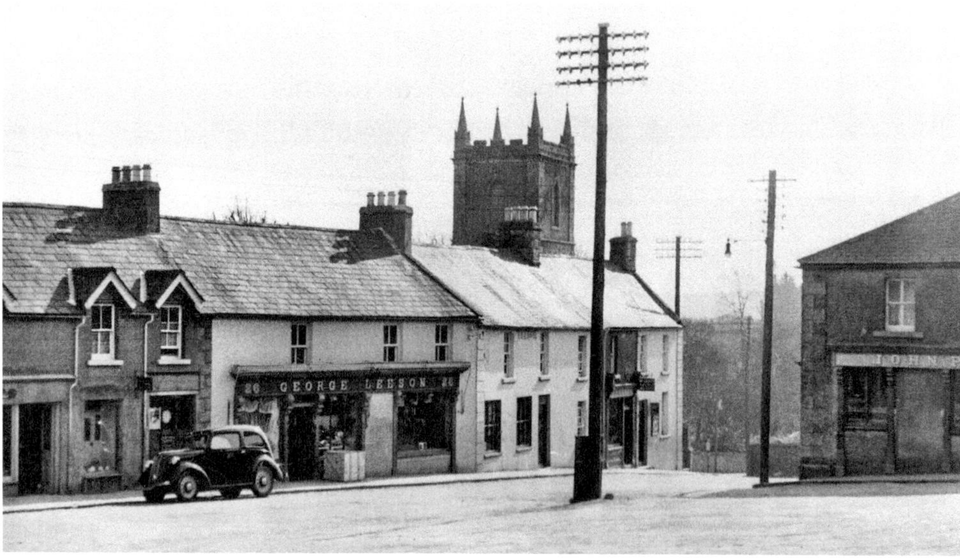

Rathdrum is a market town and popular tourist centre. In the early 1900s, the town was an important centre for the woollen trade. The card shows the Market Square with the tower of St Saviour's church in the background, *c.* 1950s. Charles S. Parnell was baptised at this church on 9 August 1846. A car is parked outside the draper's shop owned by George Leeson. Market Square has been used for shooting scenes in many Irish films over the years. The telegraph poles shown on the postcard had to be taken down and wires placed underground to enable scenes from earlier times to be filmed. In 1995, the actor Liam Neeson played Michael Collins. In one memorable scene from the film, he addressed a large crowd in Market Square while standing in front of the Railway Bar.

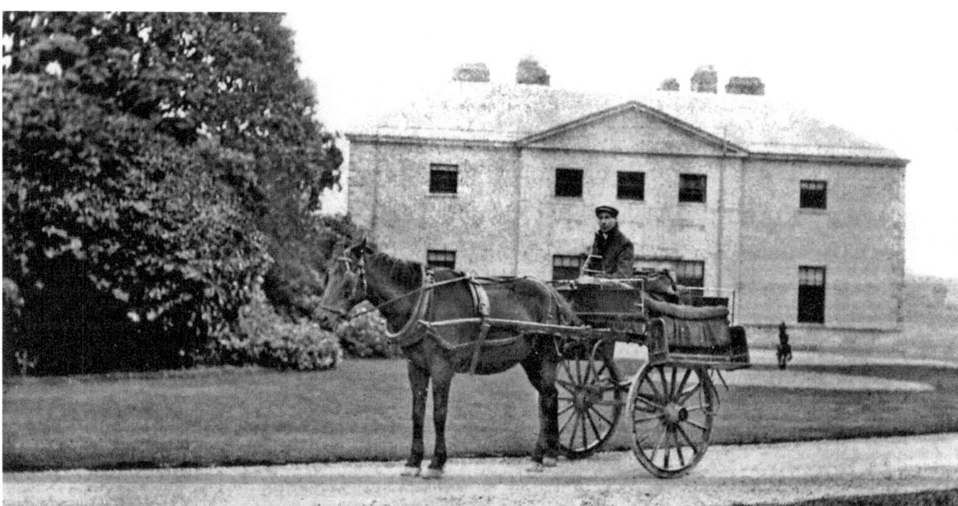

A sidecar sits outside Avondale House, Rathdrum, which was the birthplace and home of Charles S. Parnell. The fine Georgian house, designed by the English architect James Wyatt, was originally built in 1777 for Samuel Hayes, a barrister who represented Wicklow in the Irish House of Commons. When he died in 1795, the house passed to the Parnell family.

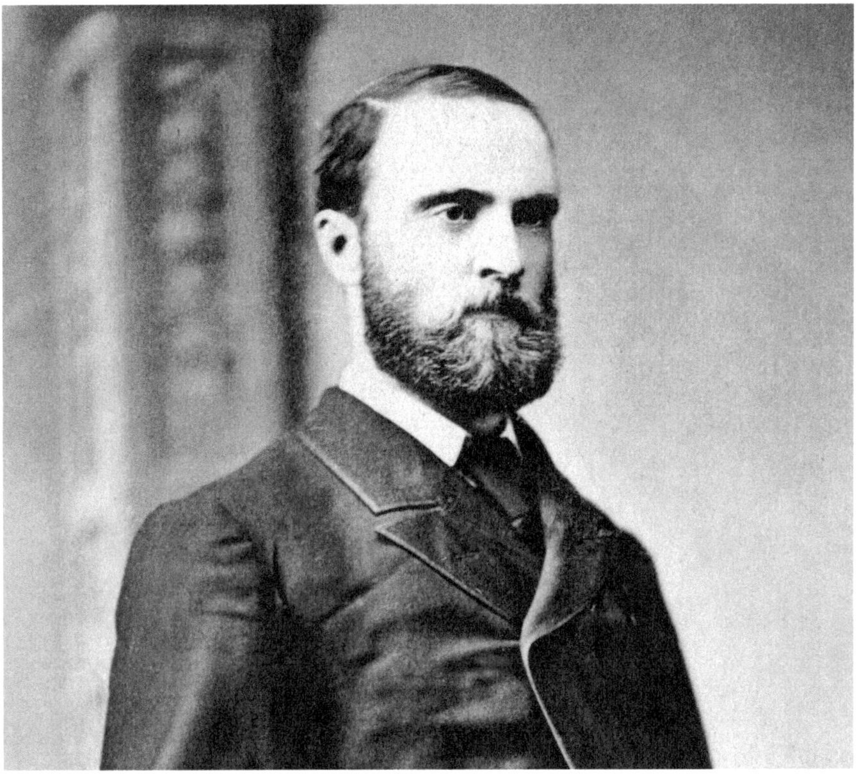

Charles S. Parnell was born at Avondale House in 1846. He was one of eleven children. In his infancy, the Great Famine (1845-50) devastated County Wicklow. In fact, over 8,000 people are buried in the famine graveyard at Rathdrum. However, Charles had a privileged life. He hunted with the Wicklow Harriers and went to Cambridge University. In 1875 he was elected MP for County Meath. He brought public attention to the Irish Question and was a strong supporter of the Land League, which was founded in 1879 by Michael Davitt. The aim was to reduce the power of the landlords in Ireland.

Obstructive tactics in parliament led by Parnell and the use of the boycott against landlords in Ireland eventually led to reform with a series of land acts, which gave more security of tenure for tenants and fairer rents fixed by the courts. Parnell wanted Home Rule and self-government for Ireland. In 1882, he founded the Irish National League to push for Home Rule even ahead of land reform. He became popularly known as the 'Uncrowned King of Ireland'. Prime Minister William Gladstone saw that some agreement with Parnell and his party would help bring peace in Ireland and the first Home Rule Bill, proposing setting up a parliament in Dublin, was introduced in 1886. However, all went wrong when Parnell was named as co-respondent in a divorce case by Captain William O'Shea, with whose wife he had been having an affair. Parnell did not contest the action. In Victorian Ireland, this was not thought proper and the affair drew strong criticism from the Church and split the Irish Nationalist Party. Gladstone said that he would not support home rule for Ireland with Parnell as leader and asked him to resign. Without the full support of his party, Parnell had little choice. He resigned and married Catherine O'Shea on 25 June 1891 and they went to live in Brighton. However, later that year he suffered a bout of rheumatic fever and died suddenly on 6 October 1891, aged only 45 years.

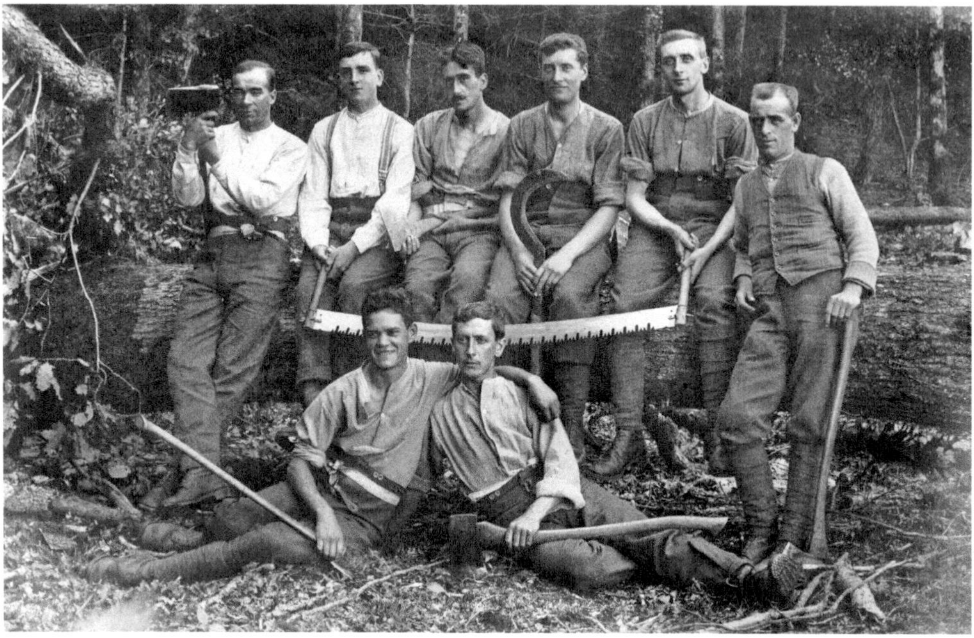

Avondale House had an estate of 200 hectares of forest and parkland with many rare trees. The first forestry school in Ireland was at Avondale. The postcard shows workers on a break from tree felling at Avon Lodge camp, Rathdrum in September 1916. The local photographer was T.D. Plunkett.

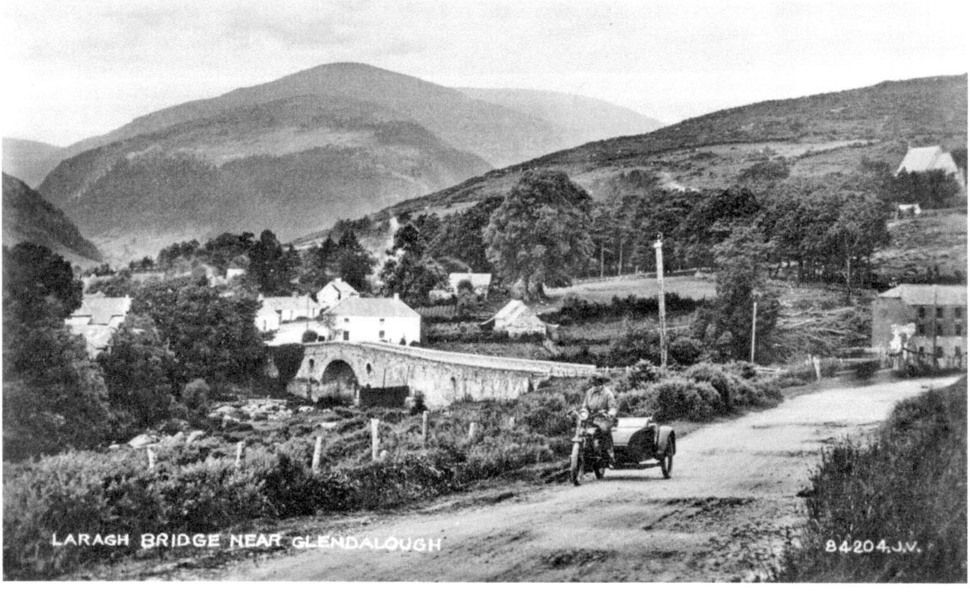

Laragh is a place where many roads meet as the mountain ranges and the glens converge. To the north is the Sally Gap, to the west are Glendalough and the Wicklow Gap and to the south is Glenalmure Valley. In this picture, a motorcyclist with sidecar is passing Laragh Bridge on his way to Glendalough.

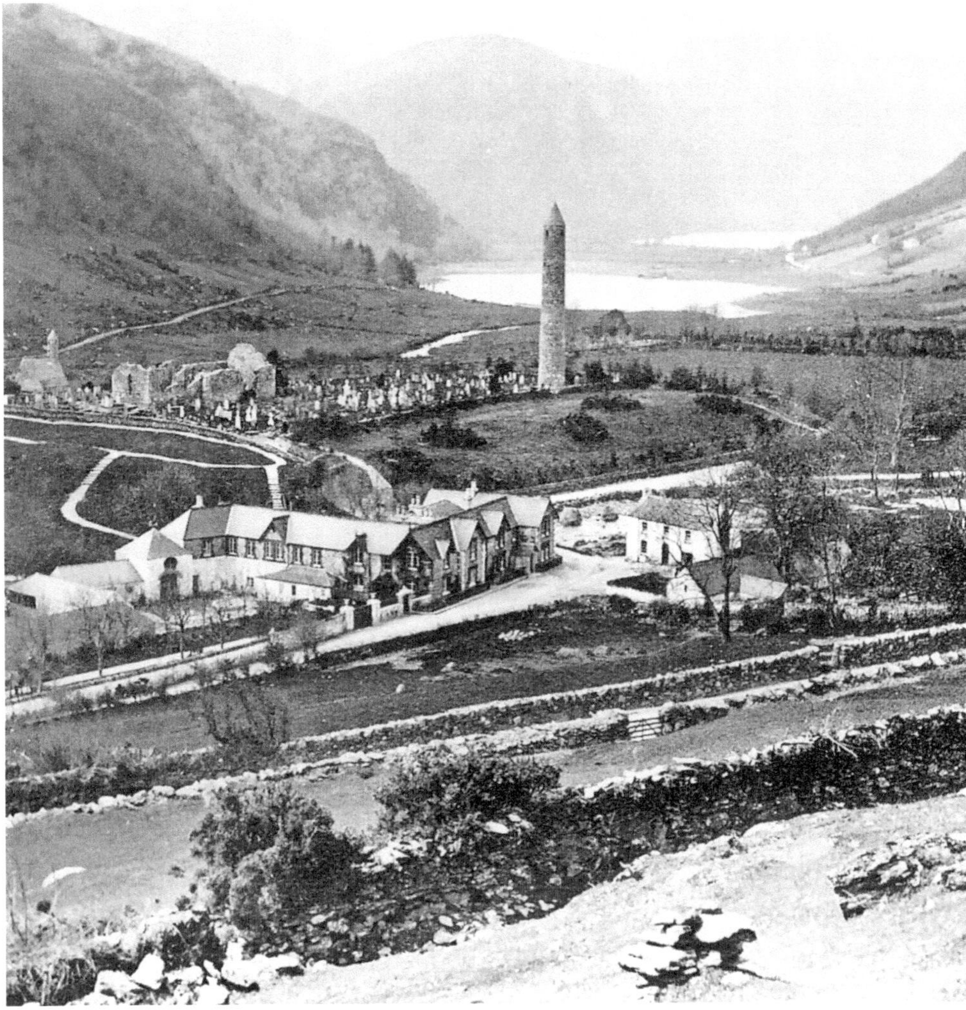

A view of Glendalough, *c.* 1890, showing the Royal Hotel, the monastic settlement founded by St Kevin in the sixth century and the Upper and Lower Lakes. It is a historic area with ruins of early Christian monastic churches, a round tower and a medieval cathedral.

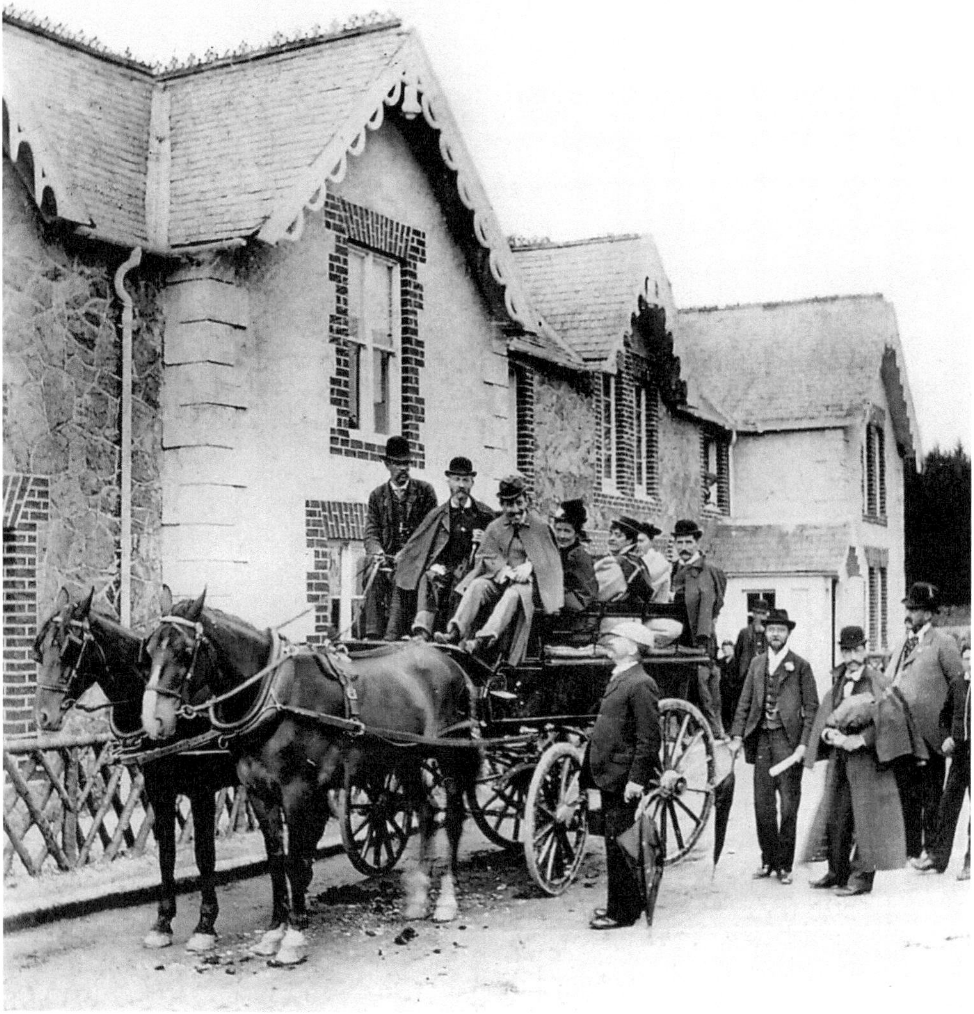

A crowded horse-drawn carriage outside the Royal Hotel, Glendalough, *c.* 1890. The carriage is preparing to depart on a sightseeing tour around the local beauty spots and historic sites. More hotel residents wait for the next carriage. The glaciated valley with the two lakes is famous for its wild beauty.

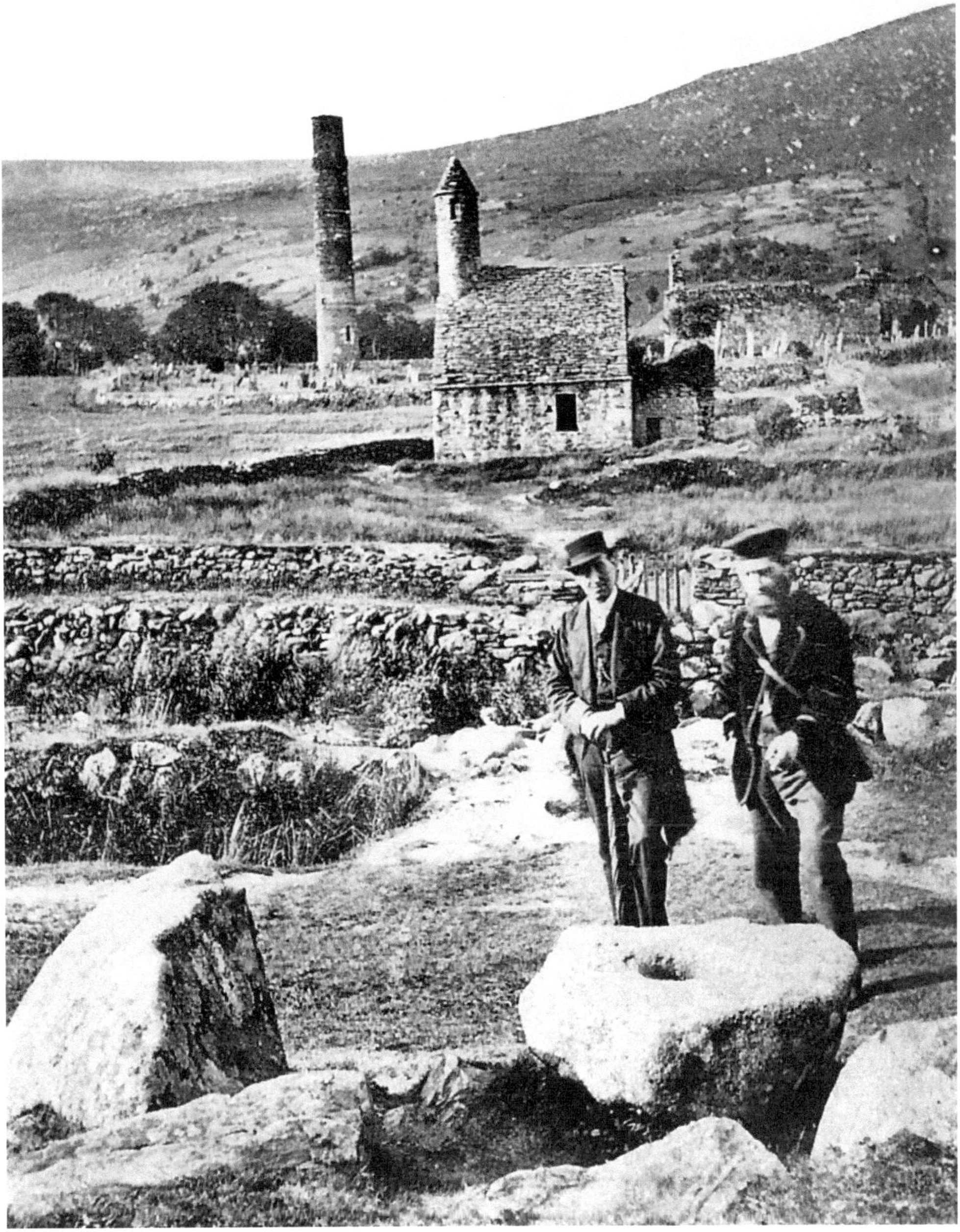

Visitors to Glendalough standing by the Deer Stone, which has a cup-like hollow and may well have been an early baptismal font. Directly behind them is St Kevin's church (known as St Kevin's Kitchen), which was built in the twelfth century, and the large Round Tower, which was the bell tower of the cathedral and a place of shelter in time of attack. The Round Tower has no conical cap, which must have fallen in, and this dates the picture to between 1860 and 1876, as it is known that the conical roof on the Round Tower was rebuilt in 1876 using the original stones.

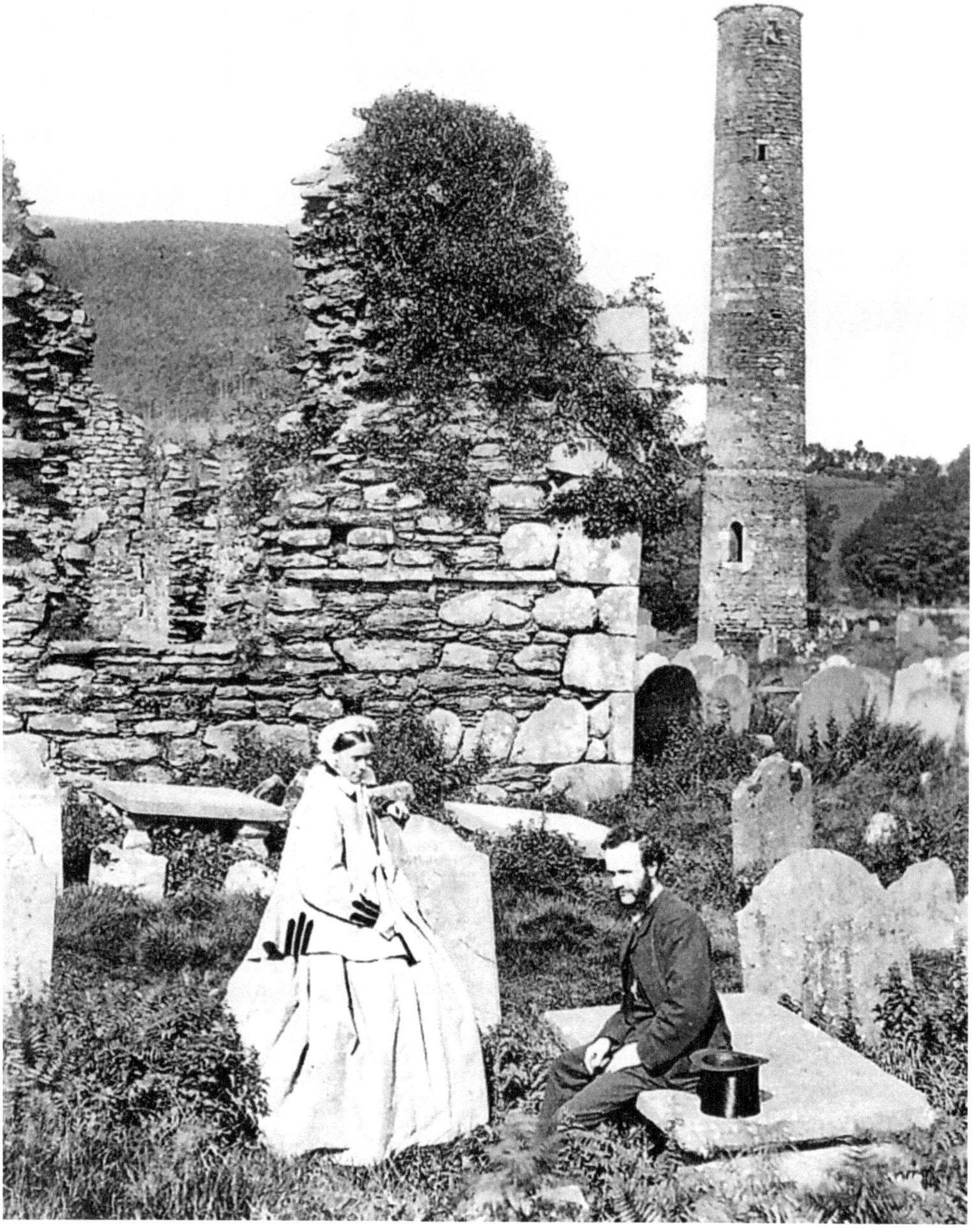

Glendalough has been attracting pilgrims to its tranquil setting since the fifth century. Considering the attacks to the settlement (particularly by the Vikings and the English over the years), it is surprising that parts of the monastery have survived, as have several churches, the cathedral and the Round Tower. This picture from 1875 shows a couple in formal dress taking a rest to enjoy the timelessness and peace of Glendalough. Certainly, it is a special place of pilgrimage, which continues to draw visitors and scholars from all over the world.

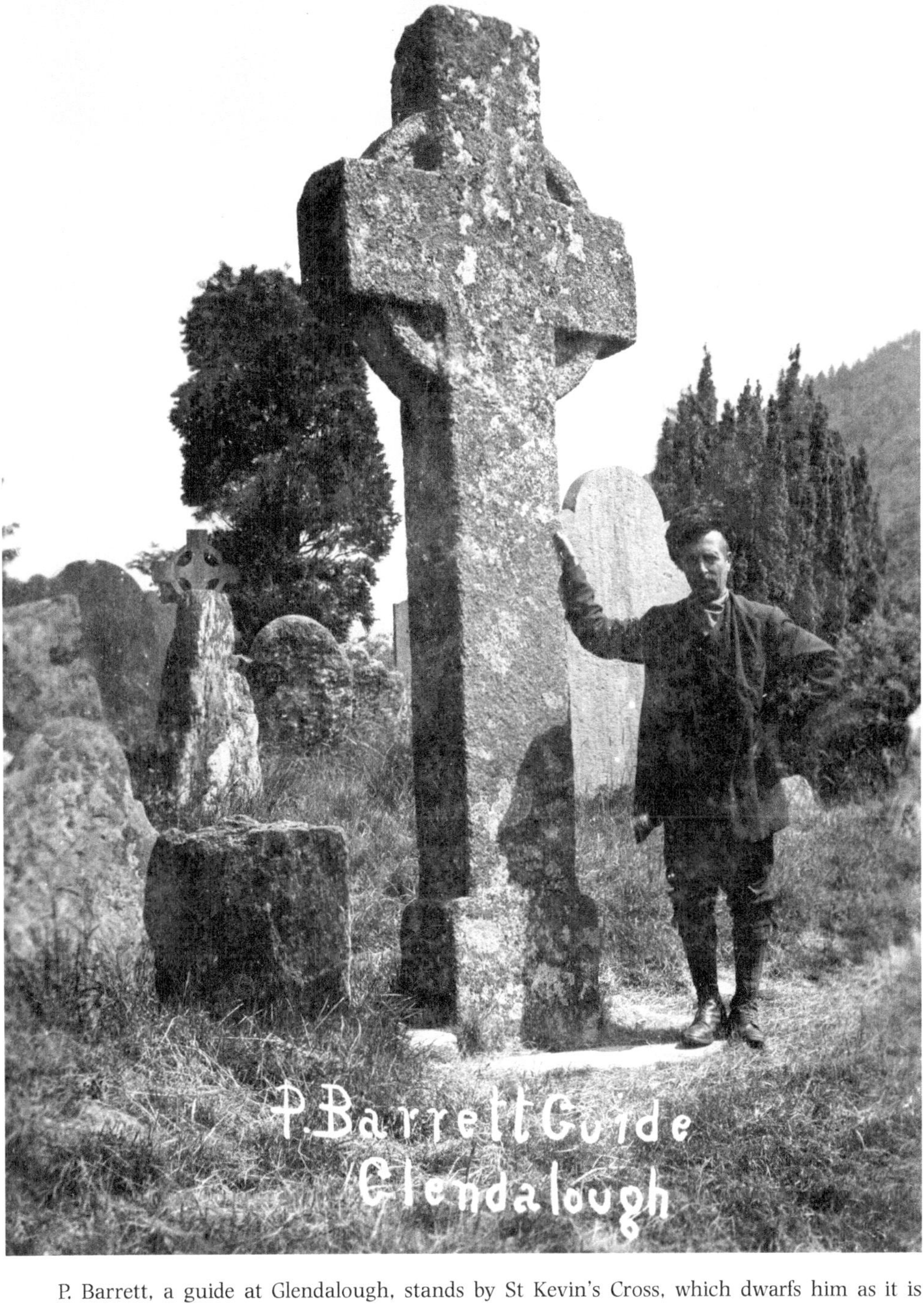

P. Barrett, a guide at Glendalough, stands by St Kevin's Cross, which dwarfs him as it is 2.5 metres tall. This high plain cross was built of local granite in the sixth century and it stands between the Priest's House and the cathedral. It is one of the oldest crosses in Ireland and with the enclosing unpierced circle representing the sun, it is intermediate between the Pagan Pillar stone and the Celtic Christian cross.

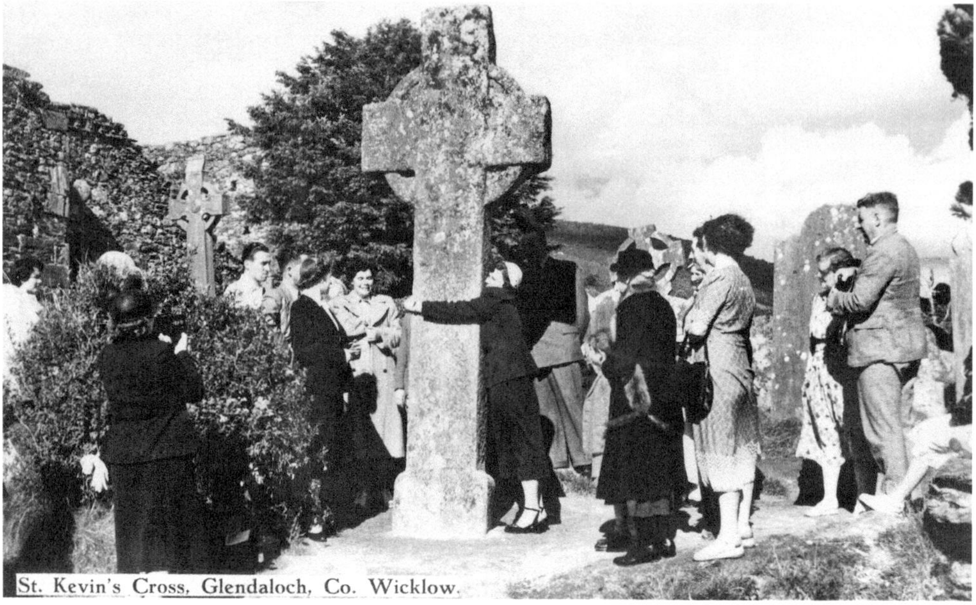

Tourists clasp the Wishing Cross at Glendalough, *c.* 1950s. All hope for a special favour as legend says that if their arms can embrace the cross and fingertips meet, they will have their wishes granted.

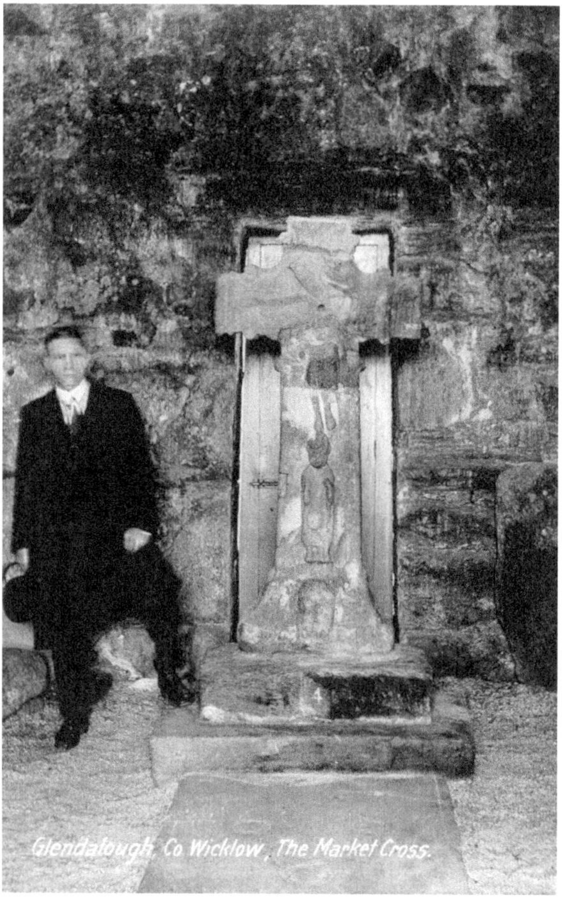

A tourist stands by the unique Market Cross in St Kevin's church at Glendalough. This ornamented cross dates to the eighth or ninth century and one Irish inscription with Greek lettering on the cross slab reads 'Pray for Bresal: Alpha Omega, Jesus Christ'. Bresal is a god in Irish mythology and alpha and omega are the first and last letters of the Greek alphabet, which represent the eternal nature of Jesus Christ.

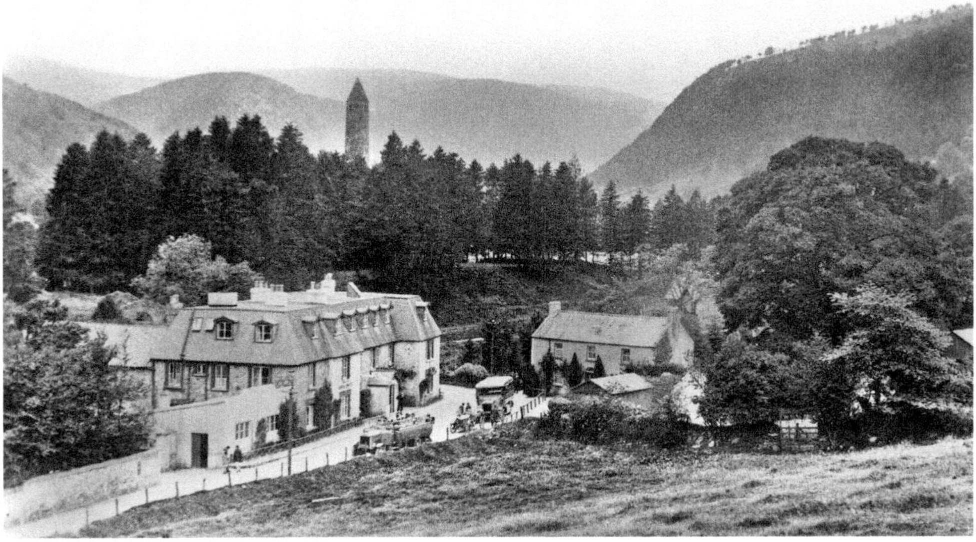

A later view of the Royal Hotel, Glendalough, showing two motor coaches parked outside. The Round Tower with its conical cap is seen in the distance. The Dublin firm of Messrs. Thompsons had two large Commer motor coaches, which were used for the popular excursion service from Dublin to Glendalough.

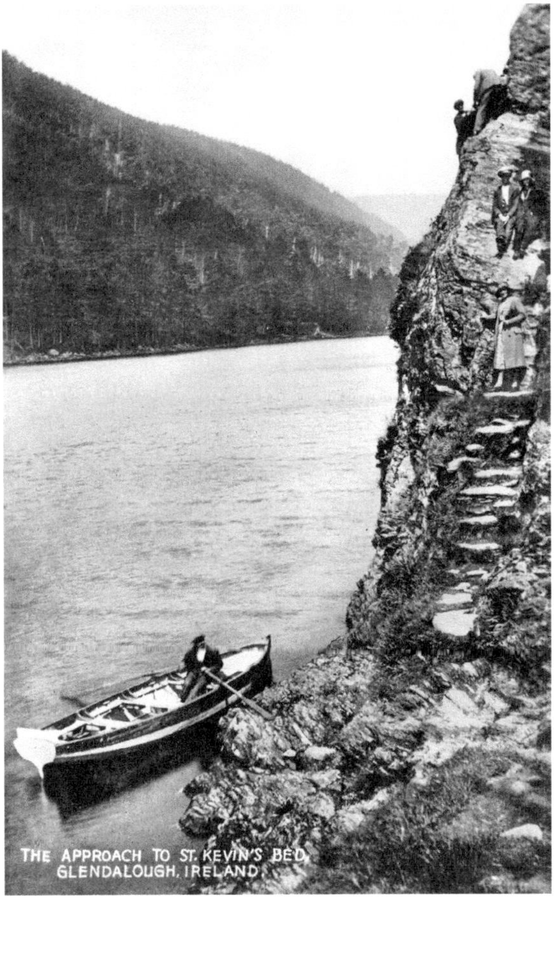

Visitors descending the steep steps on the approach to St Kevin's Bed pose for the photographer. It does not look like an easy climb. On the lake the boatman awaits the visitors' return to his boat, so that he can ferry them back across the lake.

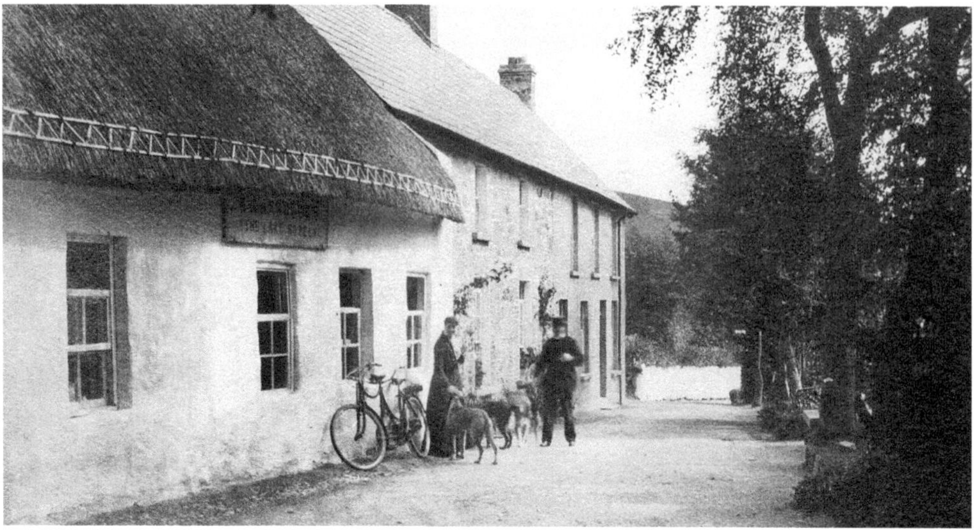

An early view of Richardson's Cottage by the lake, Glendalough, on a card posted in September 1904. The cottage was a peaceful oasis and a place to relax. However, crossroad dancing was held there for many years. This was a popular social event and the local people would gather at the crossroads for set dancing and the opportunity to meet a partner. Folklore says that if you grab a partner at the place where two paths meet and dance a jig with pure joy in your heart, fertility and abundance will soon be on its way! An attempt was made to ban crossroad dancing in Ireland by the Public Dance Halls Act in 1935. However, in this area, the practice continued up to the 1950s.

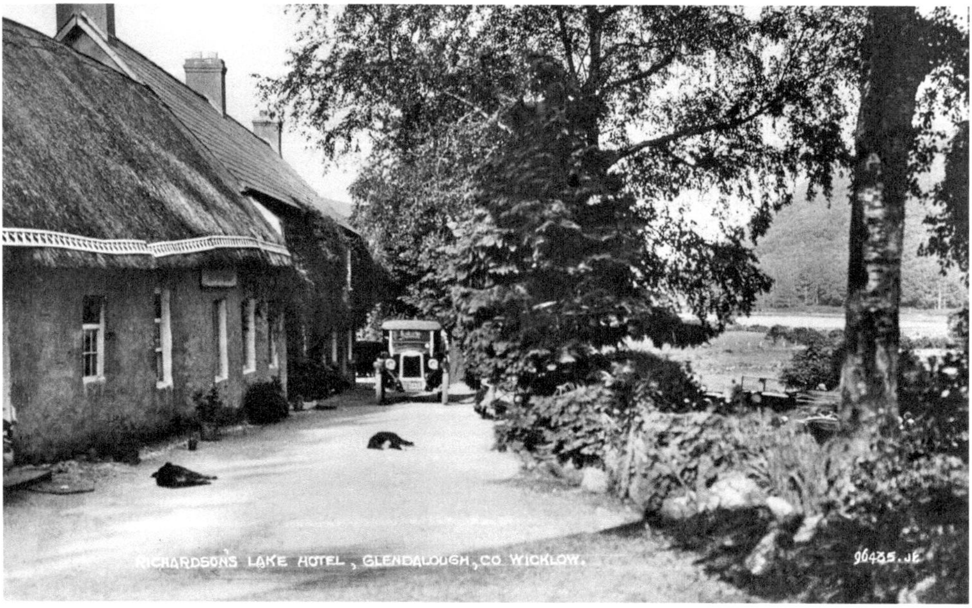

A later view of Richardson's Lake Hotel in the 1920s. An early motorcar is parked outside and there are two sleeping dogs on the road. At this time, the terrace of the hotel was used each summer for the production of plays by groups of actors from Dublin.

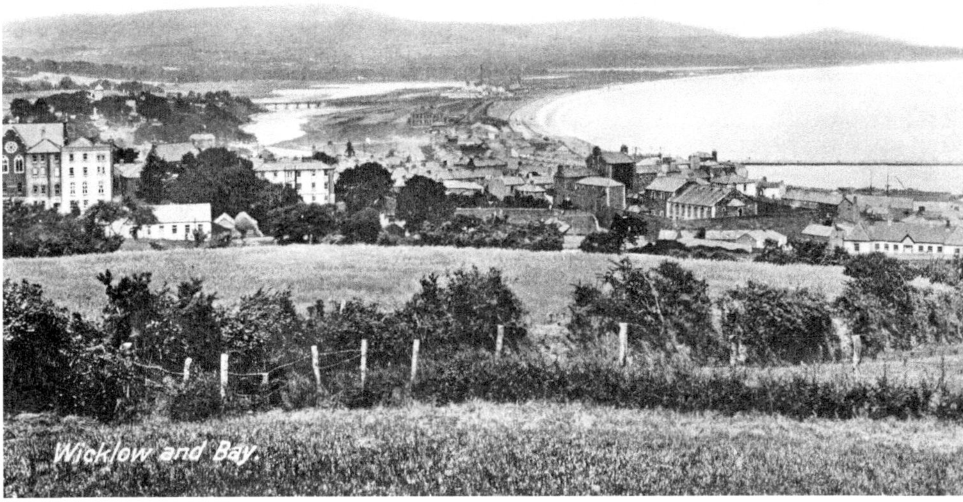

A view of Wicklow Town and the bay from the south on a postcard dated 4 June 1912. The Dominican Convent is on the left and the stone bridge over the River Vartry, which flows into the bay, is seen in the distance.

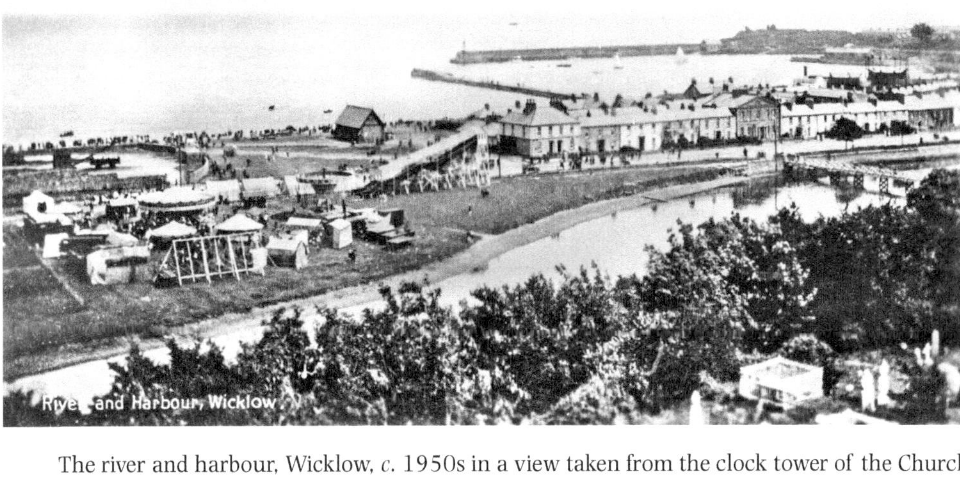

The river and harbour, Wicklow, *c.* 1950s in a view taken from the clock tower of the Church of Ireland church. A fairground with rides and roundabouts is on the riverbank. The old Lifeboat House is visible in the centre behind the fairground and some yachts sail in the harbour, which is on the right. The card was produced for McDonald's Stationers in Wicklow.

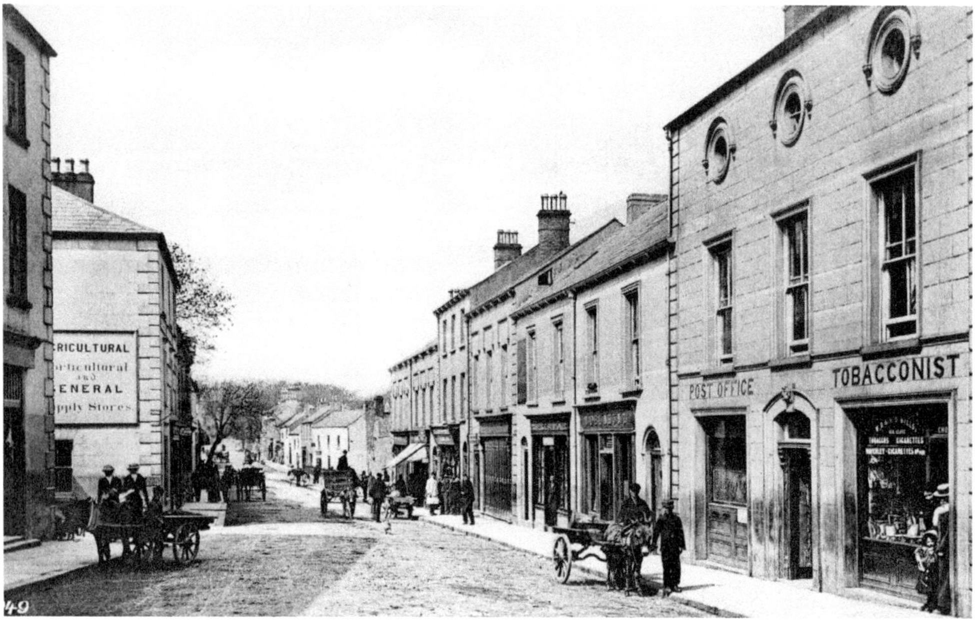

An early view, *c*. 1905, of the long Main Street, Wicklow, which runs from west to east towards the harbour. On the right, a father and son with donkey and cart stand outside the Post Office. This is a three-storey building, dating to the 1850s. It has an unusual design as there are three circular windows on the upper floor.

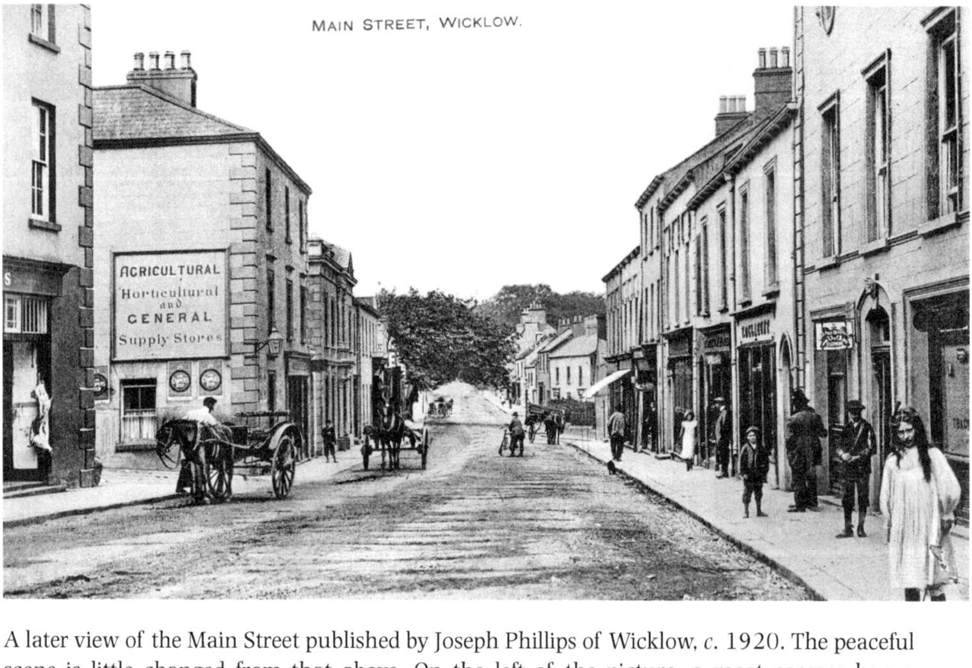

A later view of the Main Street published by Joseph Phillips of Wicklow, *c*. 1920. The peaceful scene is little changed from that above. On the left of the picture, a meat carcass hangs outside Haskins. On the right, children on the pavement are enthralled by the activities of the photographer.

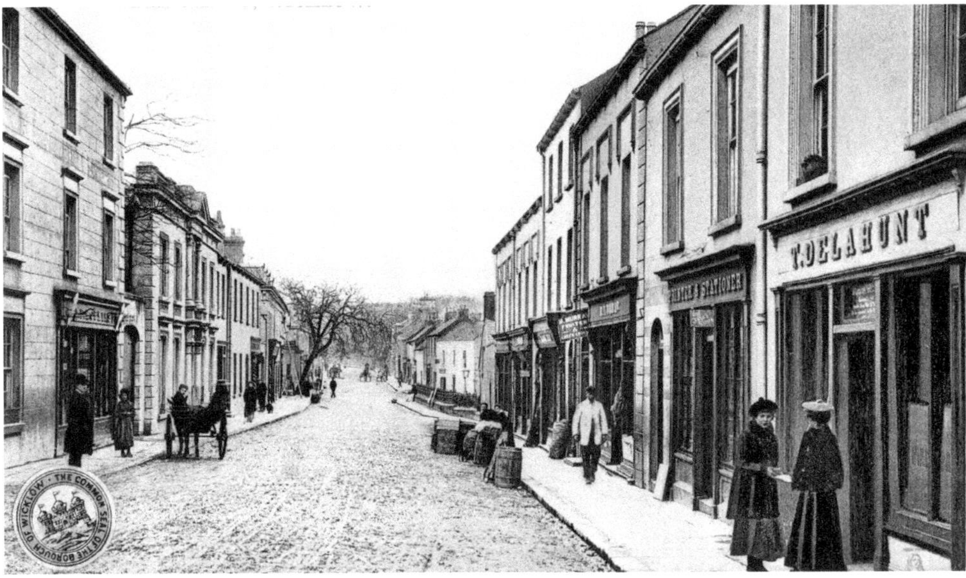

The Main Street, Wicklow on a postcard dated 20 February 1915. Two ladies stand outside T. Delahunt's shop, a grocer and grain merchant, on the right, which is next to McPhail's Printers and Stationers. On the left, in the middle distance, a pony and trap stands outside the Bank of Ireland.

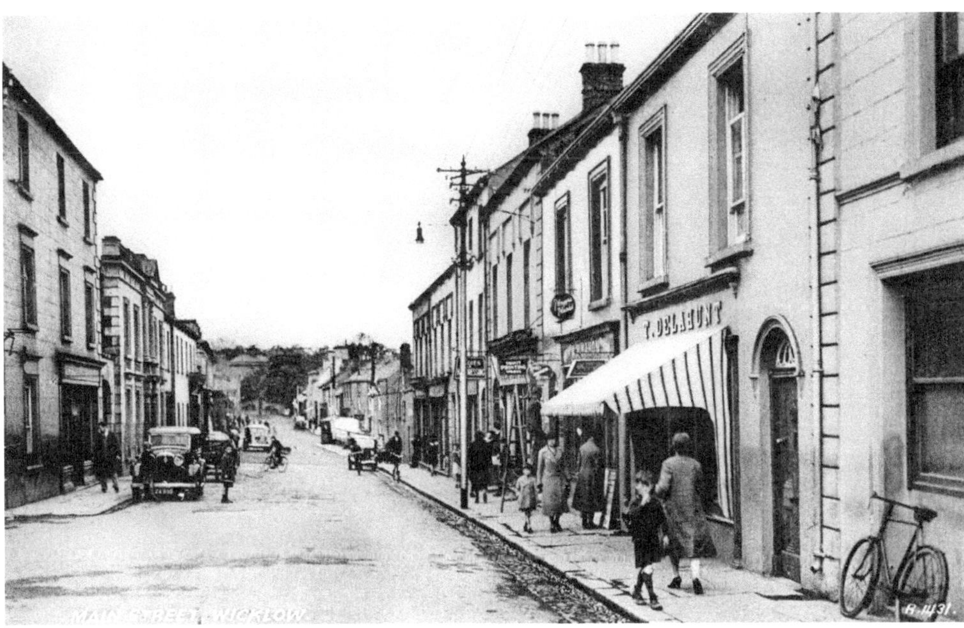

A later view of a busy Main Street, Wicklow, *c.* 1950. Motorcars have replaced horse-drawn transport and the road surface is much smoother. However, T. Delahunt's premises, on the right, is still trading. The writer of the postcard sent to Elgin in Scotland says he had a splendid day visiting Glendalough. He had crossed the lake in stormy weather, but decided not to climb up to St Kevin's Bed.

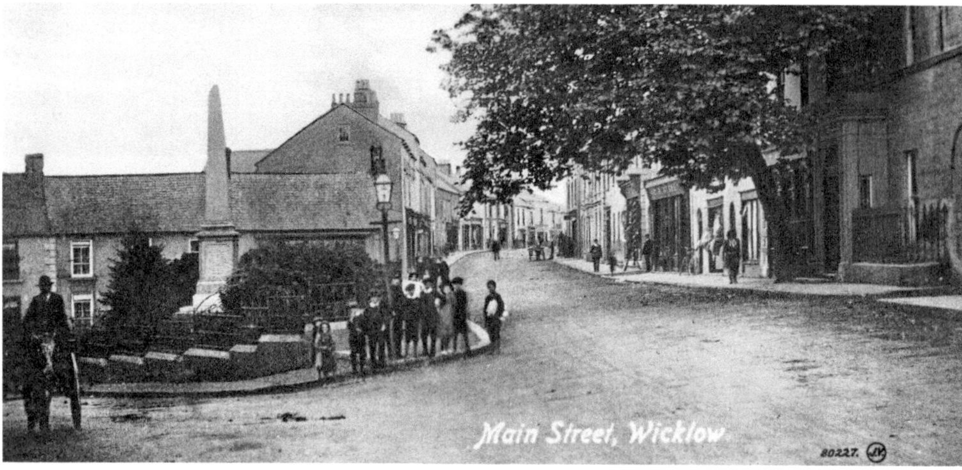

Youngsters gather on the Main Street by the Halpin Monument. The large tree on the right stands in front of Kavanagh's Green Tree Hotel, which was formerly the Fitzwilliam Arms Hotel. The tree was cut down in 1923, as it had grown too large and its roots had spread under the front door. The hotel closed in the 1950s. Captain Robert Halpin was born in Wicklow in 1836. He went to sea at an early age and worked his way up to become a respected master mariner. In 1865 he became an officer on Brunel's ship, the *Great Eastern*. In 1866, the *Great Eastern*, with Robert Halpin as Chief Officer using brilliant navigational skills, was able to lay the first transatlantic cable from Valencia in County Kerry to Newfoundland in Canada. For the first time, messages could be sent quickly across the Atlantic. He died at Tinakilly House, Rathnew, in 1894. The obelisk was erected to his memory in 1897.

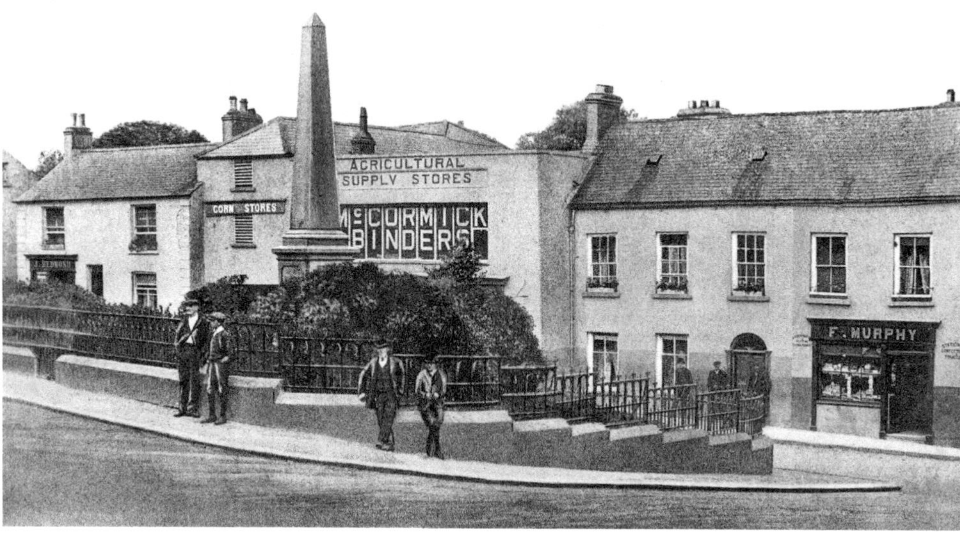

Fitzwilliam Square on a card published by Joseph Philips of Wicklow. The railings enclose the Halpin Monument. McCormack's agricultural supply stores is in the background. The stores would later become the site for the Excelsior cinema, which showed silent films in the 1920s. When this cinema closed in the late 1940s, the Rialto cinema, owned by the Clarke Family from Rosanna, Rathnew, took over the site. The Rialto finally closed in 1963.

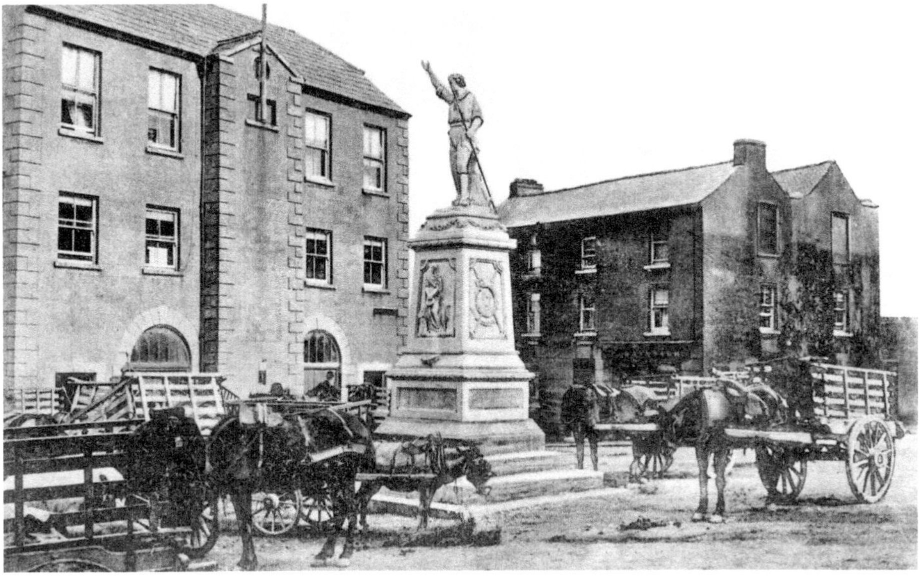

The Billy Byrne Monument, Market Square, Wicklow, on a postcard dated April 1908. The monument was erected in 1900 and shows a pike-man on a pedestal. It commemorates the Wicklow men who fought for Irish freedom and lost their lives in the revolutionary actions of 1798, 1803, 1848 and 1867. Billy Byrne was a pike-man, who was imprisoned in Wicklow Goal and then executed at Gallows Lane on 26 September 1799. On the left is the Town Hall and Market House.

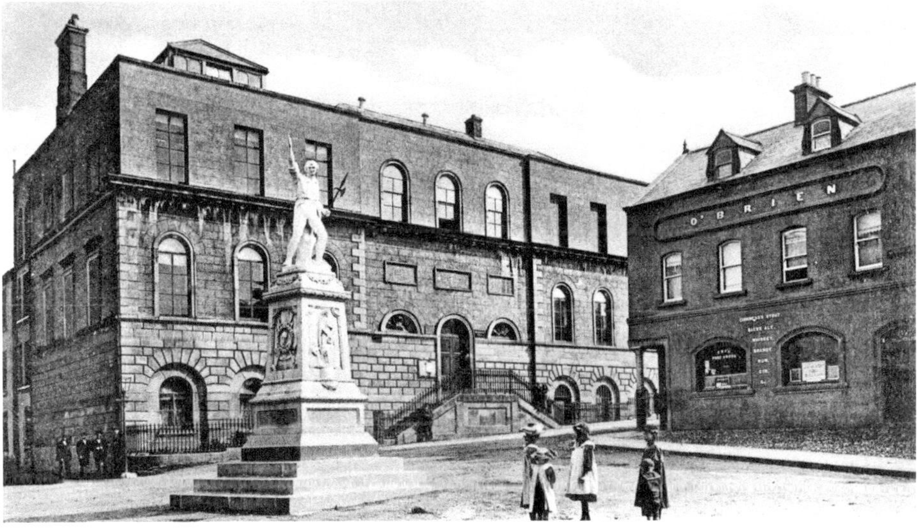

The Market Square, Wicklow, *c.* 1910. A group of children are playing near the statue of Billy Byrne while a group of men on the left lurk in a side street, probably waiting for O'Brien's Bar to open. For over a century, O'Brien's was a general grocery and spirits store as well as a public house. When executions were carried out in front of Wicklow Goal in the mid-nineteenth century, it is said that the upstairs rooms at O'Briens were rented out to give customers a good view.

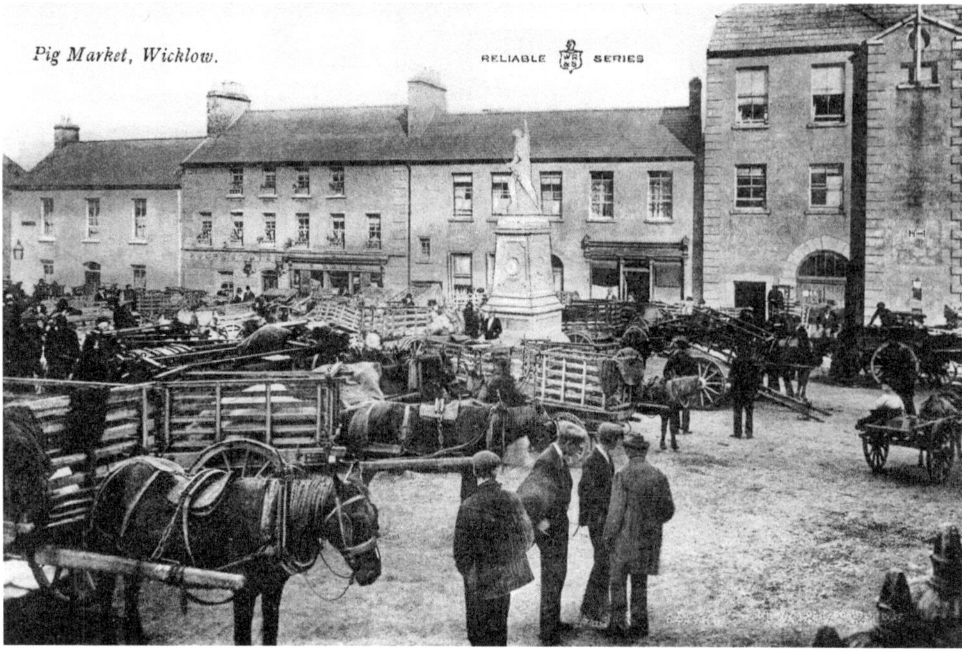

A busy day at the crowded Pig Market in Market Square, Wicklow. The farmers gather in groups, discussing their purchases and catching up on local news. The economy of these Wicklow farmers depended heavily on sales of their sheep and pigs. The Billy Byrne statue stands over them in the centre and the Market House and Town Hall are on the right.

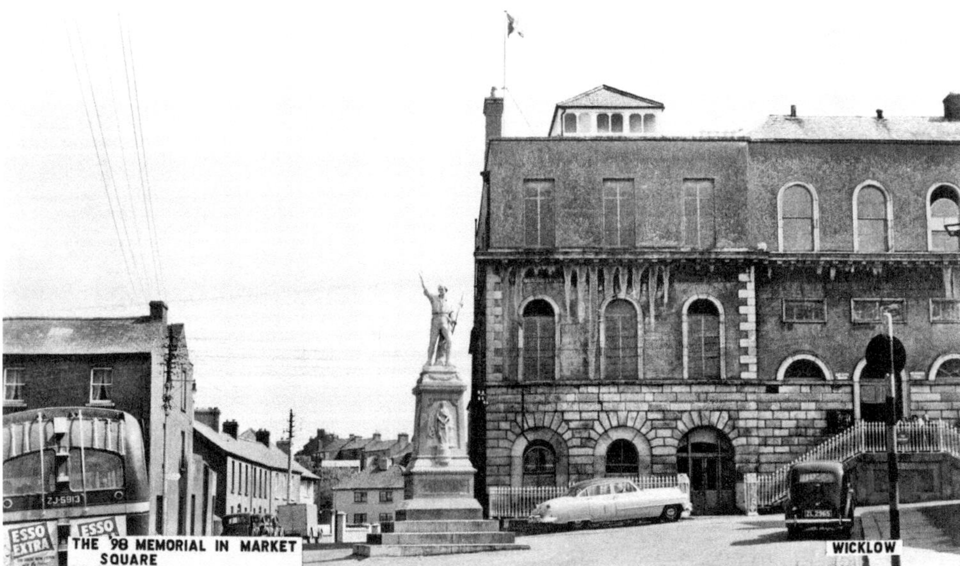

A later view of the Market Square showing a coach and some parked cars, *c.* 1950s. The courthouse, built in 1824, is in the background on the right. Many Irish political leaders – including Parnell – have stood on the steps to address large crowds in the square. The courthouse is close to Wicklow Gaol and the buildings were connected by an underground passage.

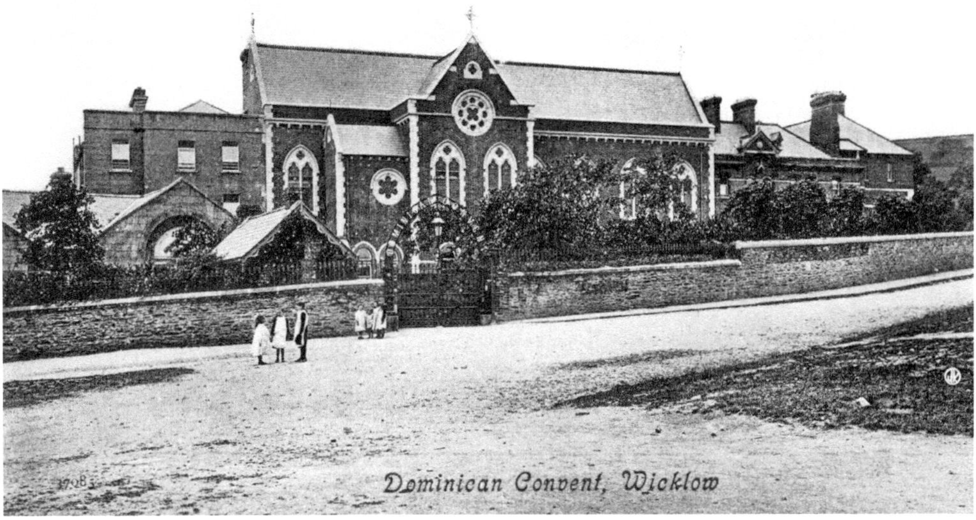

An early postcard of the Dominican Convent, *c.* 1907, showing the new chapel, which was dedicated in 1906. The convent stands at the top of Kilmantin Hill and faces Barrack Green. The National School is on the left in the foreground.

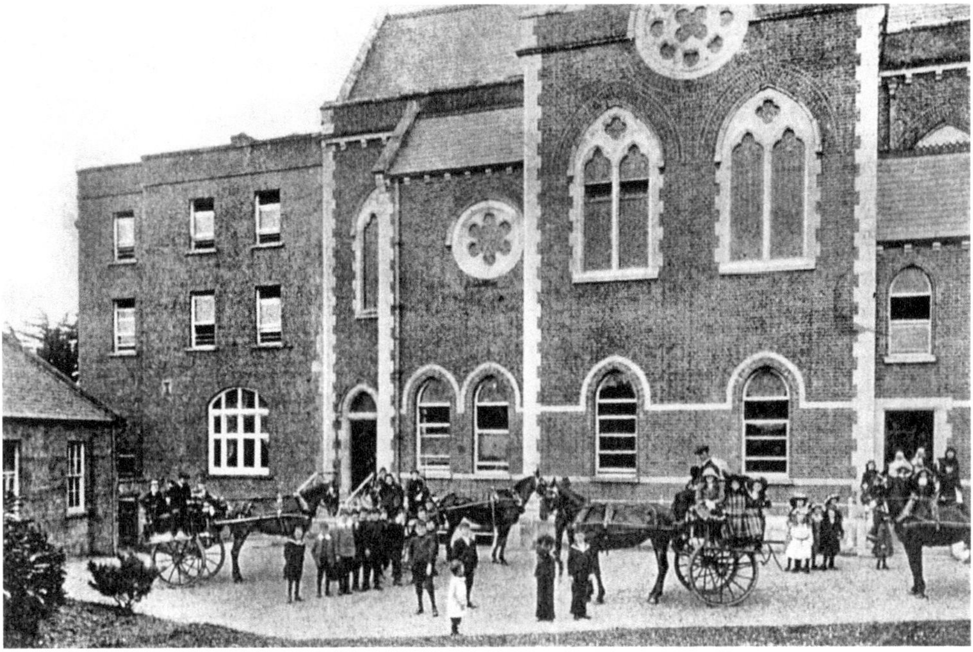

The convent was very successful and by the early 1900s it had expanded to take boarders. This postcard shows children gathered in front of the chapel being collected before departing for their holidays.

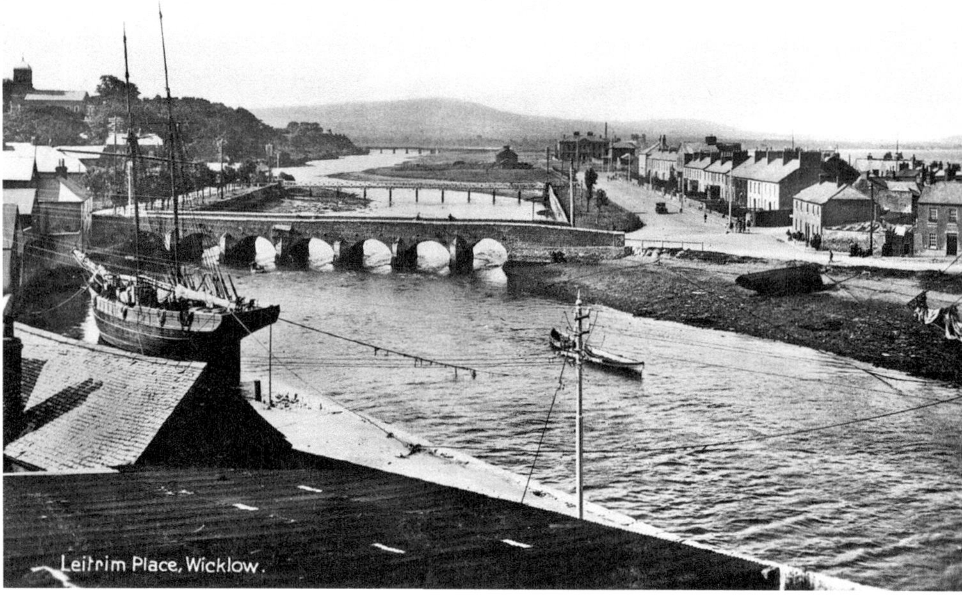

Leitrim Place, showing a ship with a tall mast berthed on the River Vartry. The stone bridge across the river was built around 1690 to provide access to the Murrough from the main town on the western side of the river. The bridge was widened in 1862. Further up the river there are two more bridges; a wooden bridge, which was replaced by the Parnell Bridge in 1947, and in the distance, carrying the railway line, is the metal bridge built in 1860.

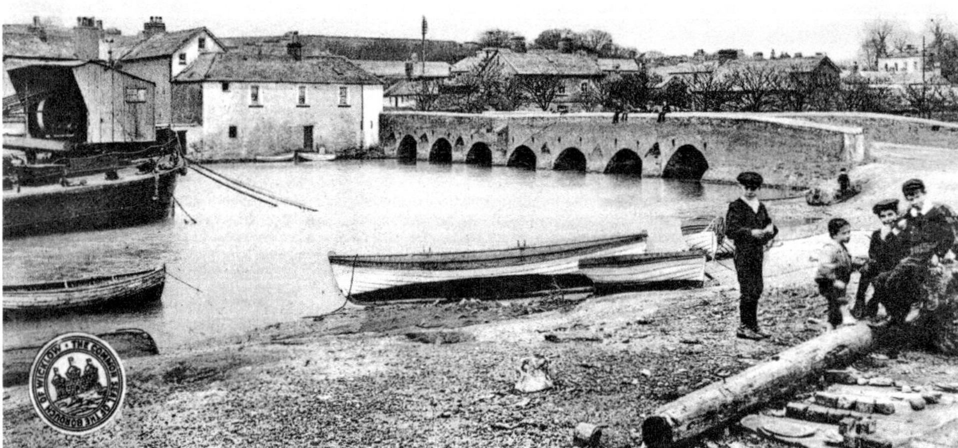

The eight-arched stone bridge, Wicklow, built around 1690, is shown on a postcard dated 10 May 1903. The dredger *Leitrim* is on the left. The tavern by the bridge, which dates back to 1702, was the birthplace of Robert Halpin.

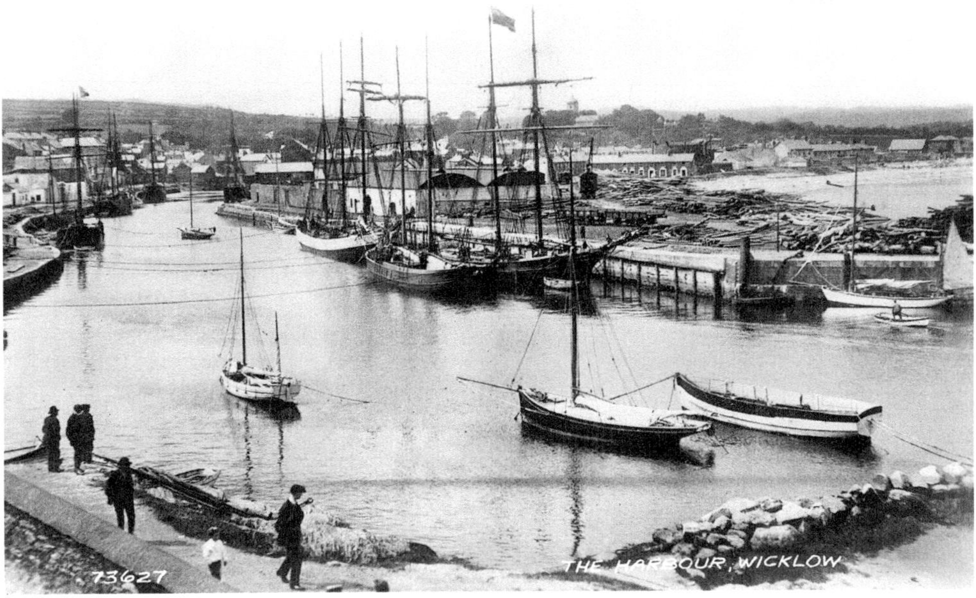

The harbour, Wicklow, *c.* 1955, which covered about 6 hectares. At that time, the harbour had east and west piers and a packet quay, which was 90 metres long. The main imports were coal, flour, foodstuffs and manures and the main exports were timber, ore, lead concentrates, oats and barley.

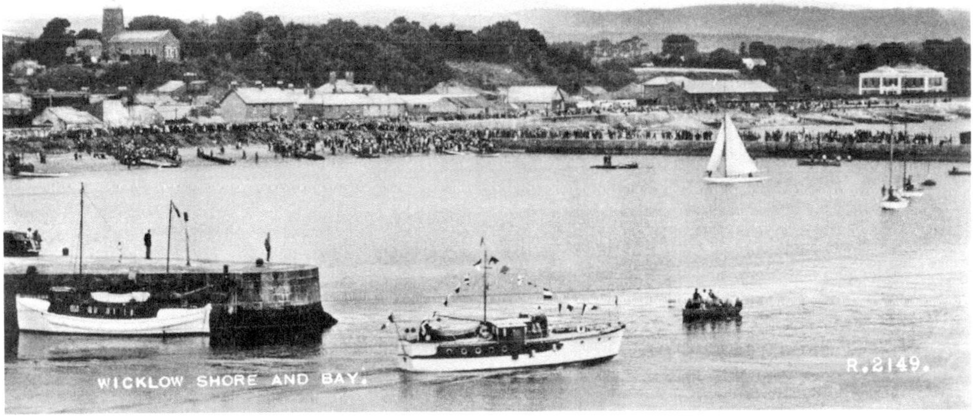

Regatta Day at Wicklow. This was an important date in the social calendar and usually took place on August Bank Holiday Monday. Visitors would come to Wicklow for the day on the cheap excursion trains from Dublin. There was plenty of entertainment with merry-go-rounds at the seafront, stalls selling refreshments, including candy floss and ice cream, and an army band playing rousing music. Large crowds stood on the shore and harbour wall watching the yachts in the sailing competitions. The Regatta flagboat is shown at the entrance to the harbour. At the end of the day, there was usually a firework display before the visitors left on the late trains to return home to Dublin.

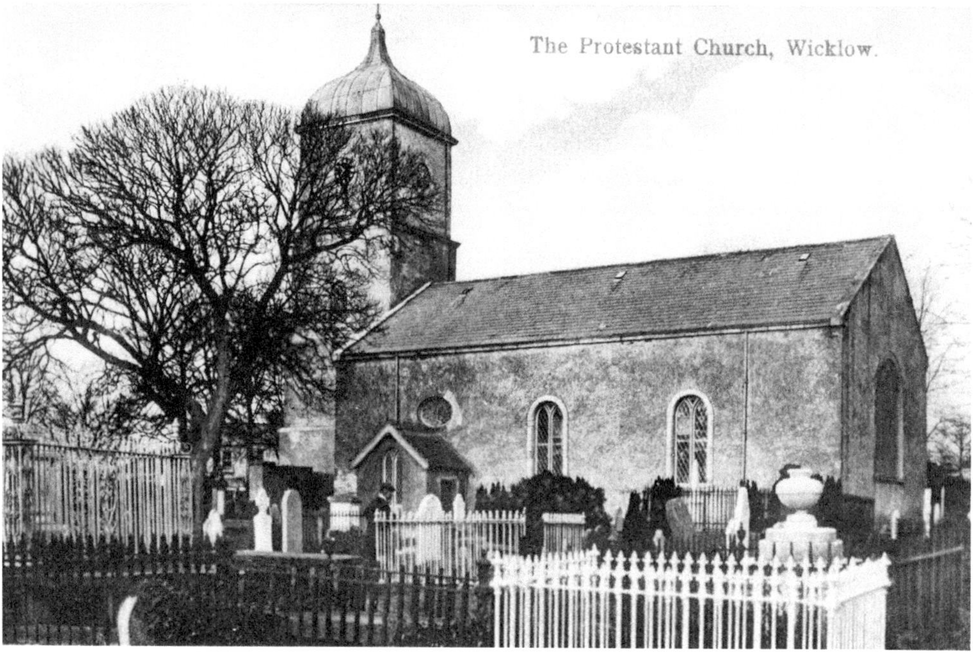

The Church of Ireland (Protestant) church, Wicklow was built on Church Hill in 1700. The church clock and bell tower were added in 1777. This was paid for by the Eaton family, whose burial vault is underneath the tower. Captain Robert Halpin (see page 60), whose grave is marked by a high Celtic stone cross, is buried in the graveyard.

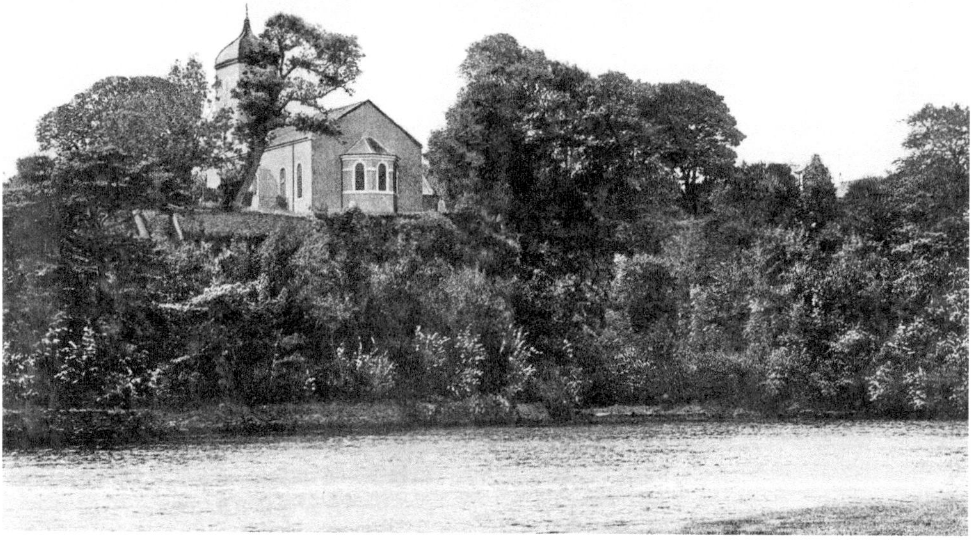

Another view of the Church of Ireland (Protestant) church, published by Joseph Phillips of Wicklow and posted in 1914. The church has a dominant position on the hill overlooking the river. Compared with the previous postcard, a new chancel can be seen at the rear of the church; this was added in 1912.

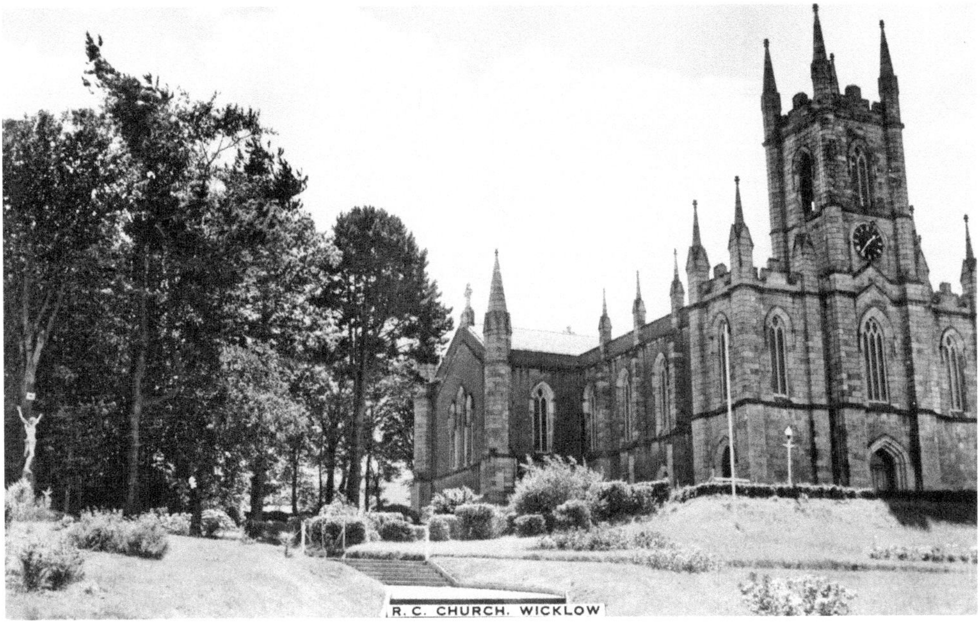

St Patrick's RC church, Wicklow, which was built in the late 1830s and finished by 1844. At that time, it had one of the largest self-supporting ceilings without pillars in Europe. In the early 1900s, stained-glass windows were made to replace the original plain glass. Of these, the best-known stained-glass window was designed by Harry Clarke and shows the nativity.

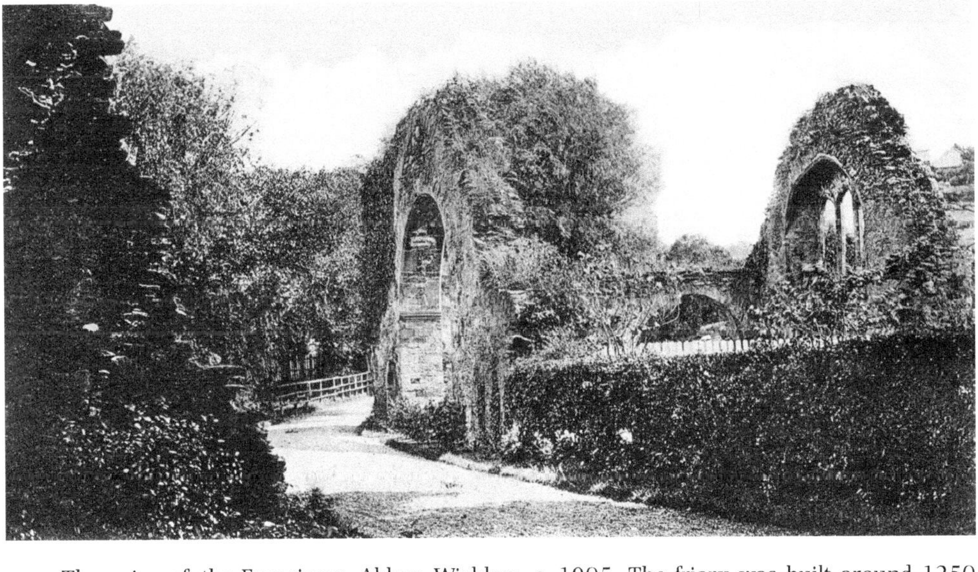

The ruins of the Franciscan Abbey, Wicklow, *c.* 1905. The friary was built around 1250 by the Fitzgerald family for the Franciscan Order. However, during the reign of Edward VI in 1552, the abbey and its land were seized by the Crown. After being used for various purposes, including use as a gaol and courthouse, it was abandoned in the early eighteenth century and soon became a neglected ruin.

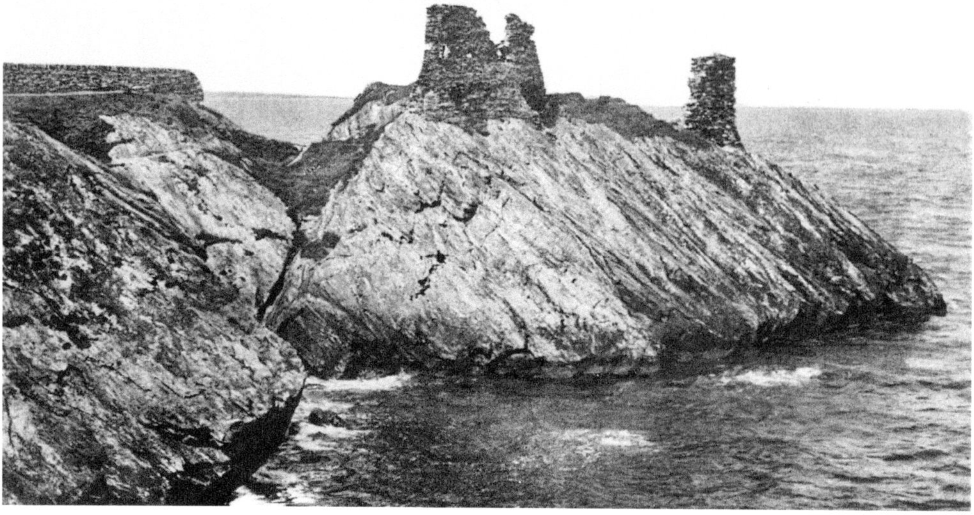

The Black Castle, Wicklow, *c.* 1910. Now in ruins, the castle was built on a rocky headland south of the Vartry estuary by the Fitzgerald family between 1178 and 1187. The situation of the castle made it extremely difficult to attack and the local clans, the O'Byrnes and O'Tooles, who regularly laid siege to the castle, usually had little success. Many prisoners were executed by being hanged over the rocks at the back of the castle. However, it was finally destroyed by fire in the rebellion in 1645 and left as a ruin. Today, because of its grim history, a wailing banshee is said to regularly appear at the castle and legend has it that the ghosts of executed men are seen wandering in the grounds.

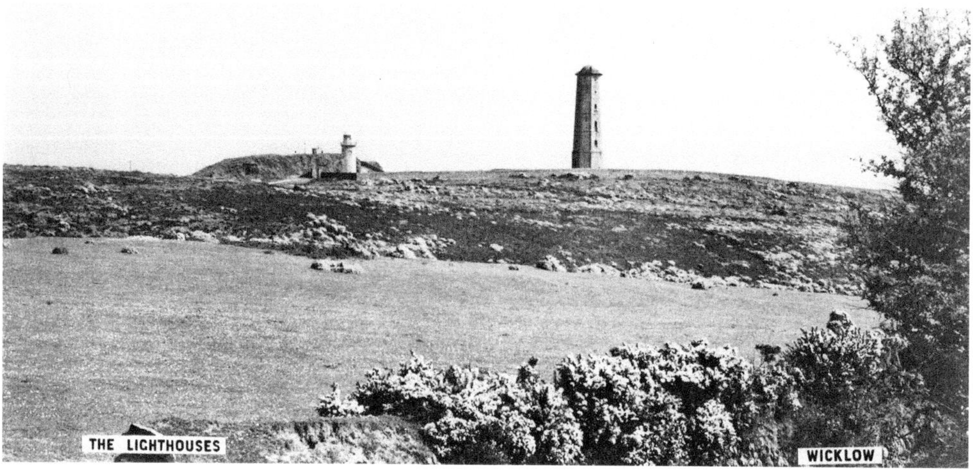

Wicklow Head is one and a half miles south-east of Wicklow town. The view shows two lighthouses, with one on the saddle of Wicklow Head above the sea and the other on the Long Hill. The octagonal lighthouse to the right on the Long Hill was one of a pair of octagonal lighthouses erected in 1781. Nothing now remains of the octagonal lighthouse, which was sited on the headland saddle. However, the old rear tower still stands as a useful landmark for shipping. The lighthouse to the left on the headland, which used oil lamps and reflectors, was brought into service in 1818.

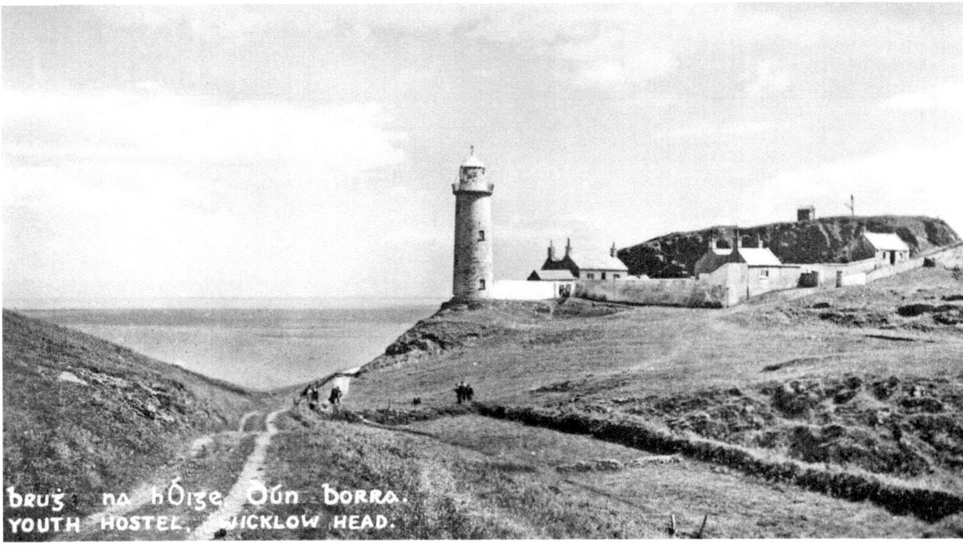

The lighthouse at Wicklow Head was converted to gas in January 1868. This continued to be used until 1906, when it was changed to incandescent paraffin. This lasted until 1976 when modernisation took place and electric power was used. A radio beacon was added in 1978. The tower and the two lightkeepers' cottages attached to it overlooked the sea but also had great views of the Wicklow Mountains and countryside.

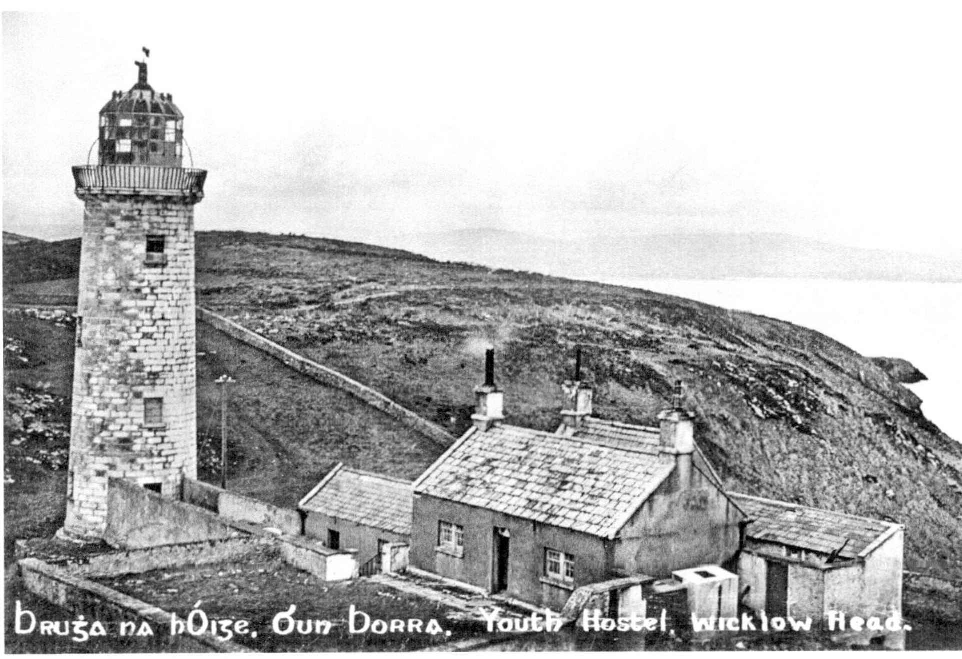

A closer view of the youth hostel at Wicklow Head. From 1934 to 1939, the buildings at the lighthouse were used by An Óige as a very popular youth hostel. In 1939, at the start of the Second World War, they were requisitioned by the Irish Government and used as a lookout post on the coast until the war ended in 1945.

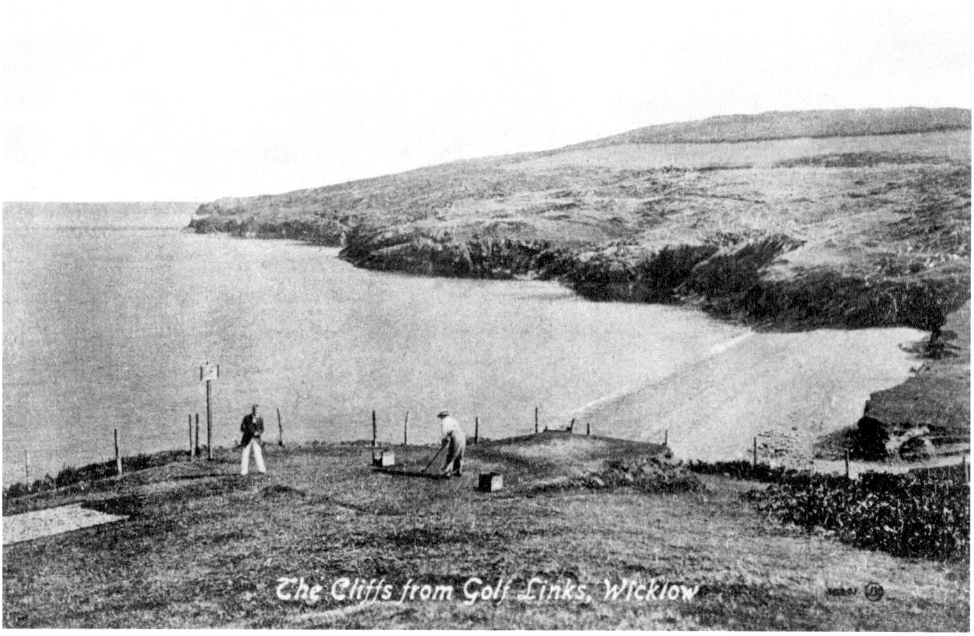

A view of the cliffs from the golf links at Wicklow on a card dated 28 June 1917. The course was designed by famous Royal Dublin professional Michael Moran and has outstanding views of the Irish Sea, cliffs and strands to the east and the Wicklow Mountains to the west. Playing a round of golf at Wicklow was challenging and said to 'fully box the compass whatever the prevailing wind'.

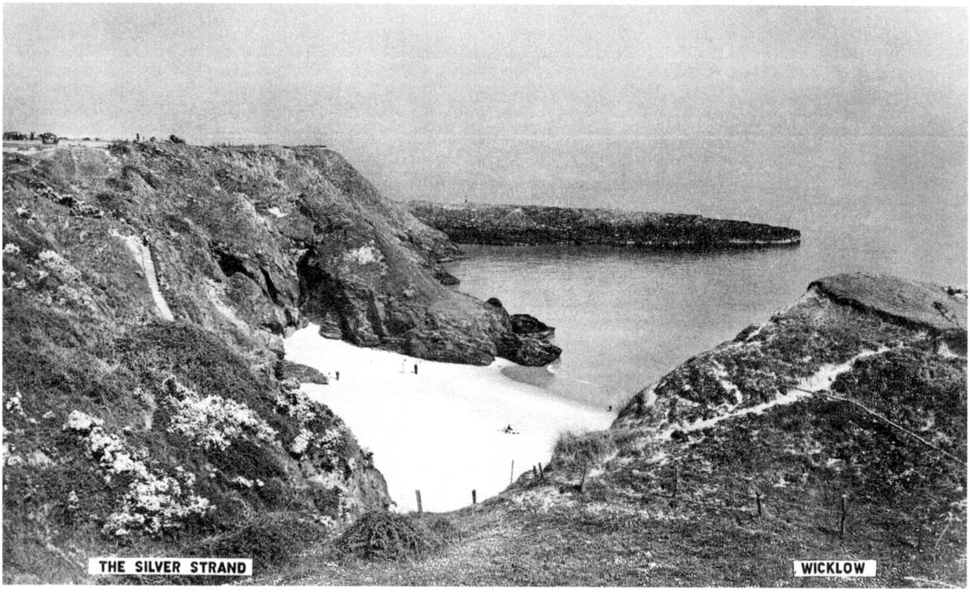

About 2 miles south of Wicklow is the popular Silver Strand. There is a golden stretch of sandy beach some 365 metres in length, lying between sheltering headlands. In good weather, visitors flock to the beach, which has excellent safe bathing.

4

RATHNEW, ASHFORD, NEWCASTLE & ROUNDWOOD

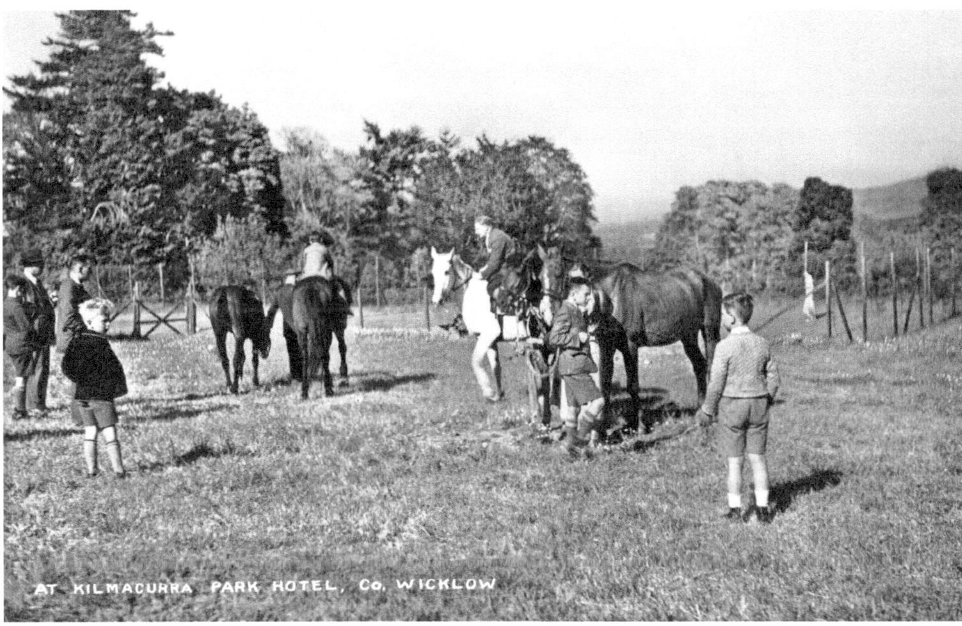

The Kilmacurragh Park Hotel had a good reputation. The hotel offered home-grown food and the finest continental cuisine. It had a walled garden and there were sporting facilities for young people. The renowned arboretum was planted during the 1850s by Tom Acton. There was also a ballroom in the garden behind the house in which the Shamrock's Ceili Band from Arklow would often play. The photograph shows youngsters being given lessons in horse riding.

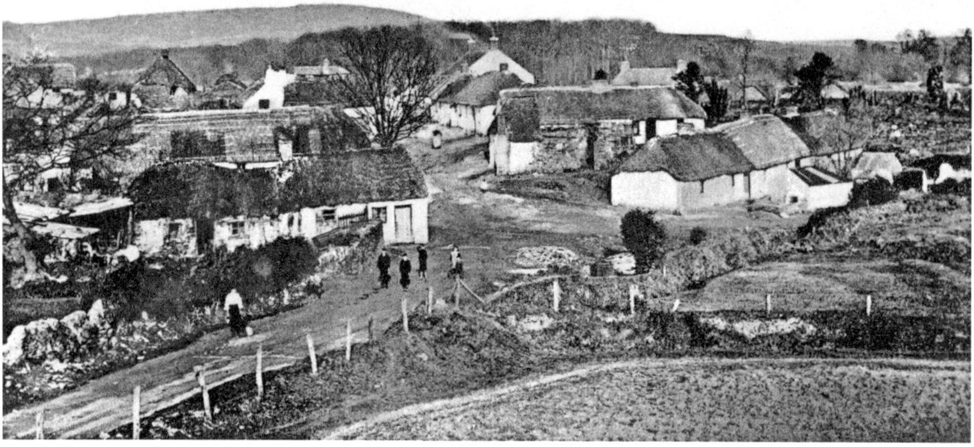

Rathnew Village, *c.* 1910, which was often called the 'thatched city', as so many houses were packed together on the area known as the Rathnew Commons. In the 1850s, when many people were evicted from their homes and made destitute, Miss Blake from Rathdrum, the owner of the Commons, offered the site to the homeless to build simple houses for themselves. Her offer was soon accepted and many cottages with thatched roofs and walls made of a mixture of straw and clay were quickly built on the rocky ground. Most cottages were built in less than a week. The men then looked for jobs as farm labourers.

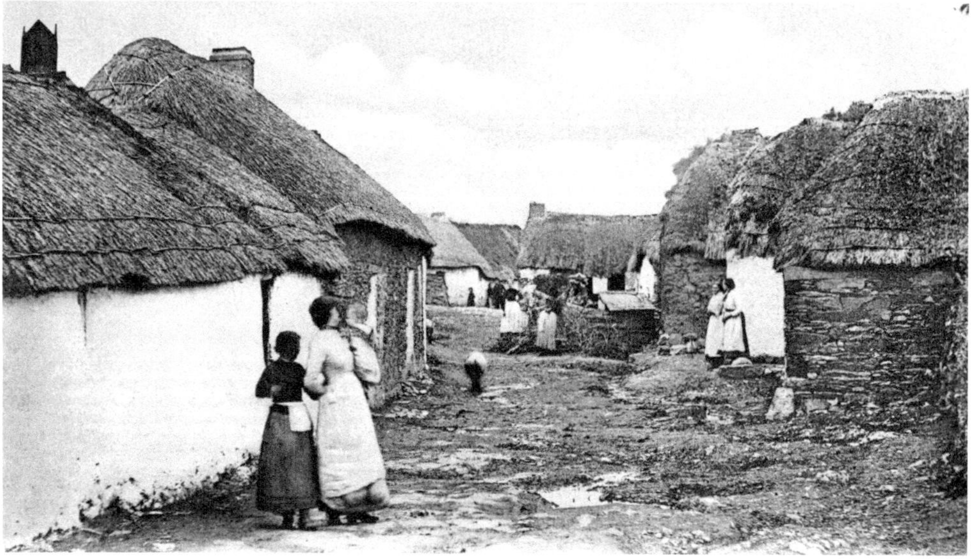

A street in Rathnew on a card dated 8 December 1903. The small thatched cottages had no planning restrictions and many face in different directions, with a front door of one cottage facing the side or back of another. However, the card shows a thriving community and the families all have a roof over their heads. Many of the cottages lasted for around a hundred years. However, people living in the cottages had no fresh water or sanitation so there was an increased risk of infection and disease. During the famine years, conditions were very bad.

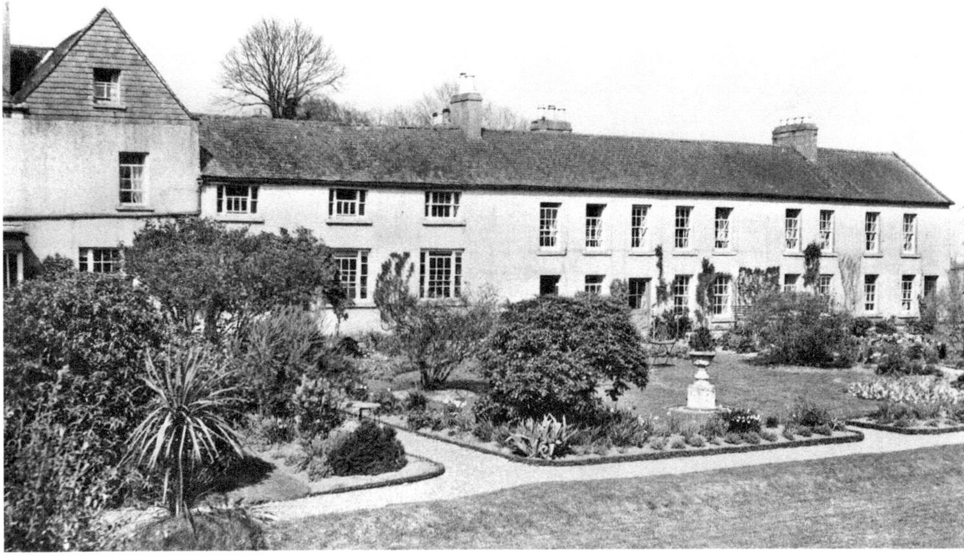

Hunter's Hotel, Rathnew, on the banks of the Vartry, is one of Ireland's oldest coaching inns, and its origins date back to around 1650. It was originally a forge and later became Newry Bridge Inn, a post house on the main Dublin Wexford Road, where travellers rested and changed horses. In 1825, the Hunter family obtained the lease on the hotel. Later, in 1858, John Hunter also obtained the lease of the Woodenbridge Hotel (see page 18) and the family ran the sister hotels for sixty years before surrendering the lease of the Woodenbridge in 1918. However, the family connection with Hunter's Hotel remained. The hotel had electricity installed in 1937 and had sixteen bedrooms by 1940. The gardens were renowned and tourists who visited the nearby Mount Usher gardens would often visit the hotel for afternoon tea. Today the hotel thrives and is a favourite haunt for celebrities.

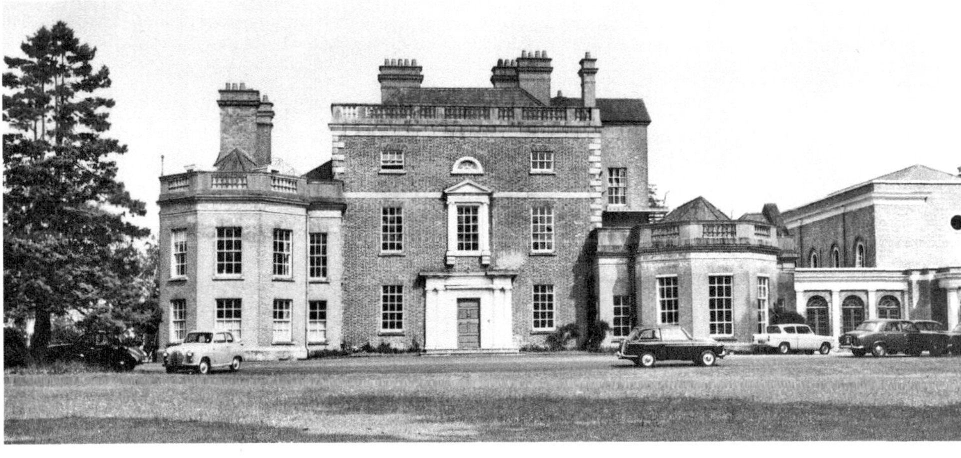

Clermont House, Rathnew, formally known as Newrath House, which is a Palladian country house built in 1730 by the first Earl of Milltown and designed by Francis Bindon. The side wings, which are different heights, were added in the 1890s. In 1956 the house was converted for use as a boarding school and the large extension shown on the right was built. The school closed in 2005.

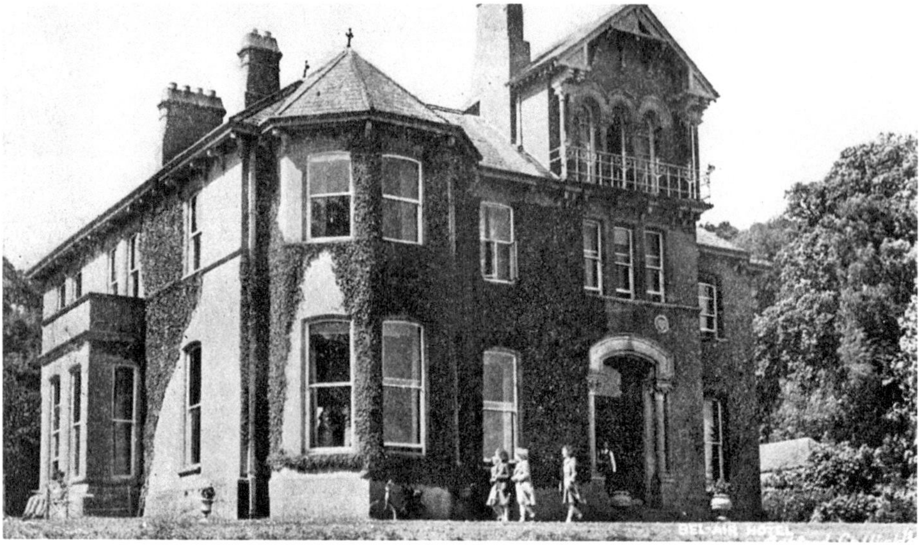

The Bel-Air Hotel, Ashford has a long history. The present house was built in 1890 after the original house known as Cronroe Manor, which dated to 1750, had burned down. Notably, the Irish patriot Sir Roger Casement spent a lot of his childhood at Cronroe. He had a career as a talented diplomat and after retiring from the Consular Service in 1914 he went to Germany, where he obtained recognition of Ireland's right to nationhood and a promise of arms. However, he was betrayed and when he landed from a German submarine on Banna Strand, County Kerry on 20 April 1916, British soldiers were waiting to arrest him. He was found guilty of treason and executed on 3 August 1916.

In August 1934, the Casement family sold Cronroe to an American, Nicholas Burns, who changed the name of the manor to Bel-Air Hotel. There have been subsequent owners and today it is a popular hotel and equestrian centre.

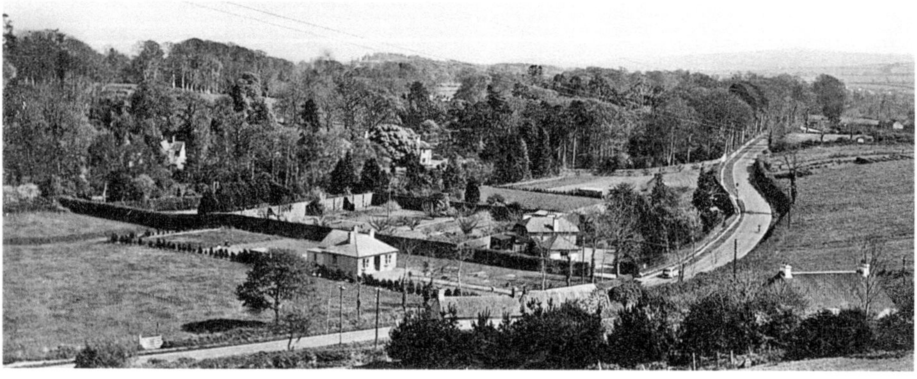

Walpoles Gardens (Mount Usher Gardens), Ashford. A Dublin businessman, Robert Walpole, purchased the land from the owner of the corn mill at Mount Usher in 1868. The Walpole family laid out gardens along the banks of the River Vartry in a natural planting style following the principles of the brilliant Irish gardener, William Robinson (1838-1935), who personally visited the gardens in the early 1880s. Today the gardens are one of the jewels in Wicklow's crown, with cascading waterfalls and plants from all over the world in an idyllic natural layout, providing pleasure for visitors in all the seasons of the year.

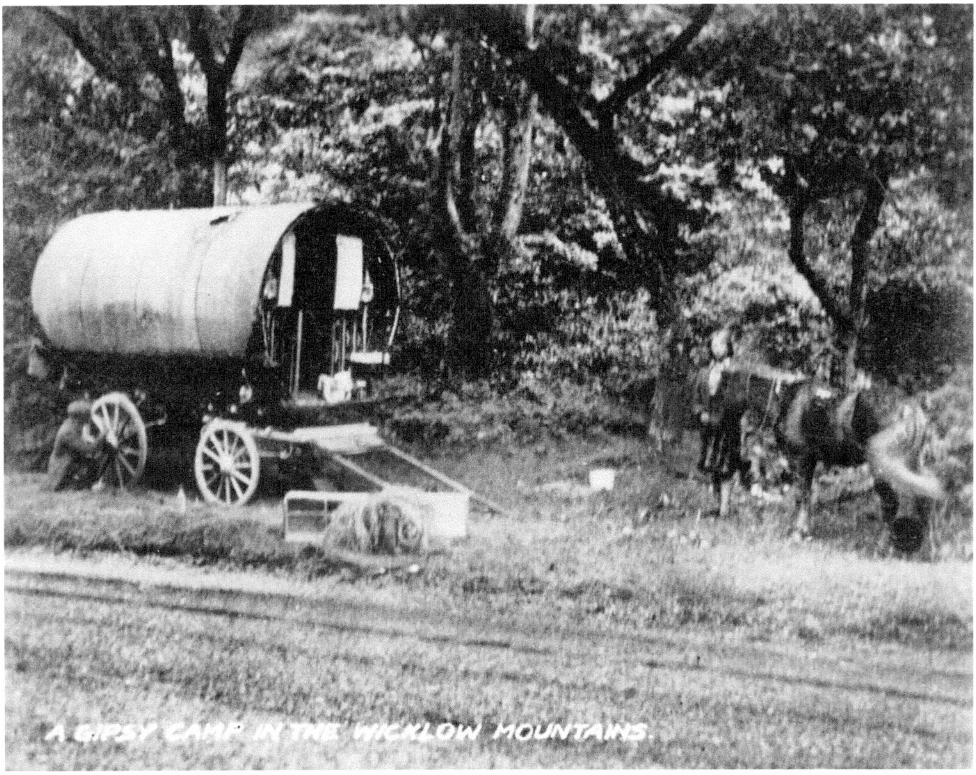

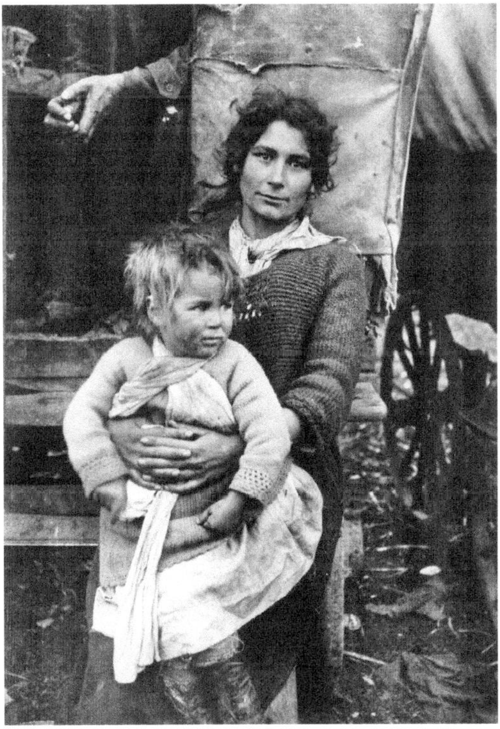

A Gipsy barrel-headed horse-caravan at the roadside in the Wicklow Mountains, *c.* 1930. Irish travellers date back to the eleventh century and have their own separate identity, culture and traditions. They journey from place to place on the country roads throughout Ireland. In the past, the travellers were often a link between isolated rural communities, bringing news, gossip, music, song and legendary tales.

Gipsy mother with a healthy, bonny-looking child.

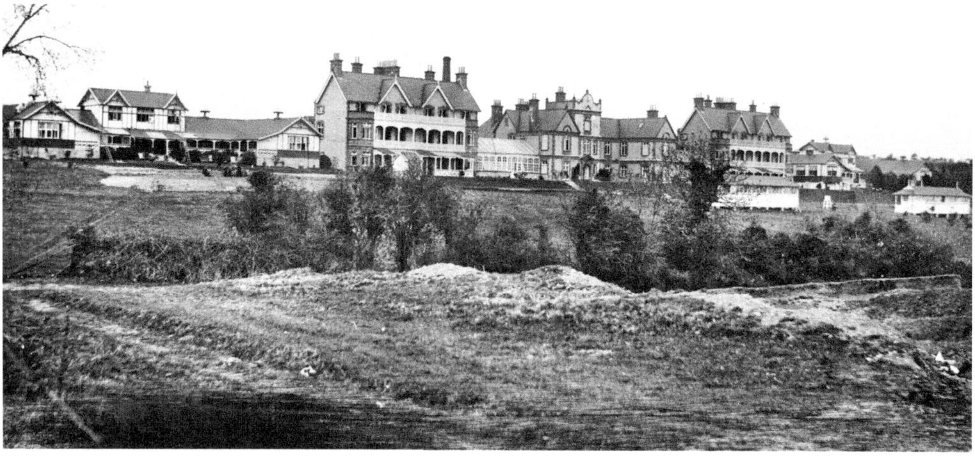

The Royal National Hospital for Consumption (Newcastle Sanatorium) opened in 1896 with twenty-four beds. It was one of the first hospitals in Ireland devoted to the treatment of tuberculosis. The sanatorium specialised in 'open-air treatment' day and night, with rest and a good diet. When patients improved, they had regular exercise. Dr John Moore reported in December 1898 that 200 patients had been treated at Newcastle Sanatorium and 164 discharged. There had been two deaths and the remaining patients showed an average weight gain of 7lbs. For the first time (in these days before antibiotic treatment), doctors now had a degree of control over tuberculosis and the sanatorium expanded. By the outbreak of the First World War in 1914 there were 125 beds. However, X-ray facilities were not added until 1935. The Irish rebel Maud Gonne Macbride suffered from TB and she was treated at the hospital with courses of creosote inhalation.

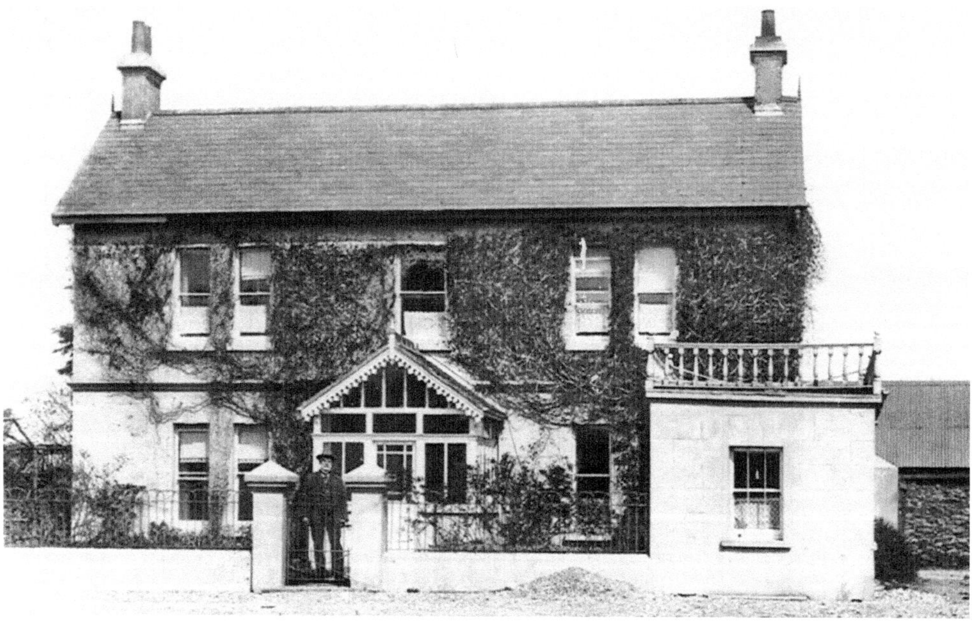

Beechmount, Newcastle, *c*. 1903. This fine ivy-covered house was built on the site of a pre-existing cottage by James Thornton, who is shown standing at the gate.

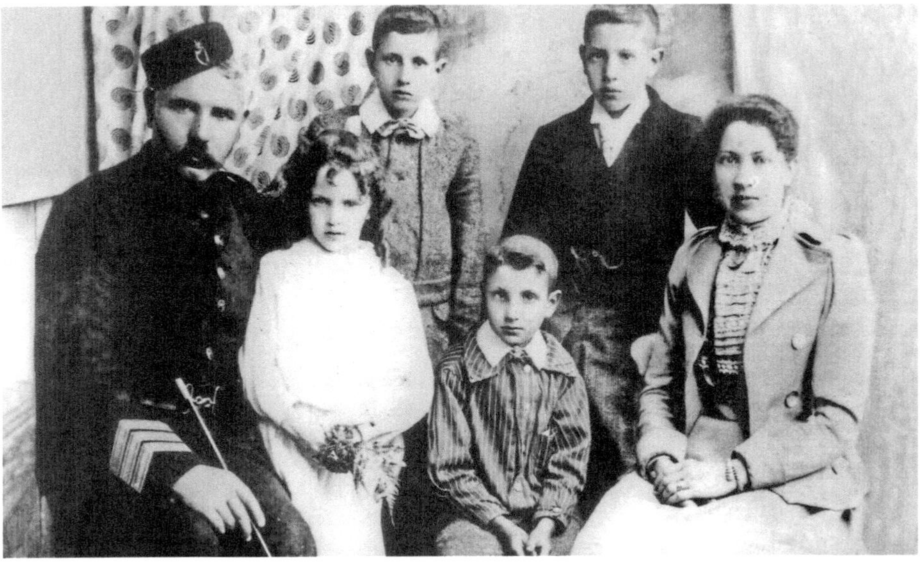

Newcastle family photograph showing, from left to right: John Leeson (Royal Irish Constabulary), Martha, who later married James Thornton (shown in the previous photograph on page 76), Charles, John and William Agar and Lucinda Daly.

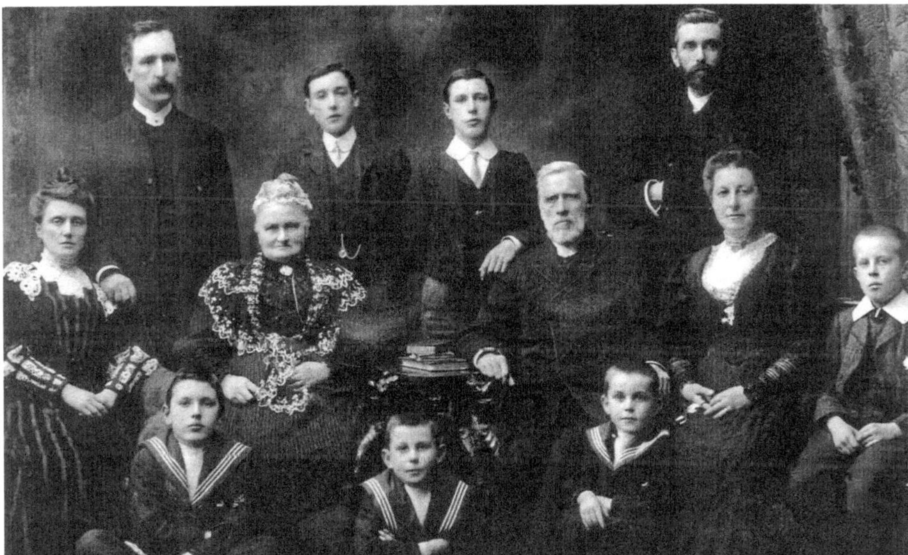

Smyth family gathering at Newcastle showing, from left to right, back row: Revd William Smyth (married to Minnie), Irvine Johnston Smyth (son of William and Minnie), who died at Gallipoli in 1915 aged 23 years, James Smyth (son of William and Minnie), Revd John Wesley Johnston (brother of Minnie); middle row: Minnie Smyth (*née* Johnston), Irvina Johnston and Revd Irvine Johnston (parents of Minnie and John Wesley), Margaret Johnston (*née* Wilson) married to John Wesley, William Irvine Johnston (son of John Wesley and Margaret); front row: Henry Smyth (son of William and Minnie), Arthur Johnston (son of John Wesley and Margaret) and his brother, Gerard, who died aged 27 years in a motorbike accident on Sea Road, Newcastle, Wicklow.

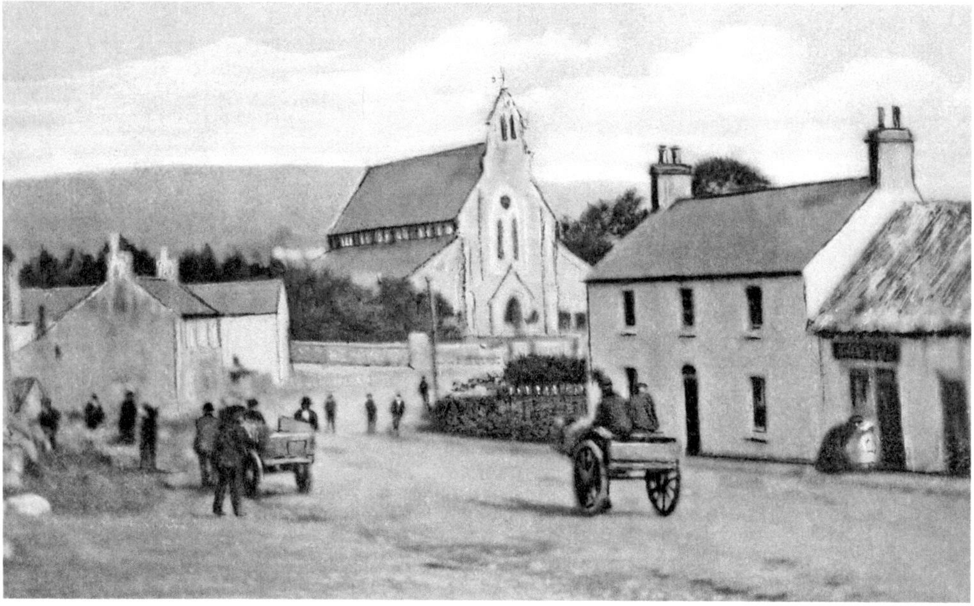

Roundwood Village, *c*. 1910, is 238 metres above sea level and is the highest village in Ireland. The writer of the postcard was attending the village fair. Roundwood is a favourite place for tourists as it is on the banks of the Vartry River and is surrounded by spectacular scenery at Lough Dan, Lough Tay and Glendalough.

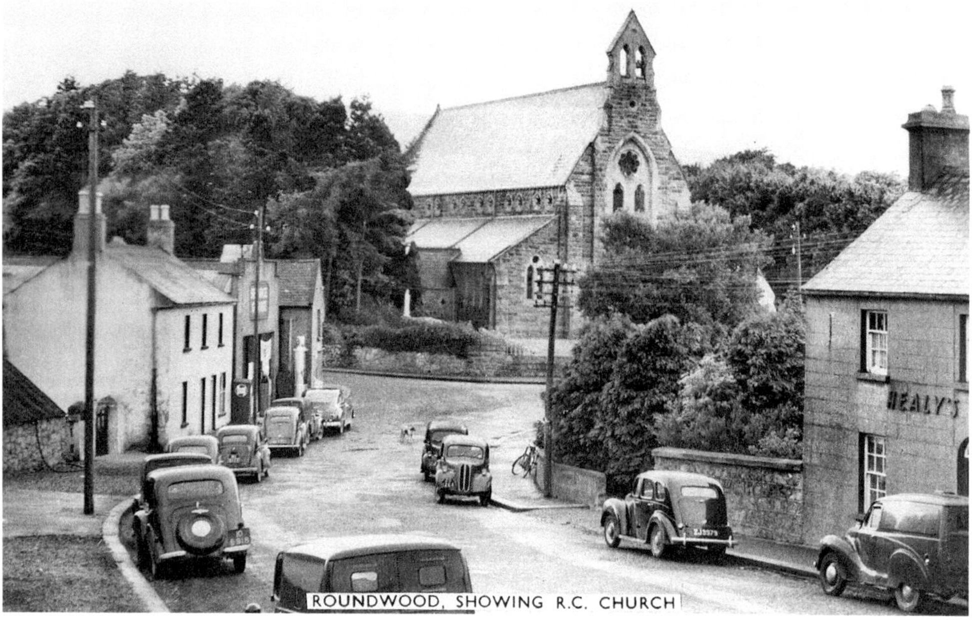

Later view of Roundwood Village in 1941, showing the Catholic church of St Laurence O'Toole. This was designed by J.J. McCarthey and built between 1867 and 1871. It is a fine example of Gothic Revival architecture. The church faces on to Roundwood's main street and Healy's pub is on the right.

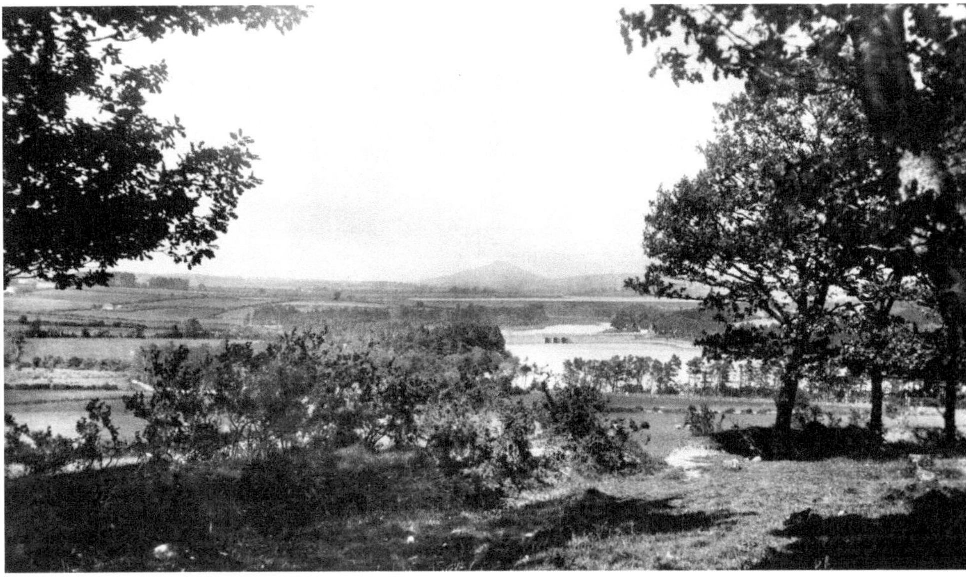

The Vartry Reservoir, Roundwood, on a postcard dated September 1933. There are actually two reservoirs together, providing a gravity supply of water for Dublin. The lower reservoir was built between 1862 and 1868 and the upper reservoir was completed in 1923. The reservoirs supplied fresh water to suburbs in South Dublin. This greatly improved public health in the area as, before the reservoir construction, drinking water for Dublin had often come from the polluted canals. In fact, there was a law attached to the agreement over the Vartry water that it could not be used for filling the canals.

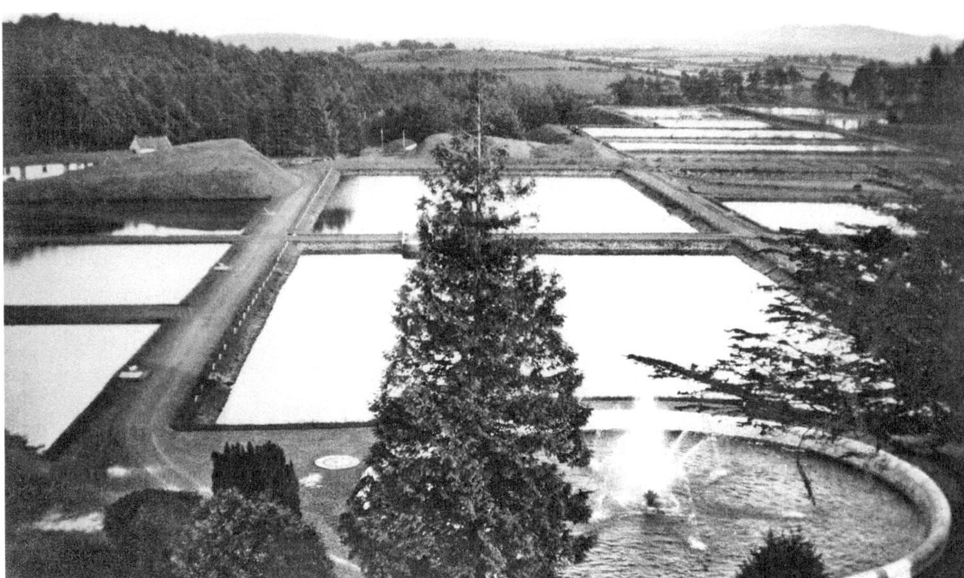

The Filter Beds, Roundwood reservoir, on a card dated 1932. Filtration helped purify the water for Dublin, reducing outbreaks of cholera, typhus and other waterborne diseases. James Joyce made several references in *Ulysses* to 'fresh Vartry water'.

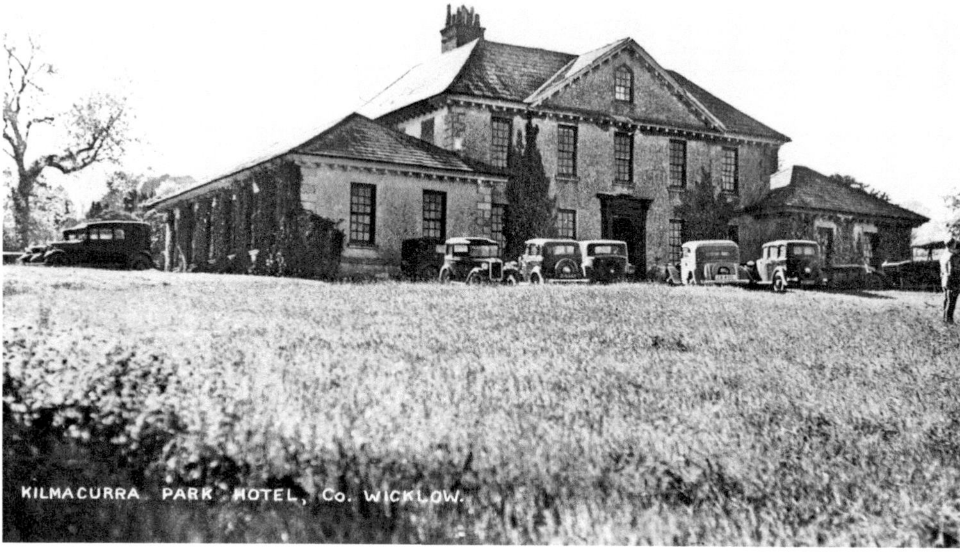

Kilmacurragh Park Hotel. The house, originally built by the Acton family at the end of the seventeenth century, was converted to a hotel in 1933. It was leased from the Actons by Charles Budina, who was prominent in the German community in Ireland in the 1930s. Under his management, the Nazi Party held some functions at Kilmacurragh. There was a Nazi Youth Camp in 1939 and a party for the sailors from the *Schleswig Holstein*, when it docked in Dublin. With the outbreak of the Second World War, Charles Budina returned to Germany and the hotel was managed by his accountant. However, when Charles returned to the hotel in 1950, there was a legal dispute over ownership. The hotel was forced to close in 1956 and soon fell into disrepair. After two fires in 1978 and 1982, the house was left derelict. However, the site, now owned by the National Botanic Gardens, has become a renowned arboretum with many botanical treasures and champion trees, which have grown from seeds planted by Thomas and Janet Acton in the nineteenth century.

5

DELGANY, GREYSTONES & BRAY

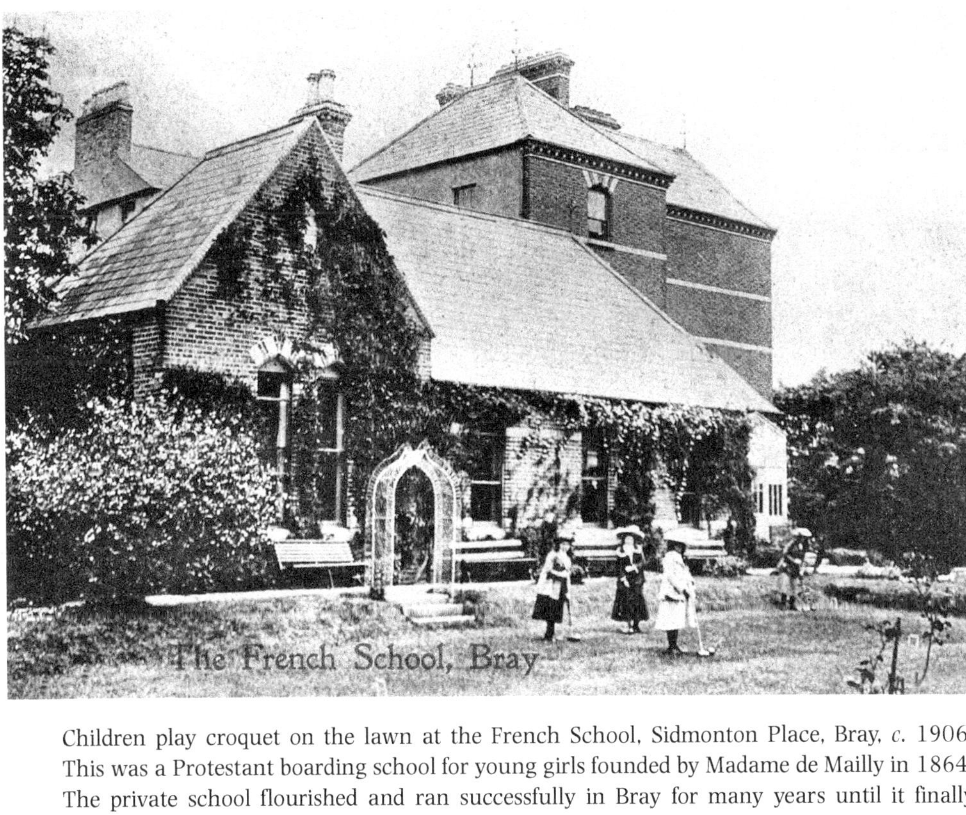

Children play croquet on the lawn at the French School, Sidmonton Place, Bray, *c.* 1906. This was a Protestant boarding school for young girls founded by Madame de Mailly in 1864. The private school flourished and ran successfully in Bray for many years until it finally closed in 1964.

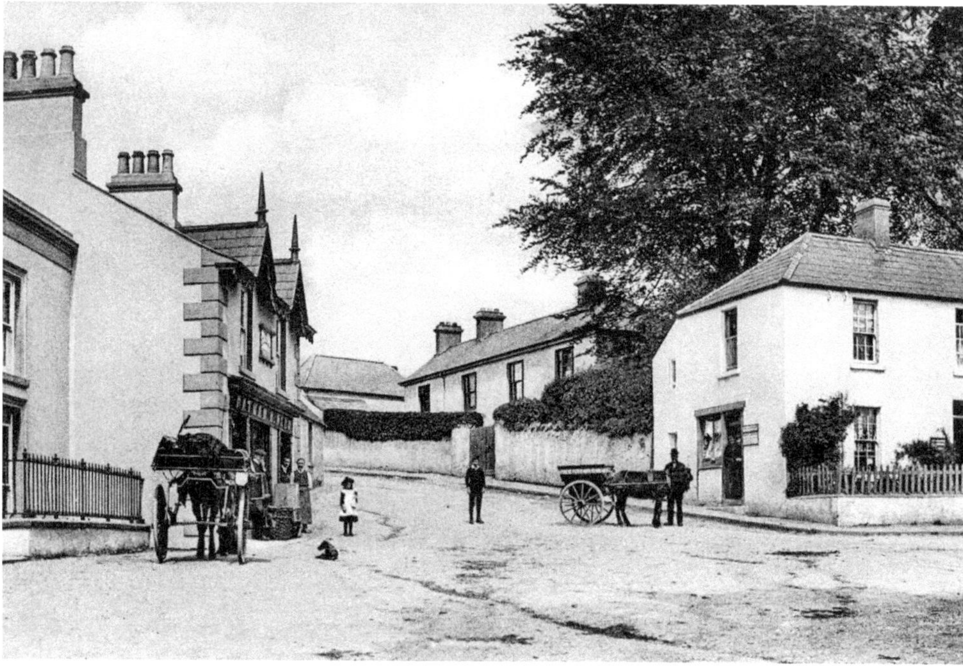

A peaceful scene in the attractive Delgany Village, *c.* 1910, showing a jarvey waiting outside the post office on the right. At that time, the postmistress was Mrs O'Connor.

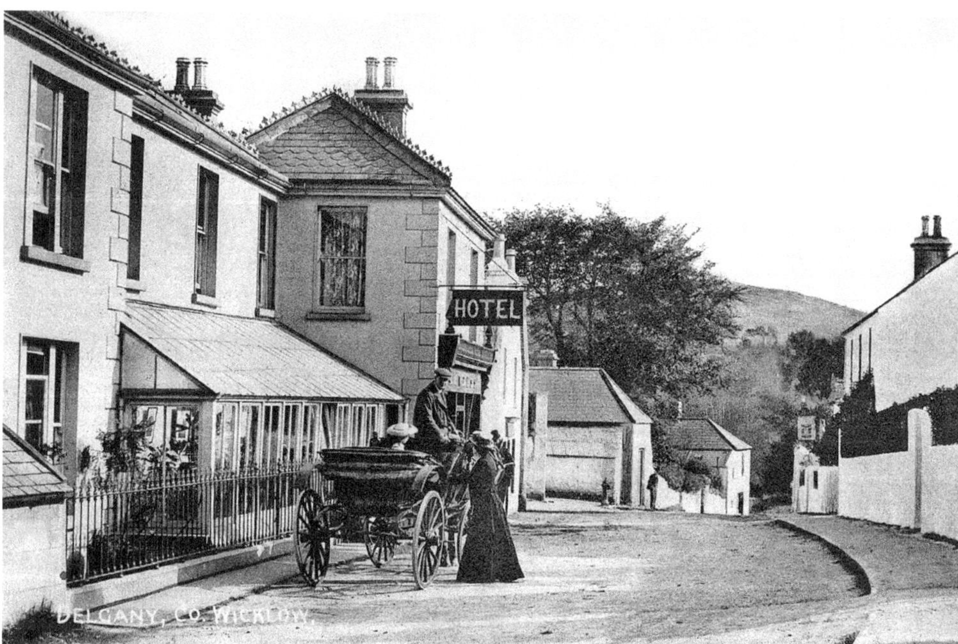

Visitors arrive at Lawless's Hotel in Delgany Village, *c.* 1910. The hotel proprietor was Thomas Lawless and he was also a family grocer and provision merchant. The hotel was popular with tourists as the village was so near to Bellevue and the Glen of the Downs.

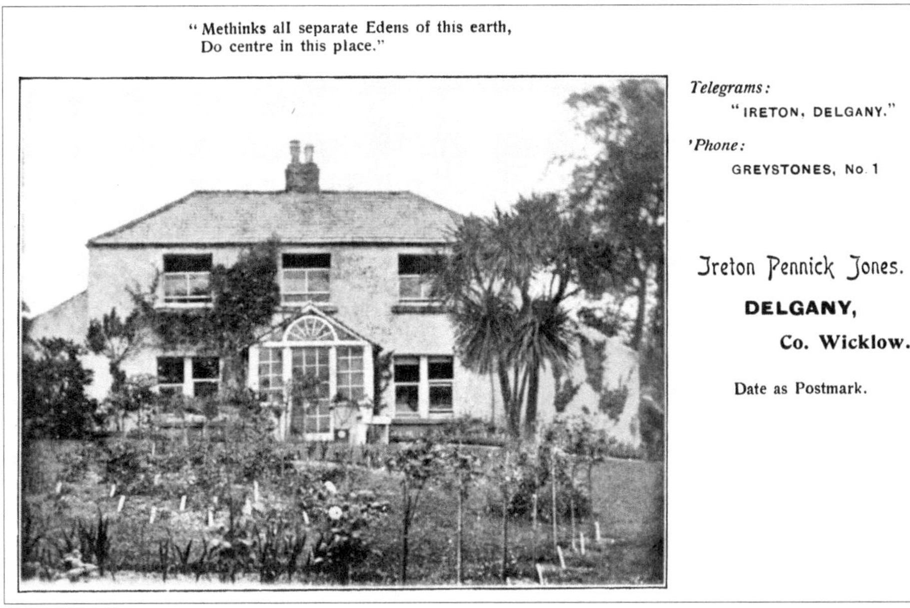

A postcard showing the home of Mr Ireton Pennick Jones, who was a nurseryman and landscape gardener in Delgany. He had a distinctive phone number: Greystones. No.1. The quotation on the card says 'Methinks all separate Edens of this earth, do centre in this place'. On 13 June 1924 in Dail Éireann, a Major Cooper asked the Minister for Defence when a gun and rifle handed over to the RIC by Mr Ireton Jones, in October 1918, would be returned to him. It seems that authority worked as slowly then as today!

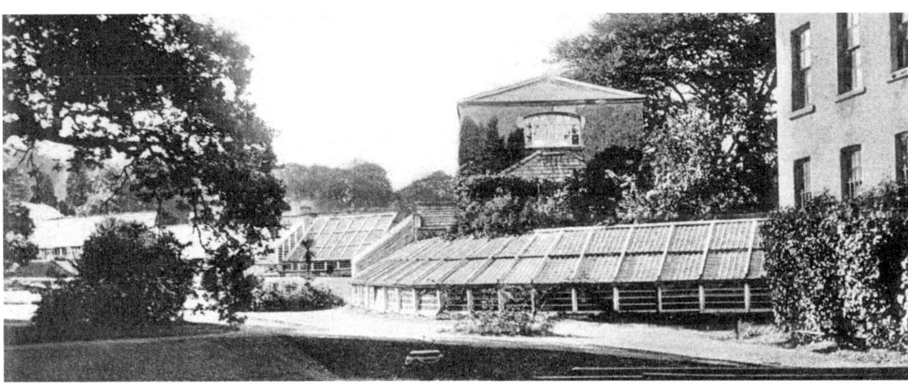

The gardens at Bellevue House on a card published by M.K. O'Connor of Delgany, *c.* 1905. The estate of Ballydonagh was purchased by David La Touche in 1753 and in the following three years, he built Bellevue House. He also laid out beautiful gardens with winding paths and extensive glasshouses sheltering many exotic plants. Over the years the La Touche family were known for their hospitality and generosity. David's son, Peter, built the new Christchurch at Delgany in 1789. During the famine years they helped to alleviate distress in the area. They were instrumental in continuing development in Greystones. Bellevue remained in the La Touche family for many years until the early 1900s, when financial problems necessitated the sale of land to the Holy Faith Sisters to build a school. However, problems continued and the family left the house in 1913. Bellevue deteriorated and had to be demolished in the 1950s.

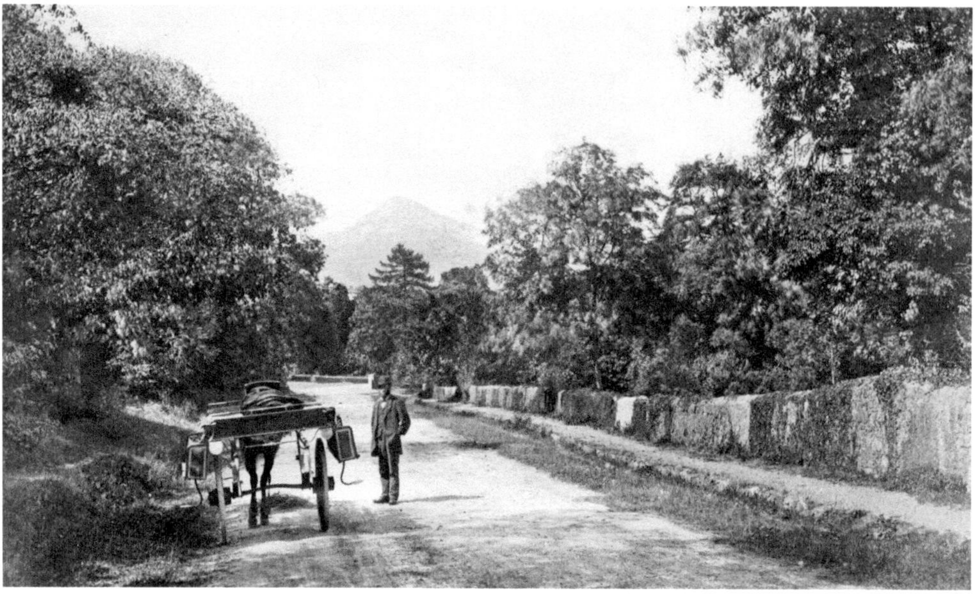

Jarvey and jaunting cart in the Glen of the Downs, County Wicklow in September 1871. The Big Sugar Loaf is in the distance. The Glen, a ravine over a mile long with steep wooded sides, was a preferred haunt for Dubliners, who would escape from the city to experience the delights of Wicklow. Visitors would halt at the Red Lane crossroads to picnic on the grass and some would dance at the crossroads (see page 56).

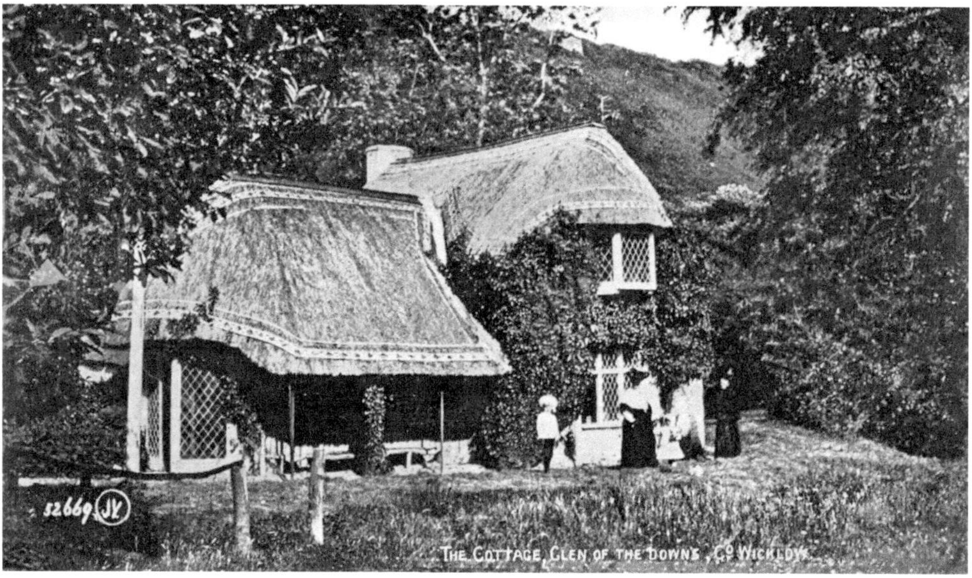

Mrs Elizabeth La Touche with her family on a card posted in March 1918. She is standing outside her picturesque thatched cottage in the Glen of the Downs, which was near the northern entrance to Bellevue. The cottage had been personally designed by her and the ground floor was filled with mementoes brought back from foreign holidays. Upstairs was a dining room where Mrs La Touche would entertain friends to lunch.

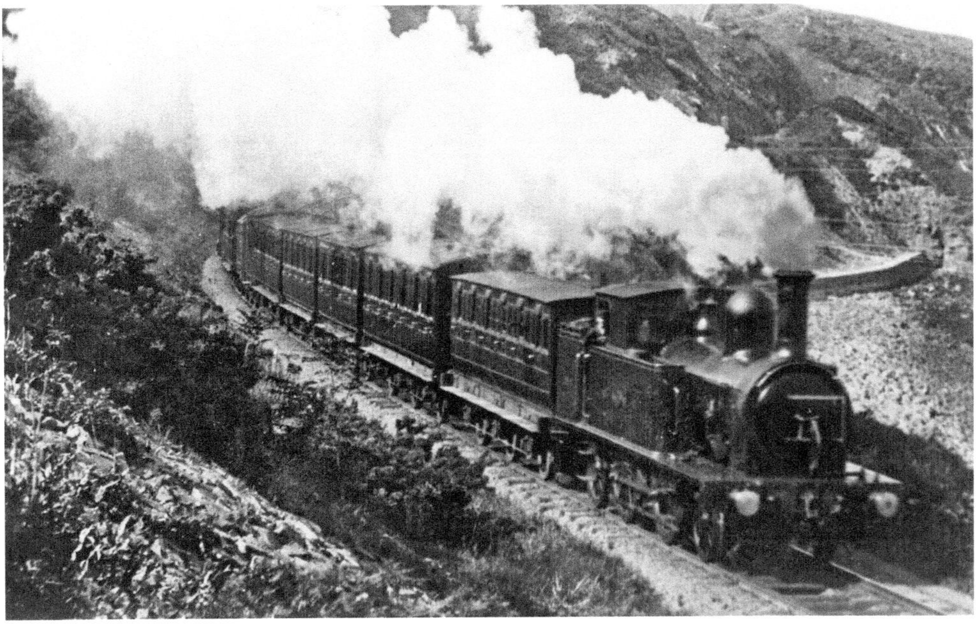

Greystones Station was opened on 30 October 1855 by the Dublin, Wicklow and Wexford Railway Company. The construction of the railway line from Bray to Greystones around Bray Head and along the sea cliffs was very difficult. However, Isambard Brunel was a brilliant engineer and using three tunnels and four trestle viaducts, he successfully completed the project. The railway revitalised Greystones. The postcard shows a steam train at Bray Head heading for Greystones.

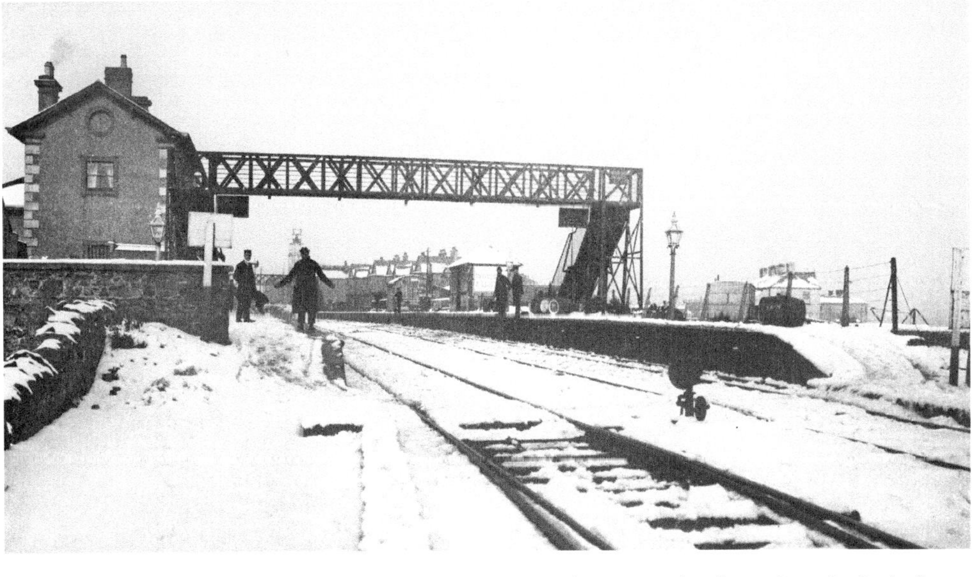

The card shows a deserted Greystones Station apart from some hardy souls on both platforms during a fall of snow in the 1950s. The railway station was built on the line dividing the estates of the La Touche family of Belleview House and the Hawkins-Whitshed family of Killincarrig House.

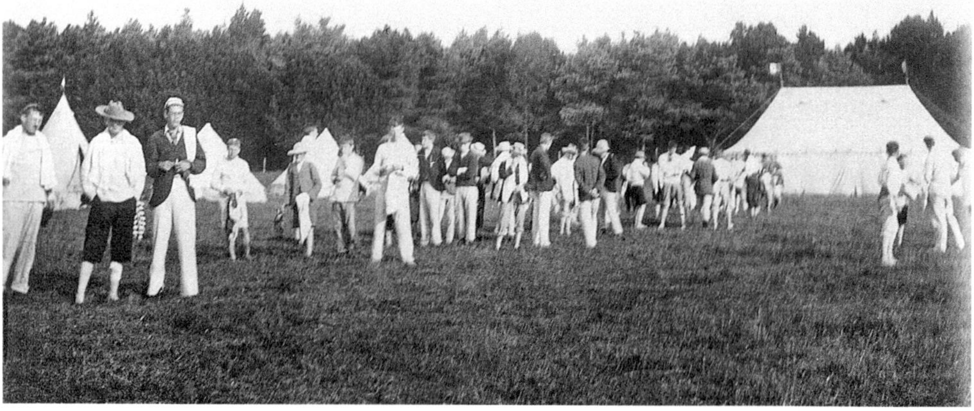

The first Boys' Brigade Camp in Ireland held at Greystones in August 1897. This was a well-organised camp with two large marquees and fifteen tents. Many of the boys had travelled on the steamer from Holyhead. The camp had a magazine – *The Camp Comet*. This included news about the camp concerts, where each 'sing-song' included a special camp song, which had the following chorus, sang to the tune of 'Mulligan Guards': 'Camp boys, camp, for thus we camp away,/ Upon the cliffs quite close to Dublin Bay;/ Och! Hear the boys bedad! They're on the way,/ With a cheer boys, cheer for Irish stew.'

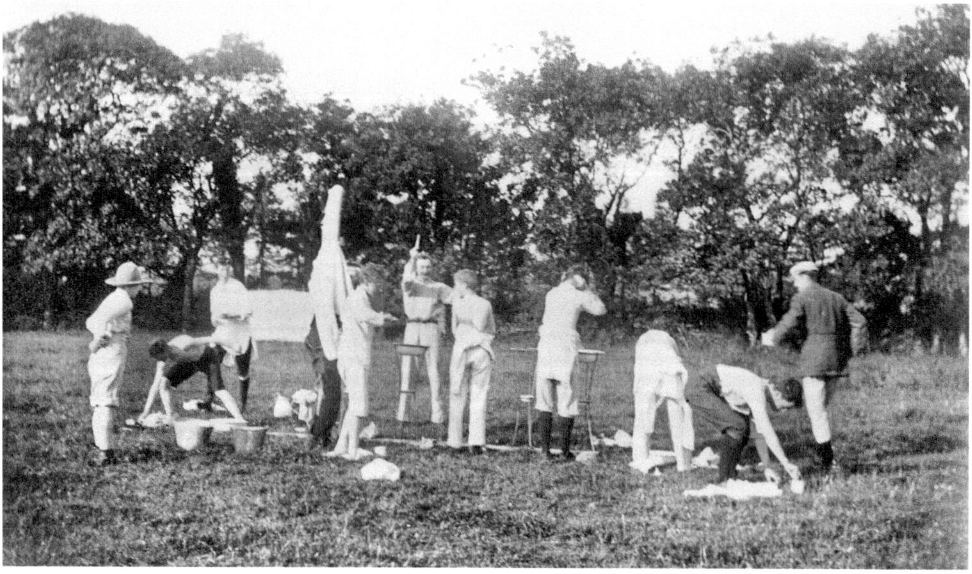

Boys having their early morning wash. The facilities at the camp were rudimentary. The boys followed a military-type regime and all were kept very active. During the week there were numerous sports including football, rounders, athletics, cycling and swimming. During the week, the camp was challenged to a game of cricket by the Wicklow County Club. It was a close game that ended with a victory for the Wicklow team by four wickets.

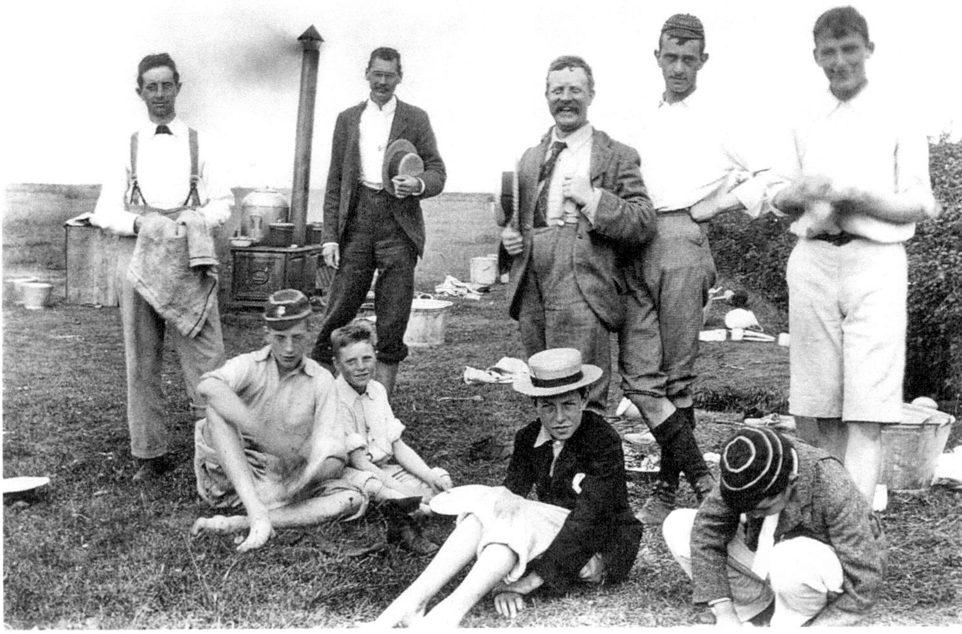

A group of the officers with some of the boys are pictured helping at the camp kitchen. They are not really dressed for camping. Most wear caps or boaters and have rolled-up trousers. The camp doctor reported in *The Camp Comet* that he had seen cases of a continuously increasing appetite in many boys and also 'sleeping sickness', when some boys had slept through the morning bugle call!

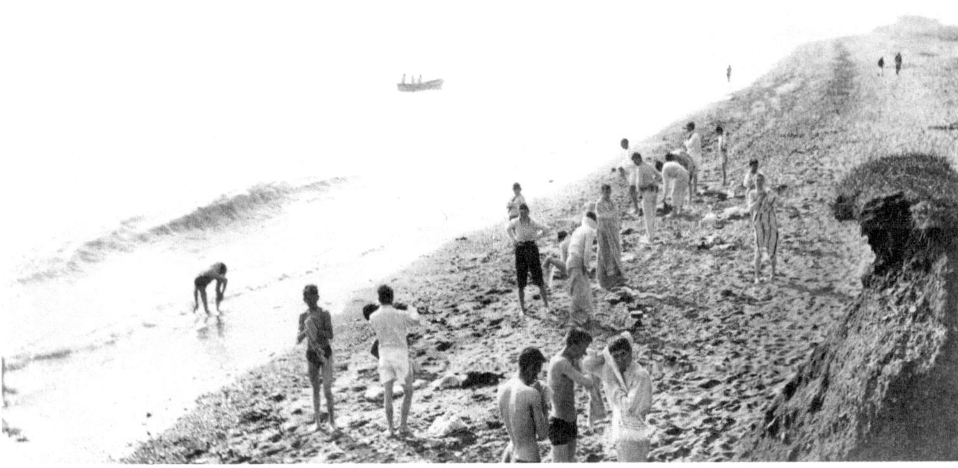

Bathing parades were held each morning. The boys would go to the nearby Greystones beach. This was a bracing start to the day, but the picture shows the boys enjoying themselves on the beach. Swimming sports were held during the week, which included diving, swimming races and water polo.

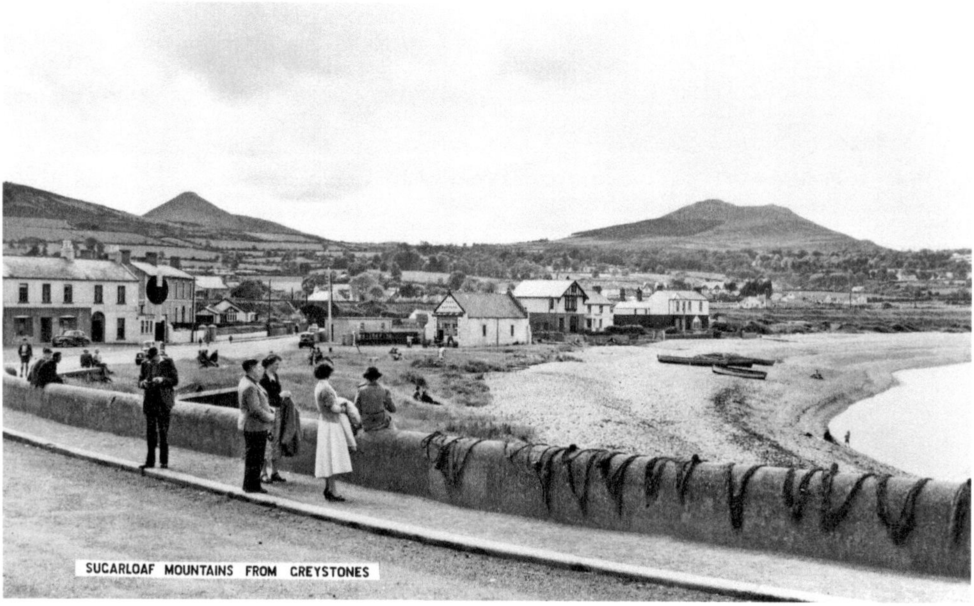

The town and the North Beach, Greystones, with the Sugarloaf mountain in the distance, *c.* 1950.

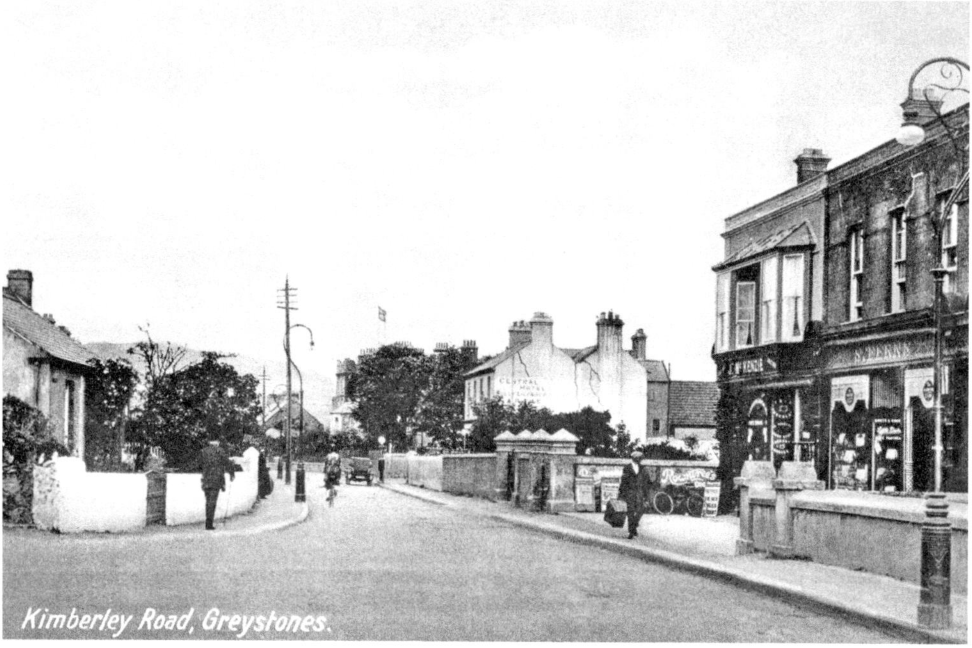

Kimberley Road, Greystones. The shops on the right are Samuel Ferns, draper, and J. McKenzie, stationer and newsagent. The next building is the Central Hotel. The sign on the side of the building says it is fully licensed and has a garage. In the distance, a flag flies over the Grand Hotel.

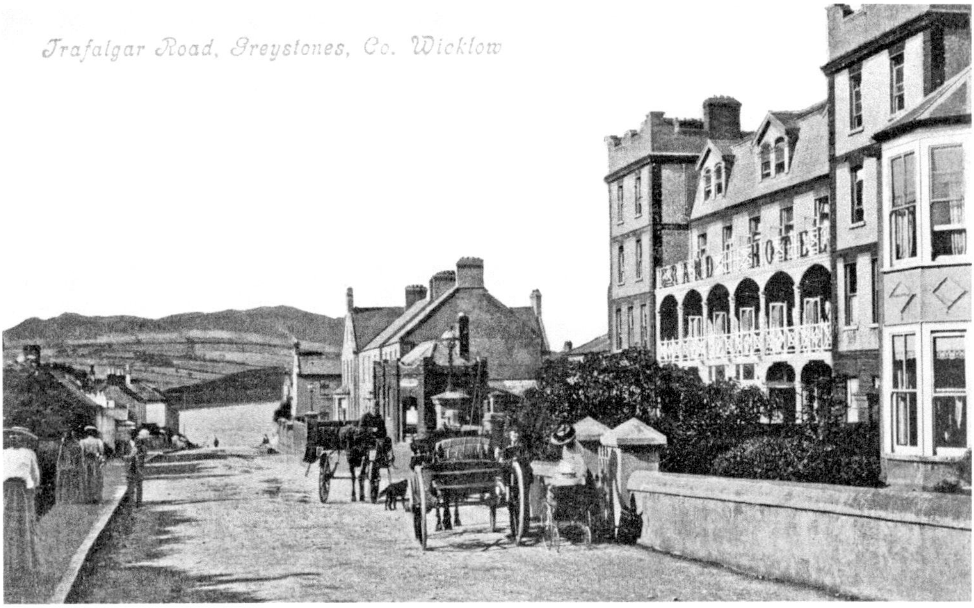

Carriages wait outside the Grand Hotel on Trafalgar Road, Greystones. The card was posted on 22 September 1908. The hotel, later named the La Touche Hotel, was built in 1890. It was very popular and attracted visitors to Greystones for over 100 years. Unfortunately, numbers declined and the hotel closed in 2004.

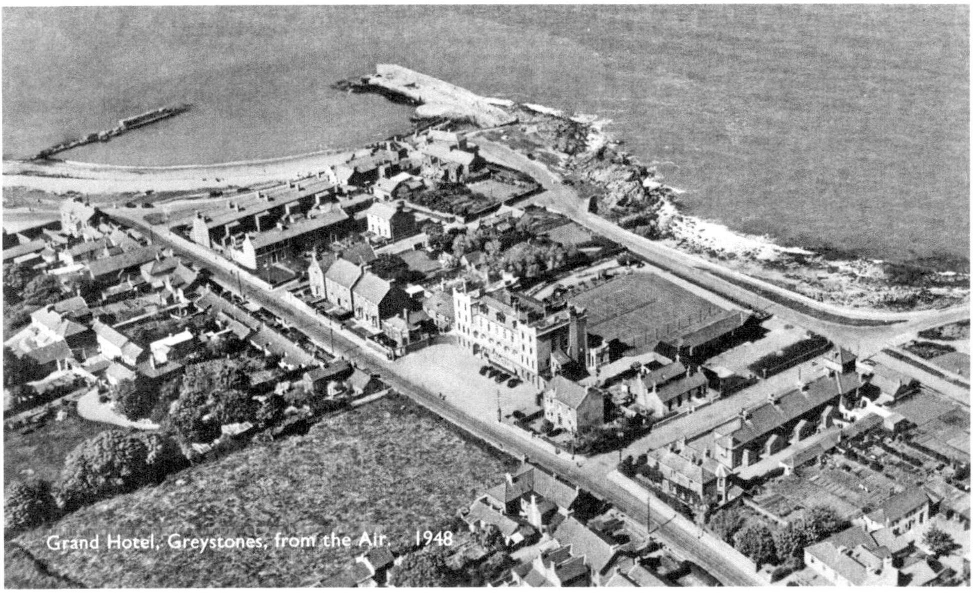

The Grand Hotel from the air in 1948. It has a superb position with tennis courts at the back of the hotel and access to the beach. The Grand Hotel has a guest list to rival many of Ireland's historic hotels. Michael Collins stayed here in 1921 on the night before he left for London to sign the Treaty. Other guests have included Samuel Becket, John Millington Synge and Brendan Behan. A regular patron at the hotel was Eamon De Valera.

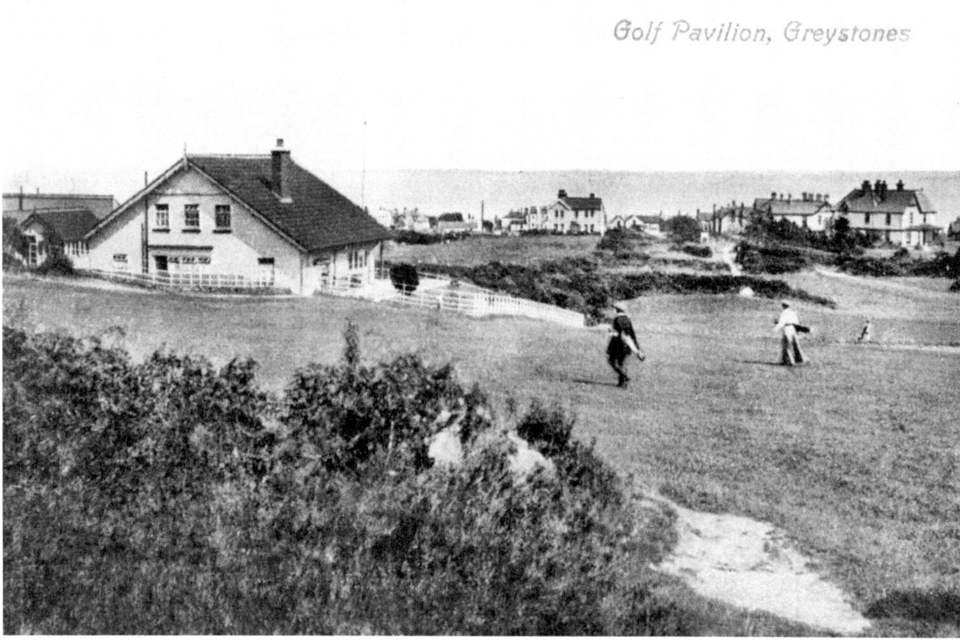

Founded in 1895, Greystones is one of Ireland's oldest golf courses. Lord Powerscourt was the club's first president. The course was originally set around Jones's Hill, a rocky prominence that provides one of the finest views in Irish golf. On a clear day, the panorama from the seventh green ranges from the Mountains of Mourne in the north to the dim outline of Wales directly across the sea. The backdrop is the Sugarloaf and Wicklow mountains. The postcard shows golfers returning to the pavilion at Greystones, *c.* 1905.

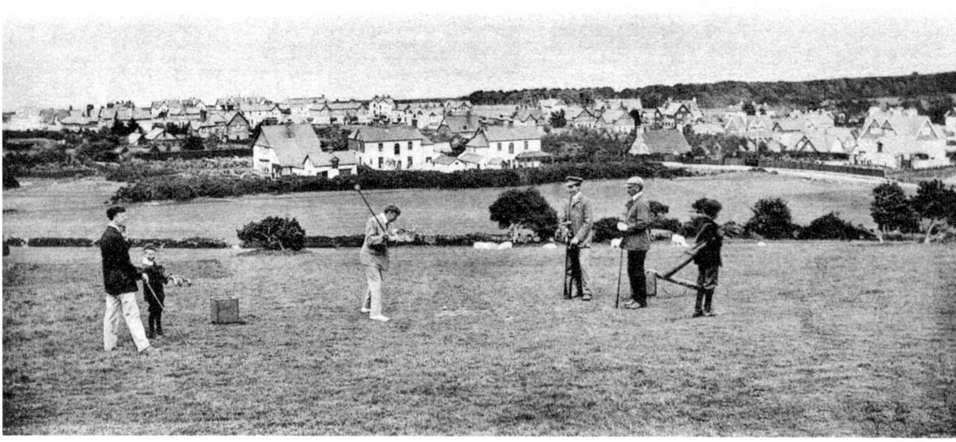

Another view of the golf links at Greystones. The card, posted in July 1905, shows a men's four-ball and says that two of the gentlemen playing golf are Mr P. Meyer and his brother. The course was originally nine holes but it was extended to eighteen holes in 1914.

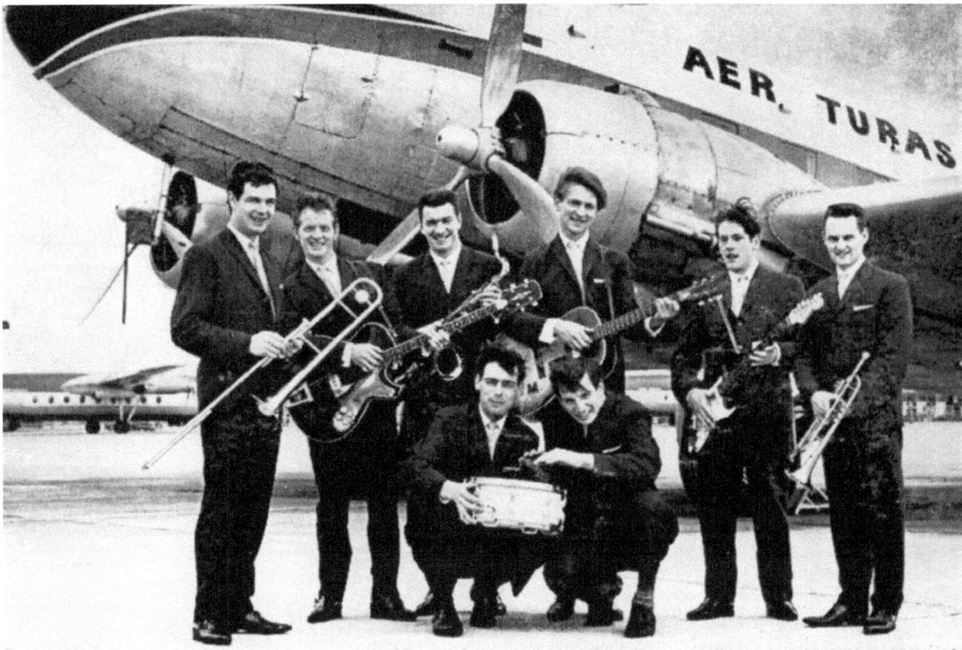

The Swinging
Singing
Sensational

JETS

GREYSTONES
Telephone 874547

The Jets Showband from Greystones pictured at Dublin Airport. The Jets (formerly The Artones) went on to form The Nevada Showband, who became one of Ireland's most popular showbands in the 1960s and '70s.

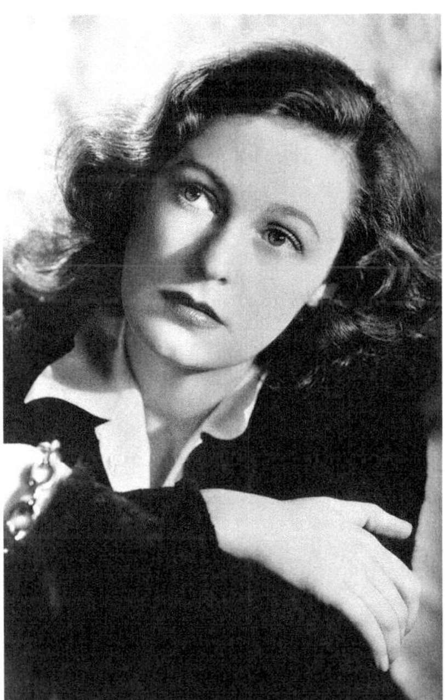

Geraldine Fitzgerald (1914-2005) was born in Greystones. She had glorious red hair and was one of the most beautiful women in British films of the 1930s. Her success led her to move to America and Broadway in 1938, where she was soon offered a film contract by the film producer Hal Wallace. She was a feisty actress, who had problems with management, but she still appeared in many films and won a number of awards. She was nominated for an Oscar in 1940 as best supporting actress for her role in *Wuthering Heights*.

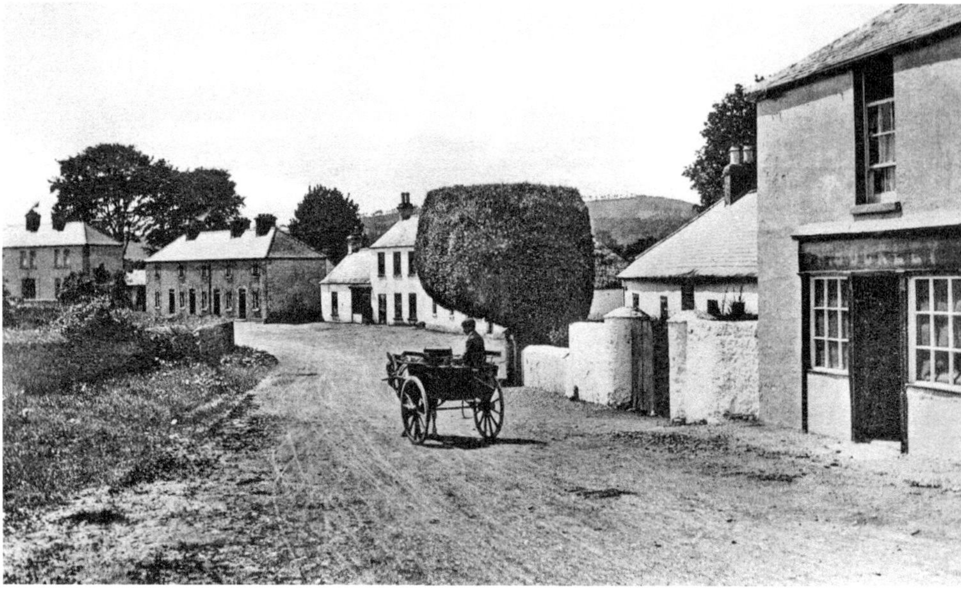

The village of Killincarrig, Greystones, *c*. 1910. The grocery and hardware shop on the right is owned by Mrs H. Buckley.

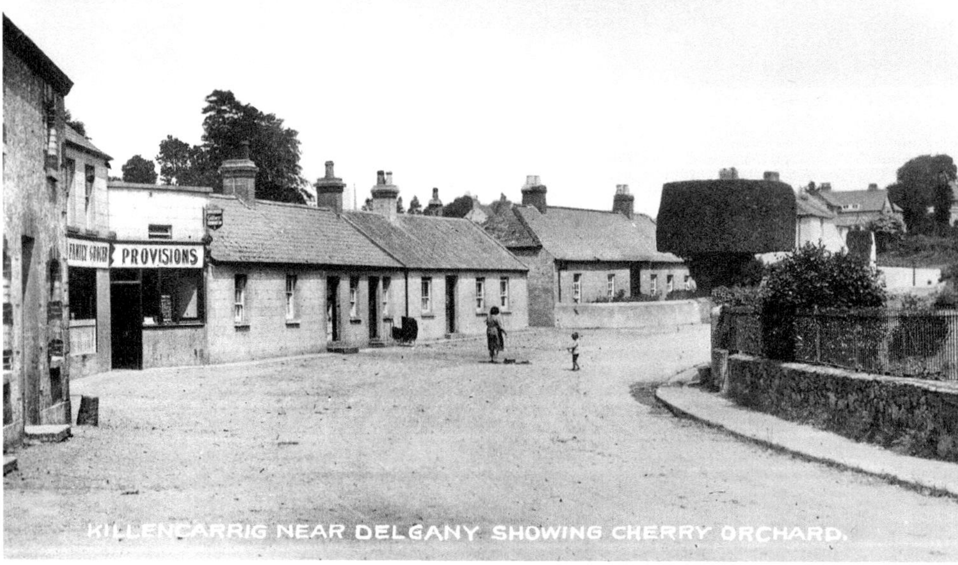

A later view of Killincarrig, showing the cherry orchard on the right. The orchard trees were grown from Spanish seeds. At this time the cherry orchard was run by Kevin and Michael Devereux, who also ran a garden nursery. They produced dessert cherries of very fine quality. Killincarrig was also famous for its superb tea rooms managed by Maeve Devereux, which attracted many visitors to the village.

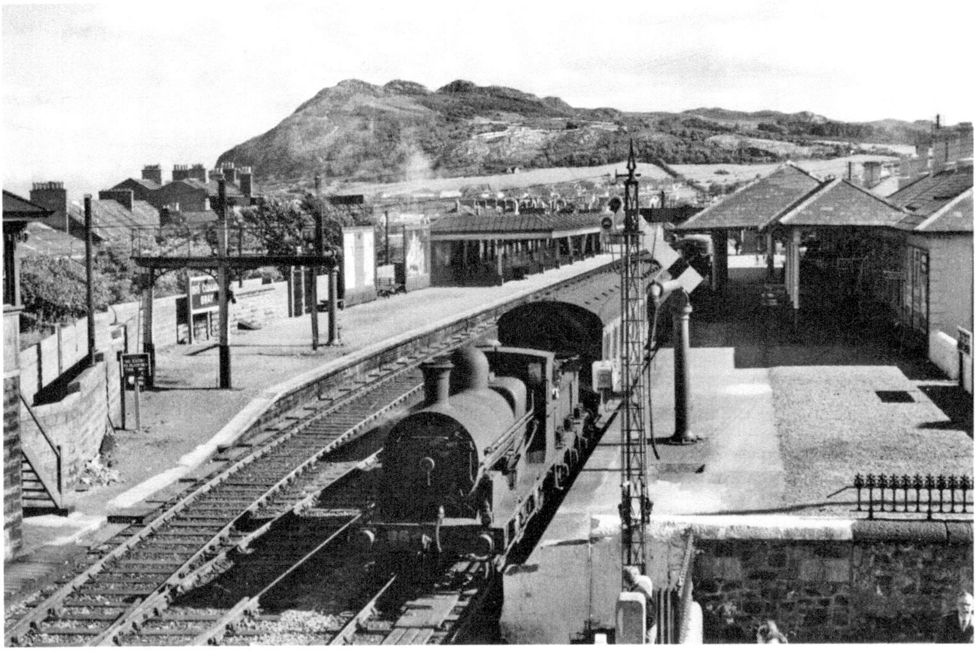

The arrival of the railway in Bray in 1854 was instrumental in making the town into Ireland's principal seaside resort. The Victorians believed in the health benefits of fresh air and seawater and flocked to Bray in great numbers. New hotels and guesthouses opened and many day-trippers arrived by train. The postcard shows Steam Train No. 254 leaving Bray Station for Amiens Street Station, Dublin in August 1956. Bray Head is in the background.

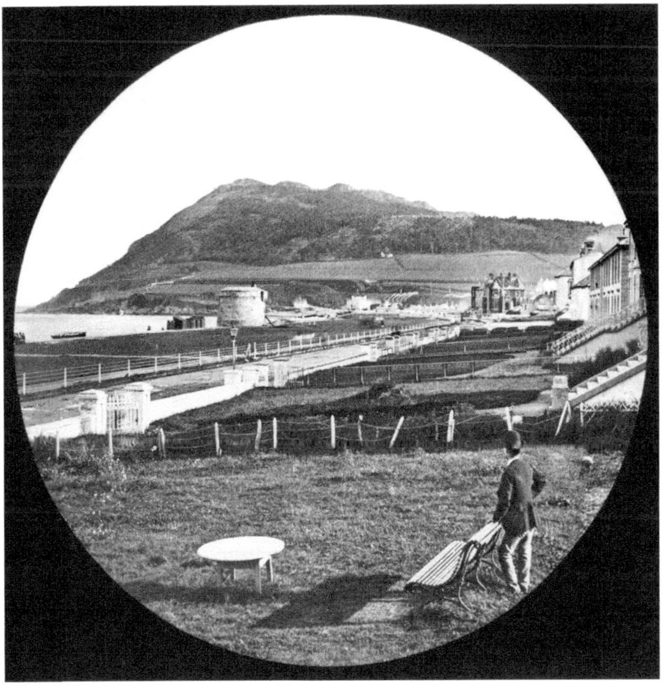

Bray seafront, showing the most southerly Martello Tower (number one) on the beach opposite the present Esplanade Terrace, *c.* 1880s. This tower was too close to the sea and was demolished in 1884. Bray had two more Martello Towers. The second tower above the harbour still stands and is now a private residence. The third tower, which was built on a headland to the north, collapsed into the sea due to coastal erosion around 1865.

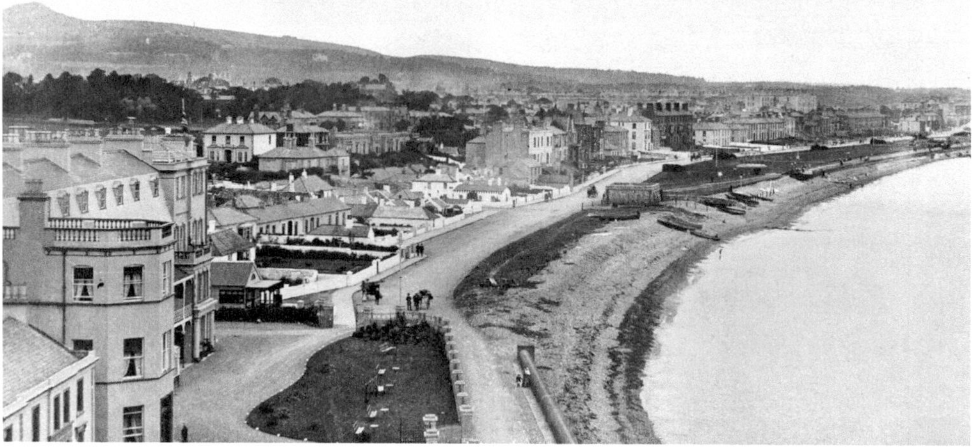

An early view of Bray seafront. The writer of the card says that 'Bray is nicer than the picture. There is a lovely prom around – indeed one of the nicest that I have ever seen'. The Bray Head Hotel is on the left.

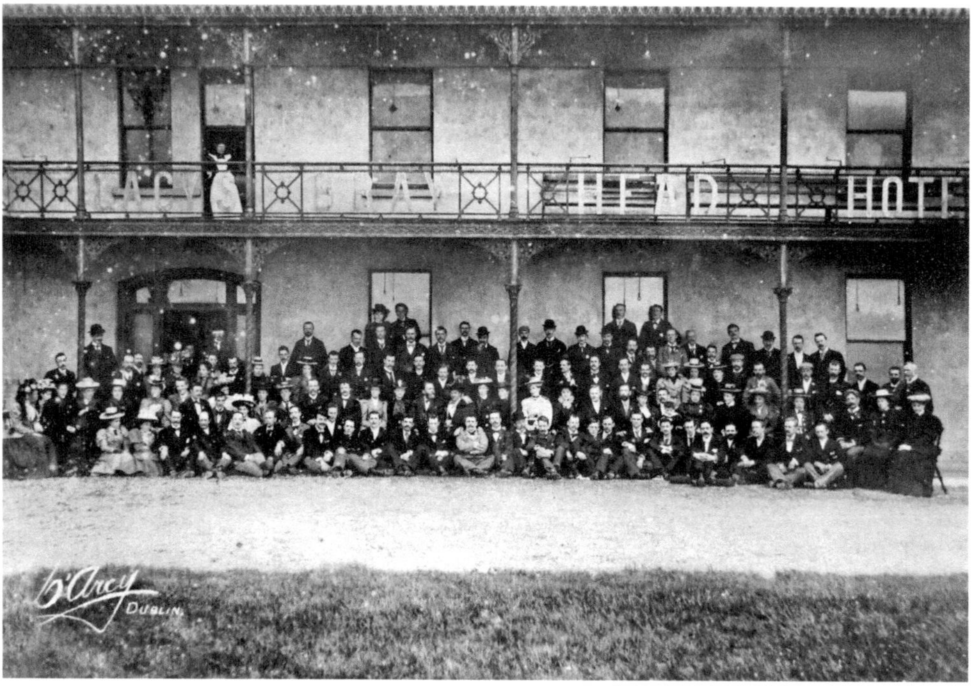

Lacy's Bray Head Hotel, *c.* 1900s, showing a large group, which looks like a company workforce on a special day out. There are some splendid hats and men in bowlers. A chambermaid looks on from the balcony. The photographer was D'Arcy from Dublin.

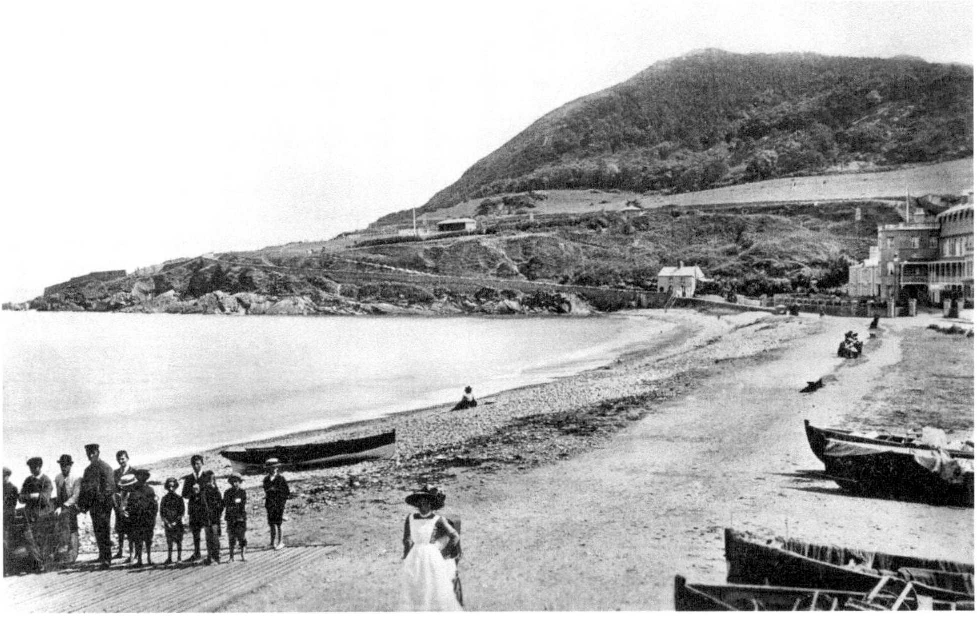

A group of children pose for the camera on the beach, *c.* 1910. Perhaps they are waiting to take a boat trip, as the waves are calm. The beach is quiet and now is a good time for the nursemaid to take the baby in her charge out in the pram to get the benefits of fresh sea air.

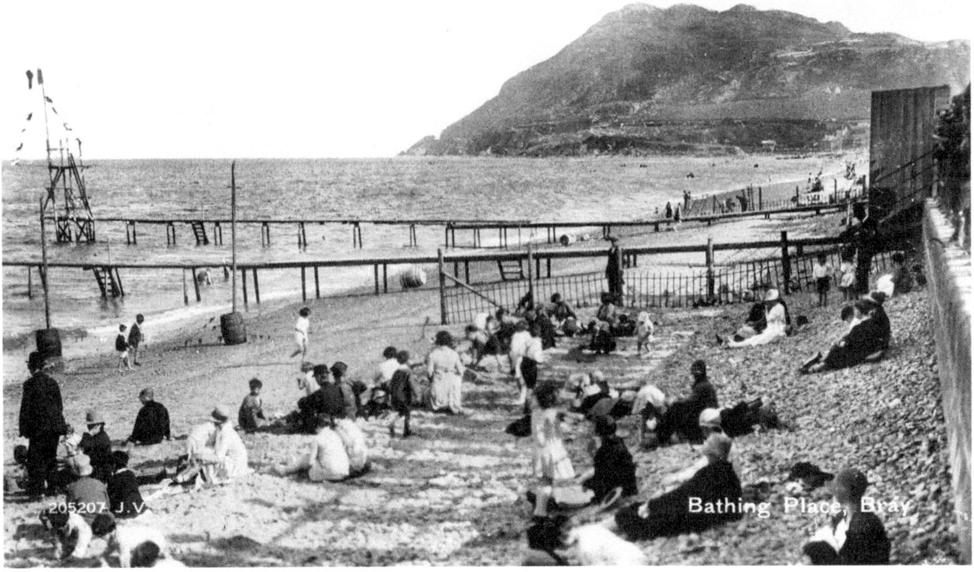

A view of the bathing place, Bray, in the 1950s, showing a crowded beach. There are fences enclosing a reserved area of the beach and the diving boards that could only be used by members of Bray Swimming Club.

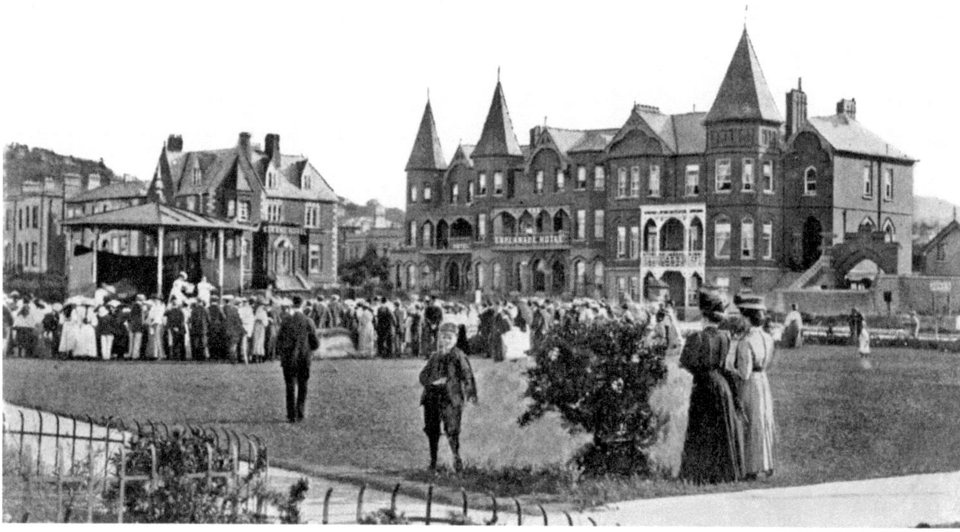

The White Coons were formed by Will C. Pepper in 1899 and entertained the crowds on the Bray seafront for many years. Here they are shown performing on the stage of the small bandstand opposite the Esplanade Hotel (formerly Lacy's Hotel). The show was free but at the end of the concert, the hat was passed around for donations towards the group's expenses, which included a payment to Bray Urban District Council for use of the bandstand.

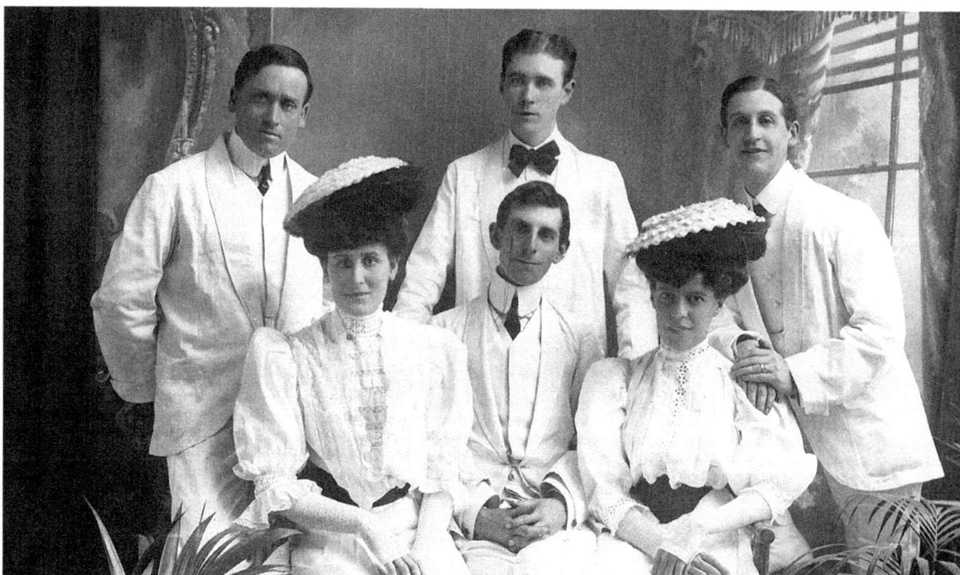

Performers in the troupe of Pierrot entertainers would regularly change. Stanley Holloway of *My Fair Lady* fame started his career with the troupe. The postcard shows Will C. Pepper's 'White Coons and Banjo Troupe' in a picture taken at Killick's Studios, Bray in 1906. From left to right, back row: James Godden, Allan Thomas and Alf Wood; front row: Ada Watson, J. Macdermott and May Windsor. The final season for the White Coons was summer 1909, as the following year they moved to the pier at Clacton-on-Sea in Essex.

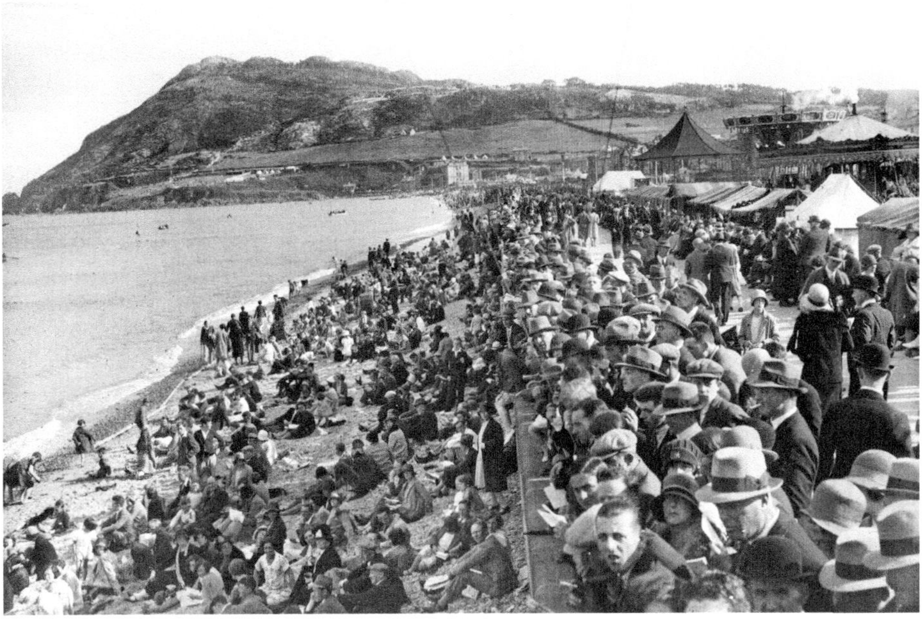

Regatta day at Bray at the height of the season in the 1950s as many day-trippers from Dublin flock to the seaside for the fresh air and entertainment. The crowds on the seashore and lining the promenade are watching the activities in the bay, including yacht races, sailing and rowing matches. Military bands played on the promenade bandstands and there were all the usual fairground amusements to entertain the crowds. At the end of the day, there would be a grand firework display.

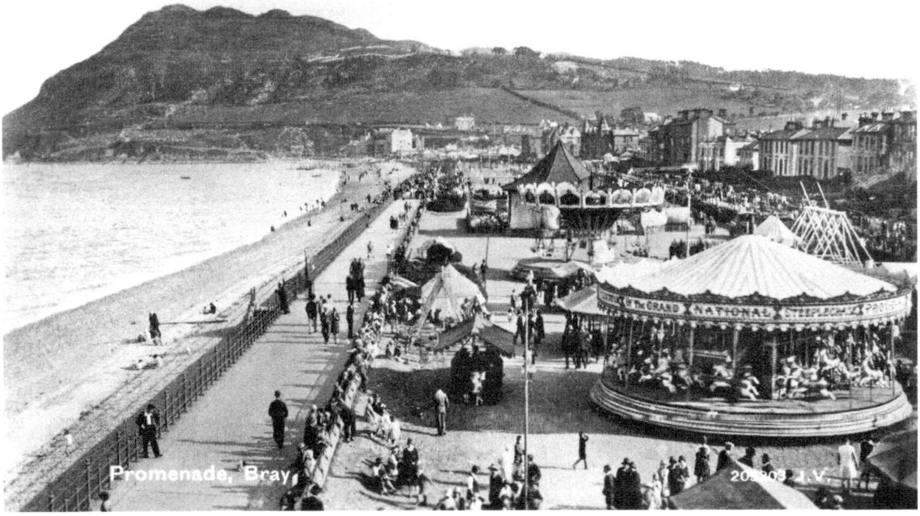

The fairgrounds on the promenade at Bray. The Grand National Steeplechase Roundabout is on the right. Among the entertainments there were many other seaside amusements including slot machines, a house of laughter, swing boats, dodgems and a ghost train. The Fun Palace, at the centre of the promenade, was said to be the biggest covered arcade in Ireland.

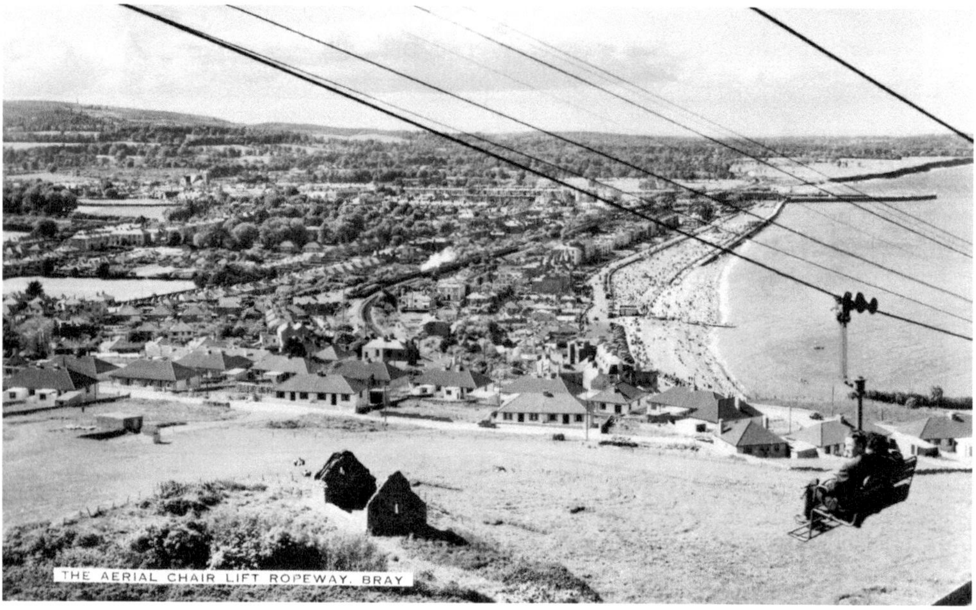

A great attraction for tourists at Bray in the 1950s was the aerial chairlift to the Eagle's Nest on Bray Head with its great panoramic views. This was built by Eamonn Quinn, who also owned the Red Island Holiday Camp at Skerries. The chairlift used electric power but was unsafe to operate in strong winds. It closed in 1970, as numbers visiting Bray and using the chairlift declined and the ride was no longer profitable.

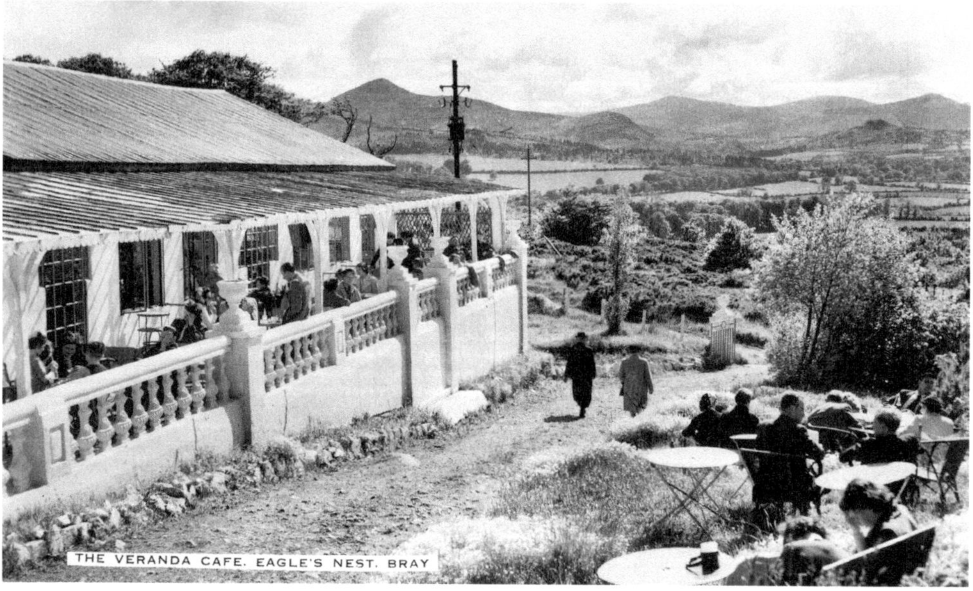

Tourists at the Verandah café at the Eagle's Nest sit outside enjoying the marvellous views. In the summer, there were daytrips by coach every Tuesday from the Red Island Holiday Camp to Bray. The trips included a ride on the chairlift and lunch at the café. In the evenings there were dances in the ballroom, which were very popular.

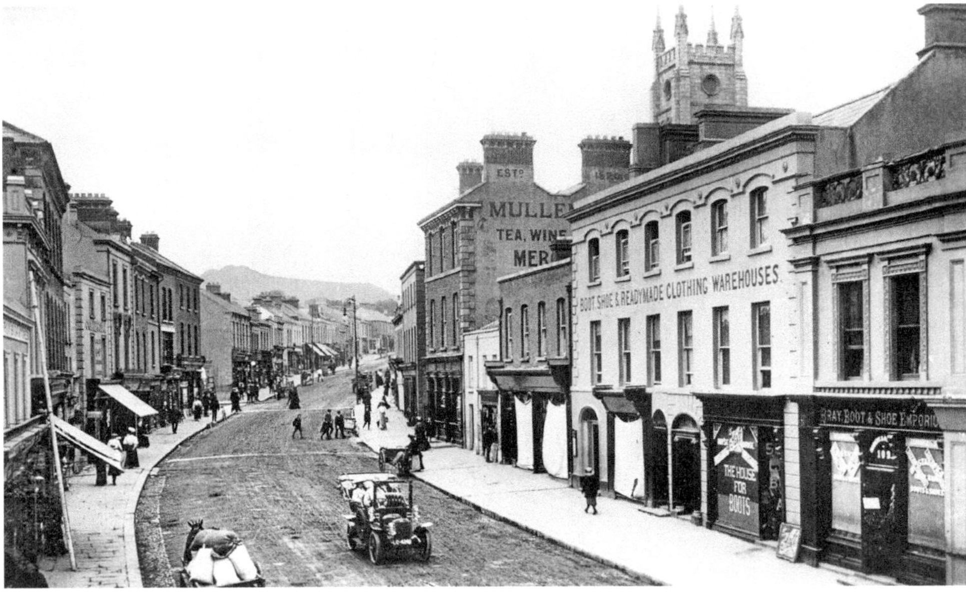

A busy scene on the Main Steet, Bray, *c.* 1910. A solitary vintage car drives up the road. The tower of the Holy Redeemer RC church is seen behind Mullen's Tea and Wine merchants. There is a fine selection of shops. On the right is the Boot Shoe and Ready-made Clothing Warehouse next to the Bray Boot and Shoe Emporium.

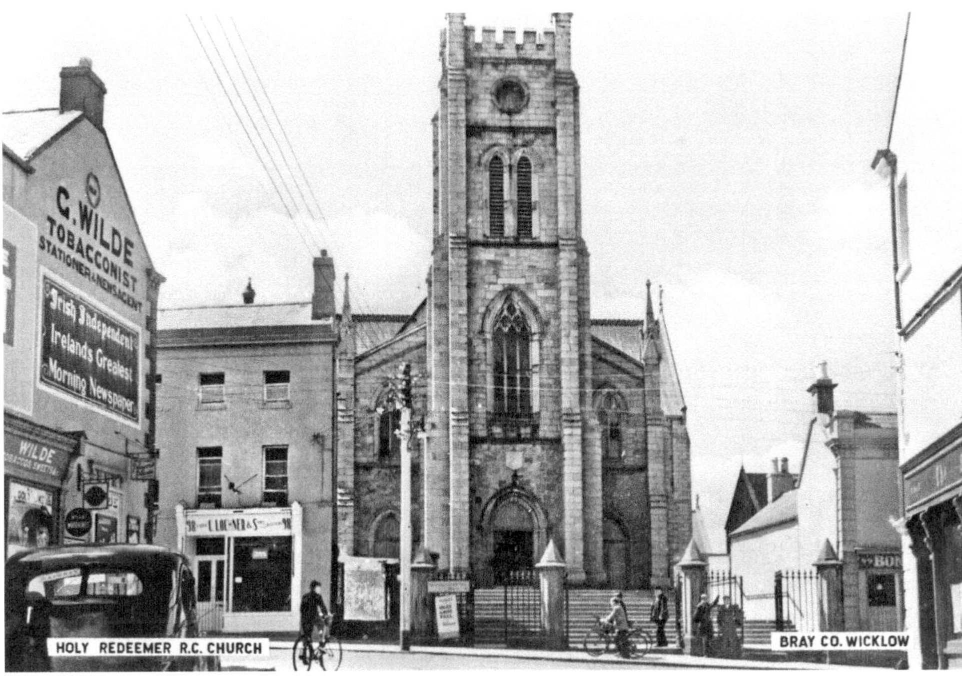

The imposing Holy Redeemer RC church with its fine steps and railings on the Main Street in Bray. The church was designed by Patrick Byrne and built in 1852. The front of the church was remodelled and extended by William Byrne in 1895-97.

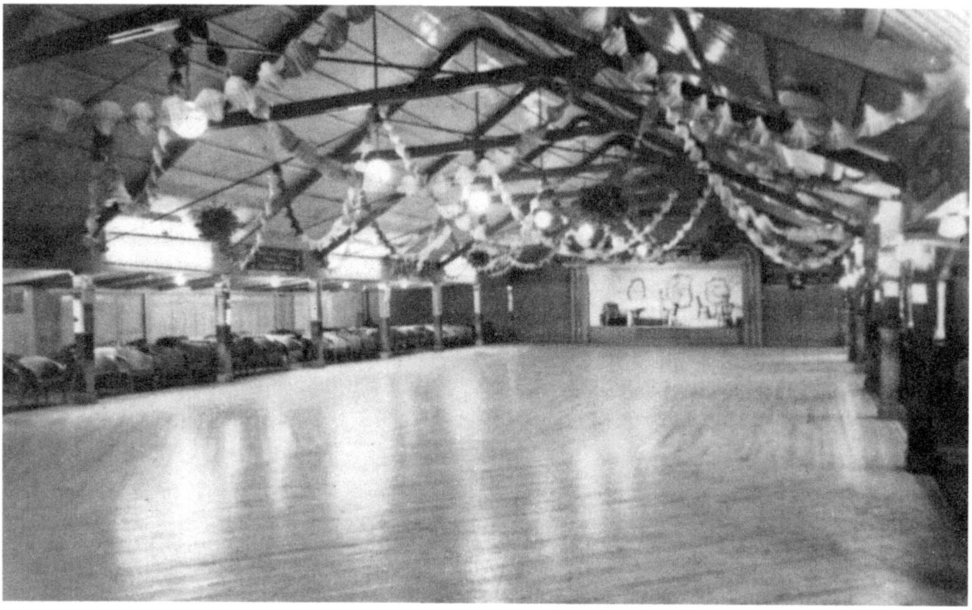

The legendary Arcadia Ballroom in Bray, known as the 'Ballroom of Romance'. It was a dancer's paradise with a fine maple-wood dance floor and a wooden ceiling. The atmosphere was great as the band played and rotating mirror balls reflected light on the dancers. In the 1940s and 1950s, it was a venue that attracted the top Irish and English bands. Crowds flocked there and for many young people it was indeed the place they first met their future partners. Unfortunately, the Arcadia burnt down in 1962. However, it was rebuilt and enlarged and many famous stars such as Status Quo, Roy Orbison, the Everley Brothers and Rod Stewart appeared there in the 1960s.

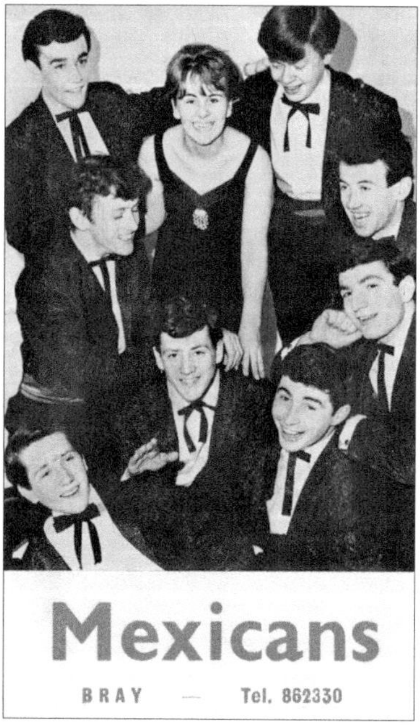

The Mexican Showband often played at the Arcadia. The group had many musicians from Bray including Mike Dunne on keyboard, Sean Owens on bass, Frank Owens on rhythm guitar, Alan Cranny on lead guitar and Desi Reynolds on drums. Tina Reynolds, born Philomena Quinn in Greystones, joined the band at the age of 17. She was a talented popular singer who became a favourite on the showband scene. She toured with the Mexicans for four years. However, after the band's manager Tom Cranny died in a car accident in 1969, the Mexicans broke up. Tina then had spells with Jim Farley's big band and the Real McCoy, before becoming the lead singer with the Nevada. She represented Ireland in the 1974 Eurovision Song Contest with her song 'Cross Your Heart', but that was the year Abba won the contest singing 'Waterloo'. Tina came in seventh place.

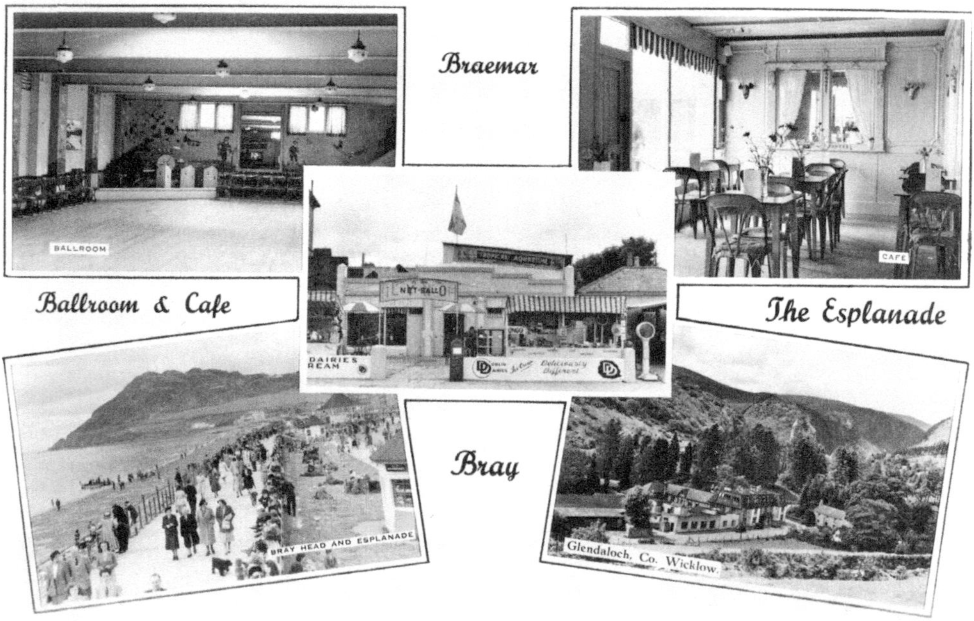

The Braemar Ballroom and Café on the seafront at the Esplanade, Bray, *c.* 1950. Dances were held in the ballroom on two nights each week, which attracted young people from Dublin, Dún Laoghaire and the surrounding areas.

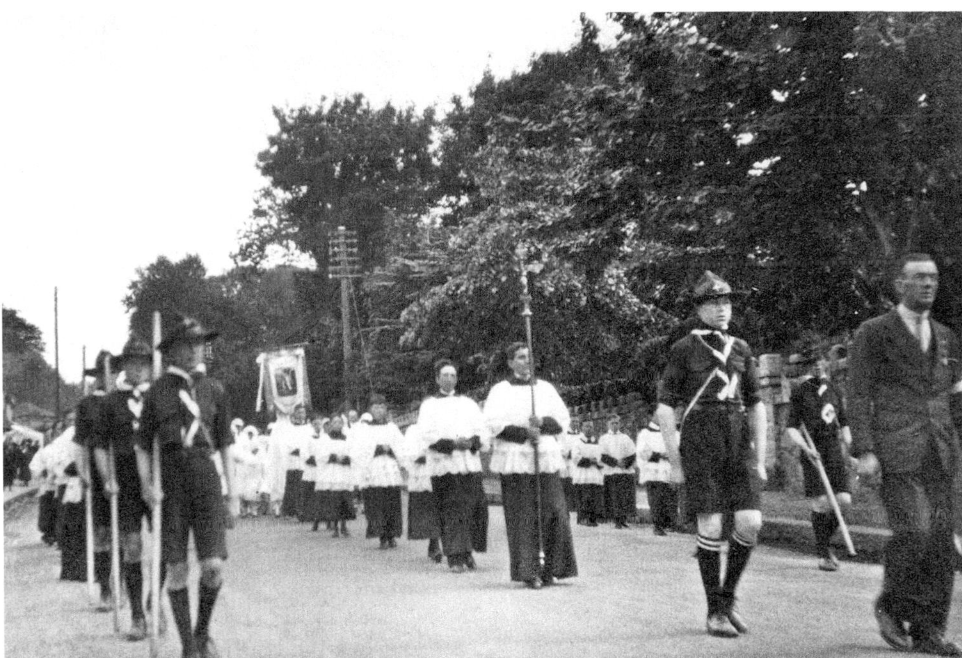

Crowds watch from the pavement as scouts escort a church procession through Bray during the Eucharistic Congress in June 1932.

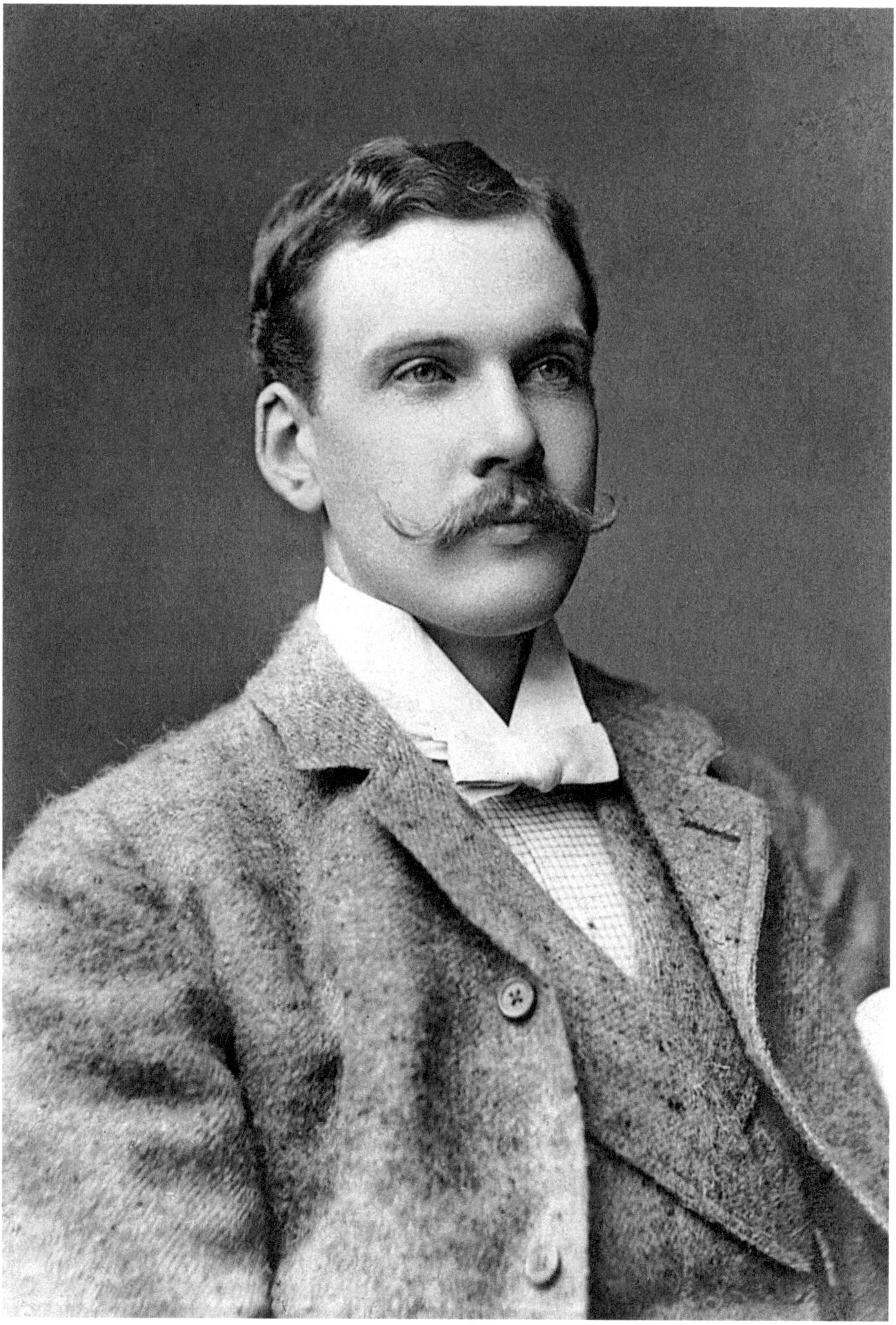

The well-known baritone performer, Mr Harry Plunket Greene. He was born on 24 June 1865 at Old Connaught House, Bray. He studied at Stuttgart, Florence and London. His public singing career began in 1888 in Handel's *Messiah*, which led to performances at Covent Garden and the major London concert venues. He became one of the leading British singers, famed for his great diction and unique interpretation of a wide variety of songs.

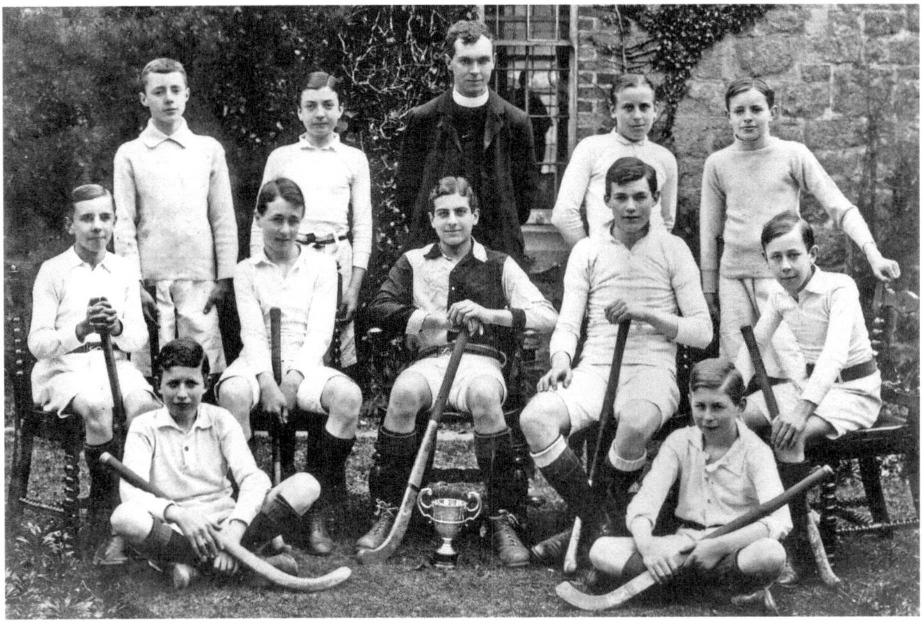

Aravon School, Meath Road, Bray, winners of the schoolboy Hockey League in 1911. From left to right, back row: Beatty, R.D. Greer, Revd F.C. Stockes, Price, O'Connor; middle row: Price, C. Gamble, W.E. Caldbeck (Captain), E.J. Lyndon, A.V. Bridge; front row: Haughton, N.V. Nunn.

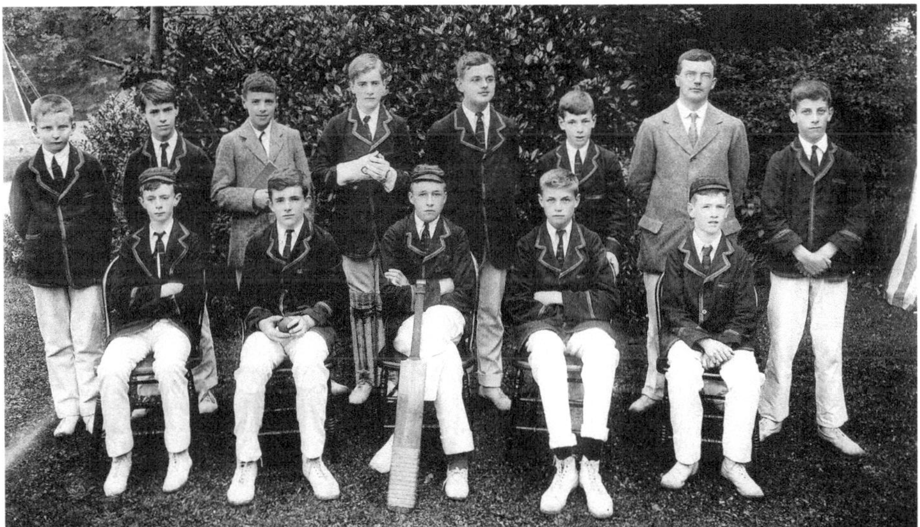

The First Eleven Cricket Team at Aravon School in 1916. Aravon School was founded in 1862 by Thomas Courtney in a house on Sidmonton Road, Bray. Four years later, the school moved to 'Aravon' on Meath Road. It was a successful private school, which expanded over the following years, although the maximum roll at any time was about ninety. Among its pupils were the dramatist John Millington Synge and the patriot Roger Casement (see page 74). In 1984, the school transferred to Old Conna Hill House, which had formerly been a hotel and home of Count Cyril McCormack.

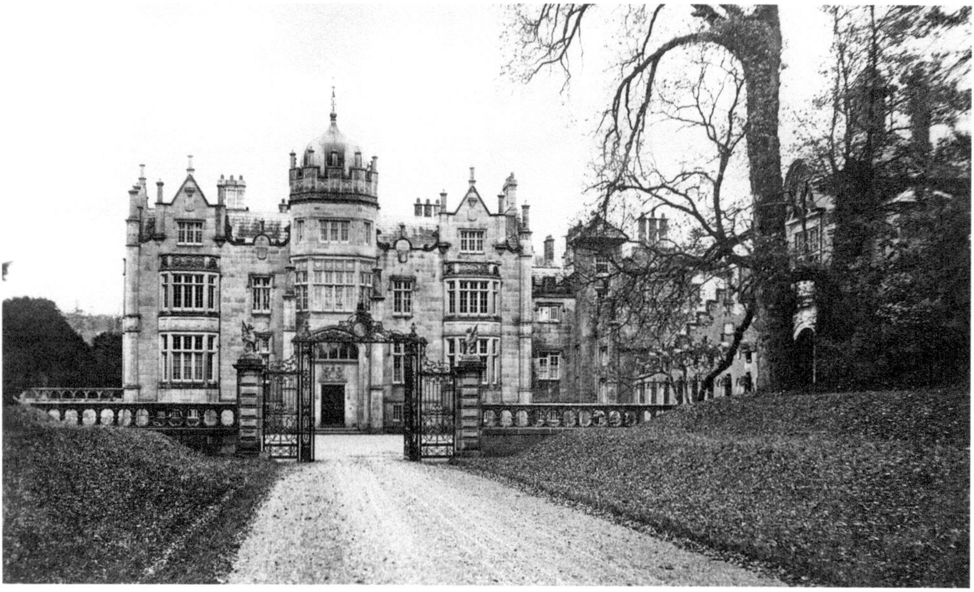

Kilruddery House, Bray. The house is an Elizabethan-Revival mansion, which has been home to the Brabazon family, the Earls of Meath, since 1618. It was rebuilt in the 1820s to the design of Sir Richard Morrison and is regarded as the best example of this type of architecture in Ireland. It has superb gardens dating back to the seventeenth century. Many eminent guests have stayed there, including King George IV in 1821 and William Gladstone in 1877.

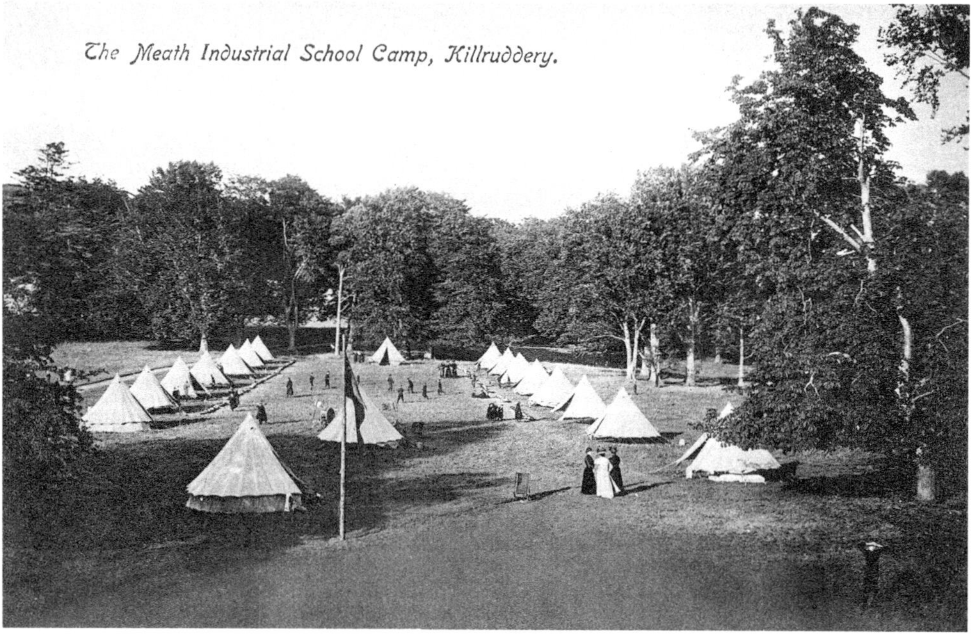

The Boys' Summer Camp for the Meath Industrial School, held on the Kilruddery Estate in 1910. The boys were kept very active and the photo, taken by Killick of Bray, shows them exercising in the middle of the field.

6

ENNISKERRY, POWERSCOURT & GLENCREE

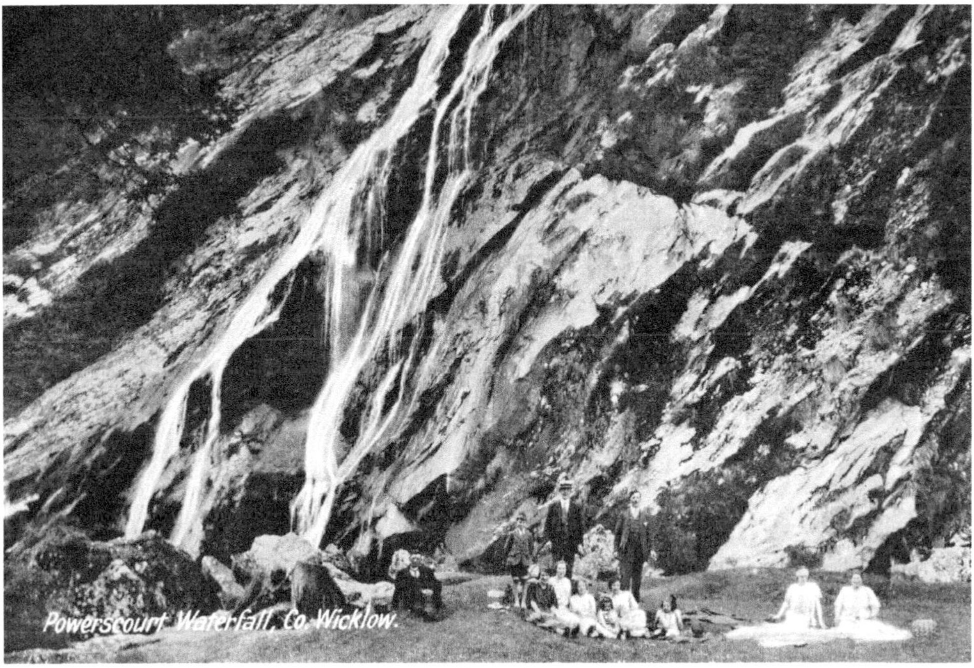

Tourists at the Powerscourt Waterfall, *c.* 1900. Certainly a spectacular attraction and a great place for a family picnic, this is Ireland's highest waterfall at 121 metres.

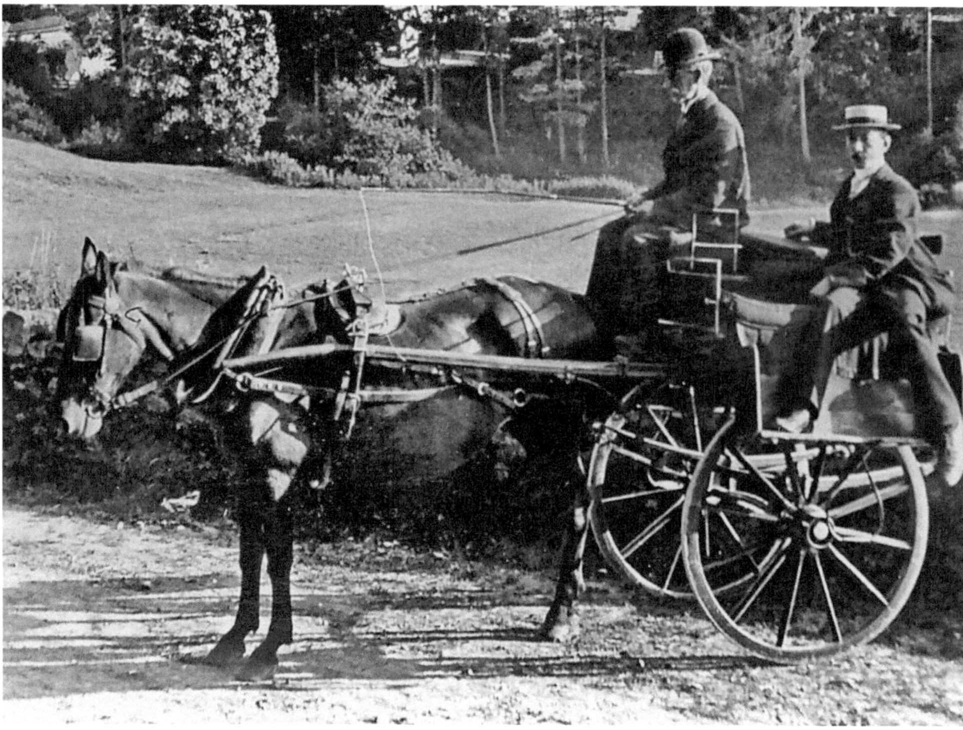

An 'outside car' with jarvey on the road to the pretty estate village of Enniskerry in 1895. The two-wheeled cart was pulled by a single horse. The tourist sits with his feet resting on the footboards outside the wheels. He has a fine view from that side of the car of the wild Wicklow scenery. Good weather was needed as there was no protection from wind or rain.

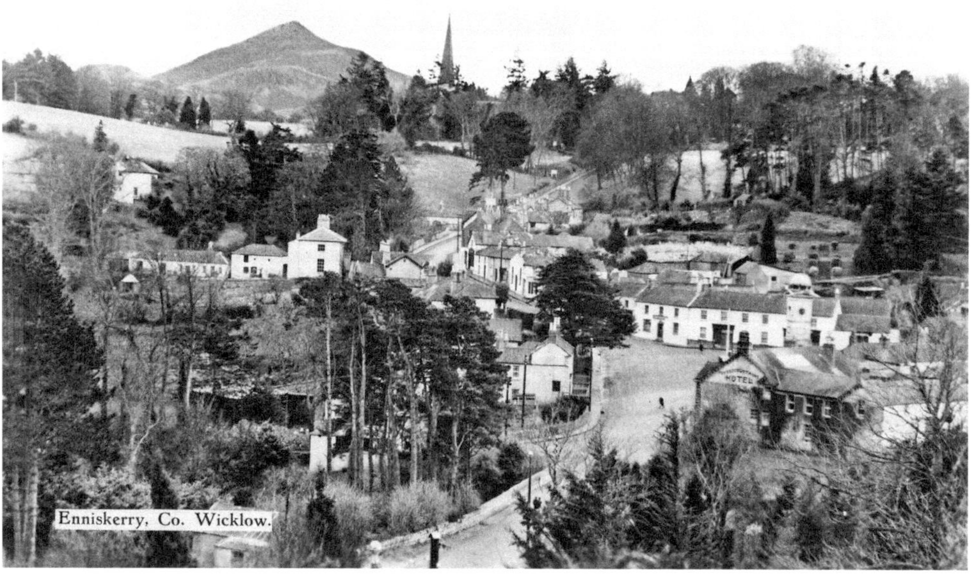

View of Enniskerry Village and church with the Sugarloaf in the distance.

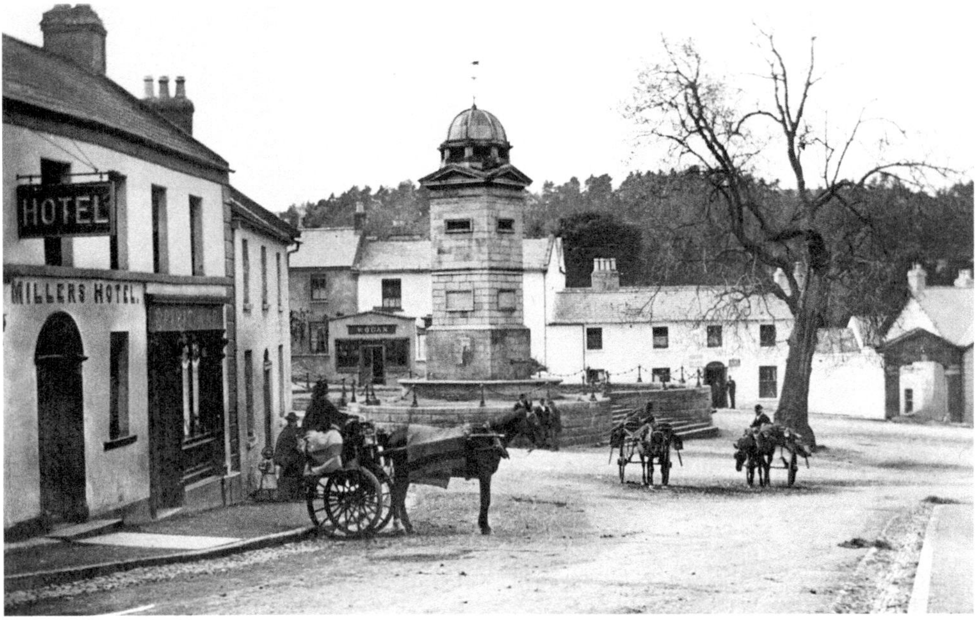

A peaceful scene in Enniskerry Village showing Miller's Hotel on the left, the Town Clock in the centre with the large tree at its base and the Powerscourt Arms Hotel on the distant right.

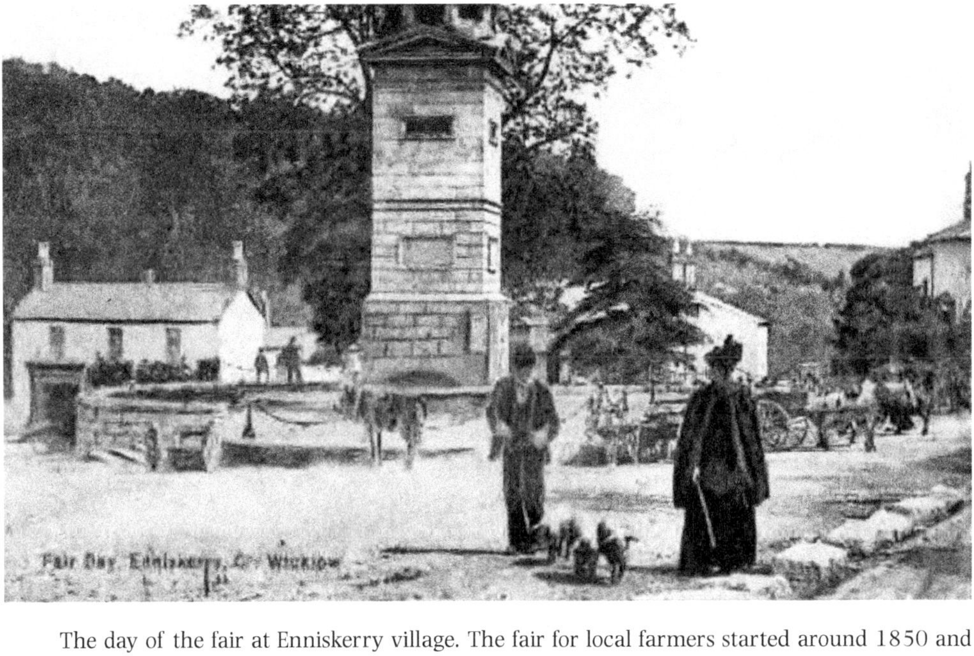

The day of the fair at Enniskerry village. The fair for local farmers started around 1850 and was held every two months. In the centre of the village is the renaissance-style, granite Clock Tower designed by John Louch, which was presented to Enniskerry on St Patrick's Day in 1843 to commemorate the centenary of the creation of the first Viscount of Powerscourt in 1743. The monument has a shamrock shaped base. The cupola was added in 1860.

An early view of the village blacksmith working at the Forge at Enniskerry, *c.* 1890. Smoke billows from the chimney and a carthorse is being shod while the owner waits. The stone smithy building with its horseshoe-shaped doorway was built by the Wingfield family around 1855. In Wicklow, the blacksmith had a traditional role in the community; he would not only shoe horses but would also repair agricultural tools and make metal gates.

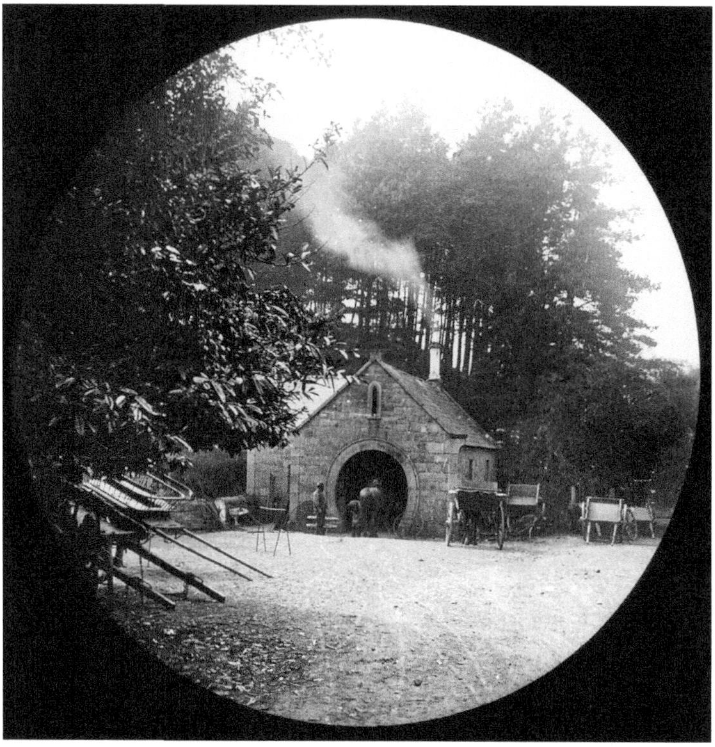

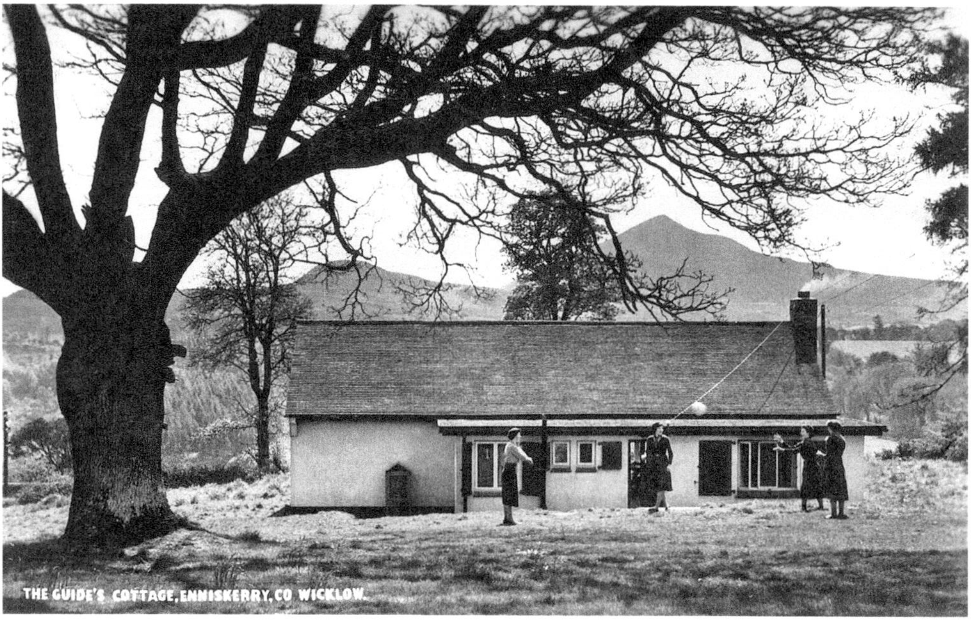

The Guides' Cottage at Enniskerry was opened on 1 July 1950. It was built in memory of Lord Baden-Powell. It was the first Guides hostel in Ireland and it was a very popular resource for the Girl Guides Association. The hostel was used to provide training in outdoor skills for leaders. Here, guides are shown drilling outside the Guides' Cottage.

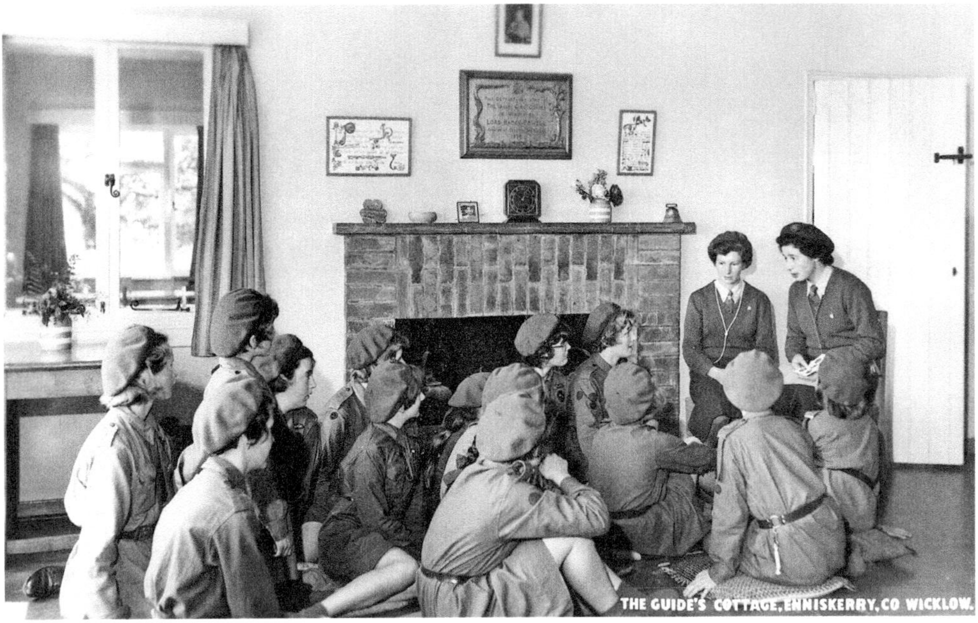

Interior view of the Guides' Cottage, Enniskerry. The Guides gather around the fireplace for instruction. When first opened, the cottage had no electricity and the guides had to use oil lamps and torches for lighting and an oil stove for cooking. Today the cottage is comfortable and does have electricity and central heating!

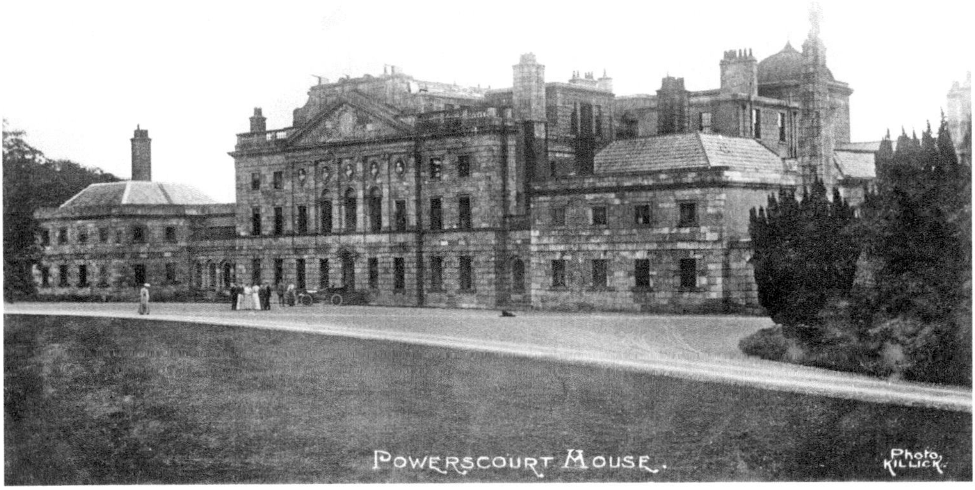

Visitors gather outside Powerscourt House, *c*. 1920s. The magnificent Palladian house and gardens were laid out, in the 6,000 hectare estate, by successive Viscount Powerscourts since 1618.

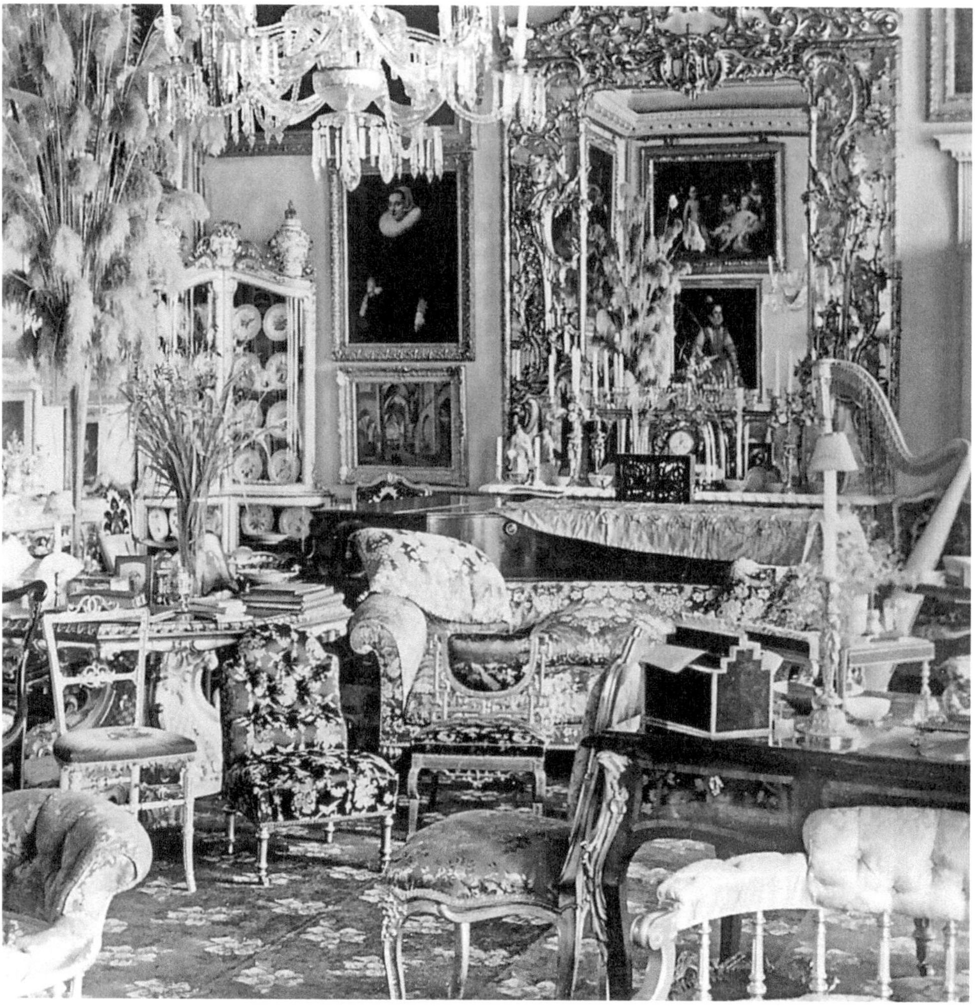

The beautiful saloon on the ground floor at Powerscourt House, showing elaborate furnishings fit for a royal palace. There is a superb mirror, a large crystal chandelier, old paintings by famous artists, a collection of porcelain and a fine Irish harp. Unfortunately, the room is now lost, as Powerscourt House was totally gutted by fire in 1974. The house has since been partially restored, including the historic ballroom, and now attracts many visitors who enjoy viewing the house and exploring the audio-visual exhibition describing the history of Powerscourt. They can also see the best of Irish products in fine design outlets and tour the magnificent estate gardens.

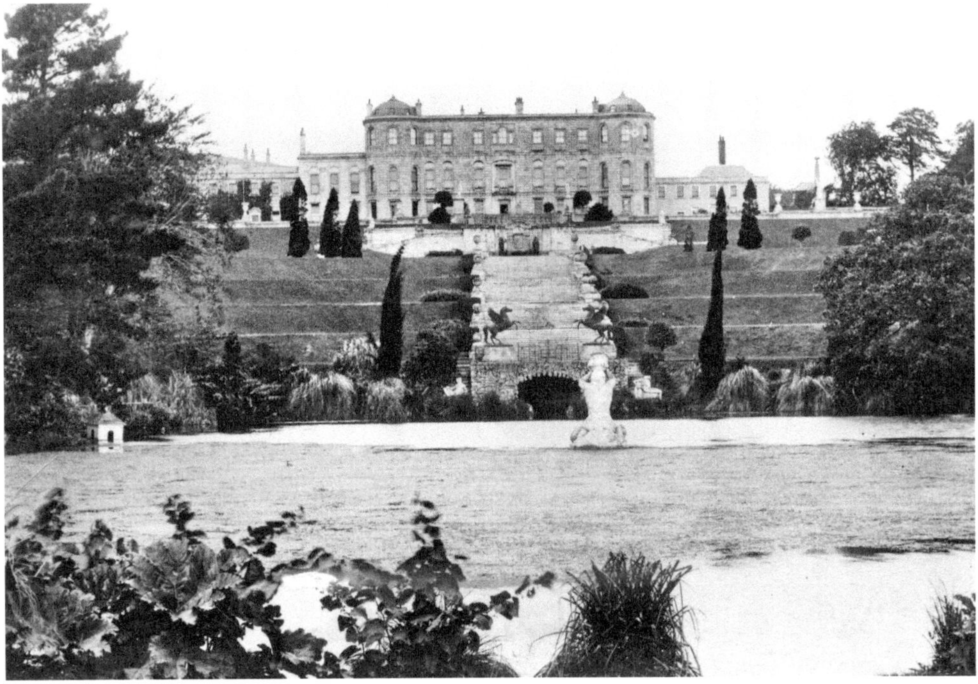

The south front of Powerscourt House, showing the terraces designed by Daniel Robertson and built between 1843 and 1867. There is fine statuary with two life-sized winged zinc horses, sculpted by Professor Hayes in Berlin in 1869, guarding the lake. The Triton in the middle of the lake is a copy of the well-known fountain in the Piazza Barberini in Rome.

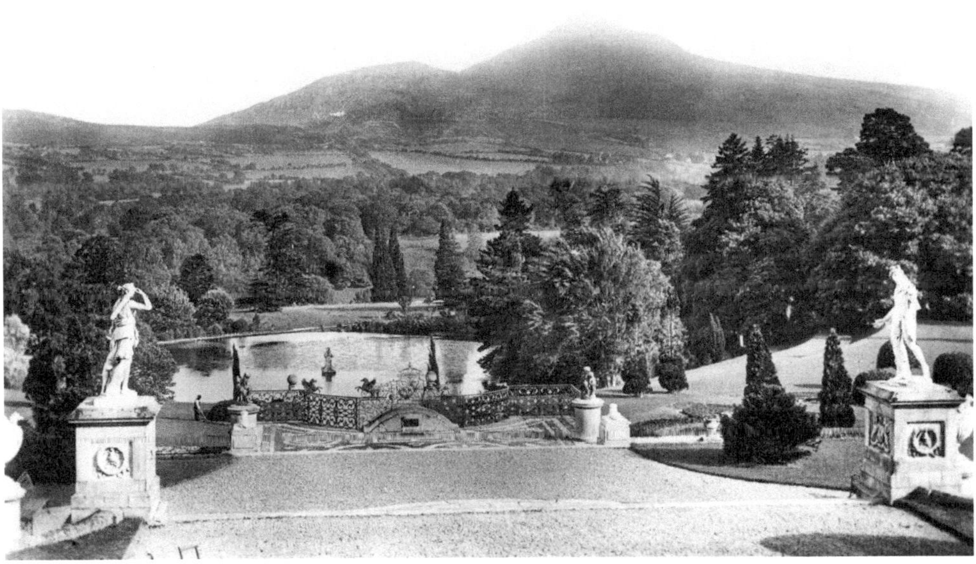

The gardens and Sugarloaf mountain from the Upper Terrace at Powerscourt House. There is a natural harmony between the terraces, statues, flowerbeds, the lake and surrounding bushes and trees.

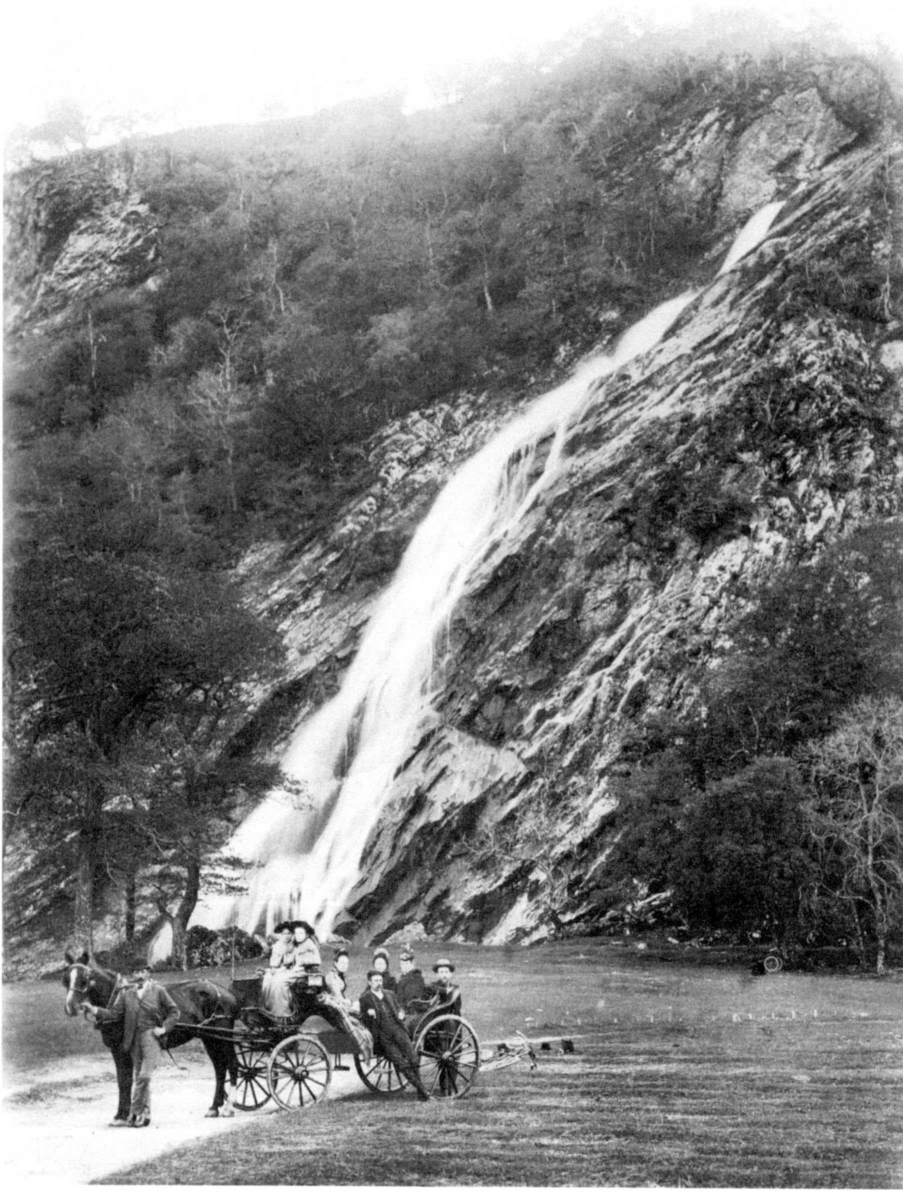

A carriage with tourists pictured at Powerscourt Waterfall, *c.* 1900. The stunning cascade of water into the Dargle Valley is set in magnificent wooded surroundings and visitors could not fail to be impressed. The photographer had one of nature's finest backdrops.

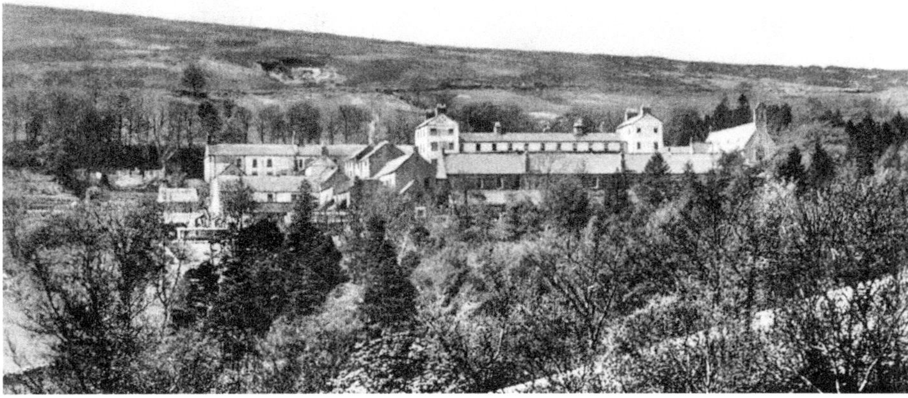

The Glencree military barracks, completed in 1806, was one of five barracks erected along the Military Road to keep local rebel insurgents under control. However, when the Napoleonic Wars ended, the military road and barracks were no longer needed. The Oblates of Mary Immaculate (OMI) established St Kevin's Reformatory School, in the abandoned barracks at Glencree in 1858. There was a strict programme of hard work and exercise for the boys, who worked on the land and grew much of their own food. However, the reformatory was a better environment than the prisons from which many of the young men had come. The school also had a band and choir, which performed at local community events. The reformatory finally closed in 1940.

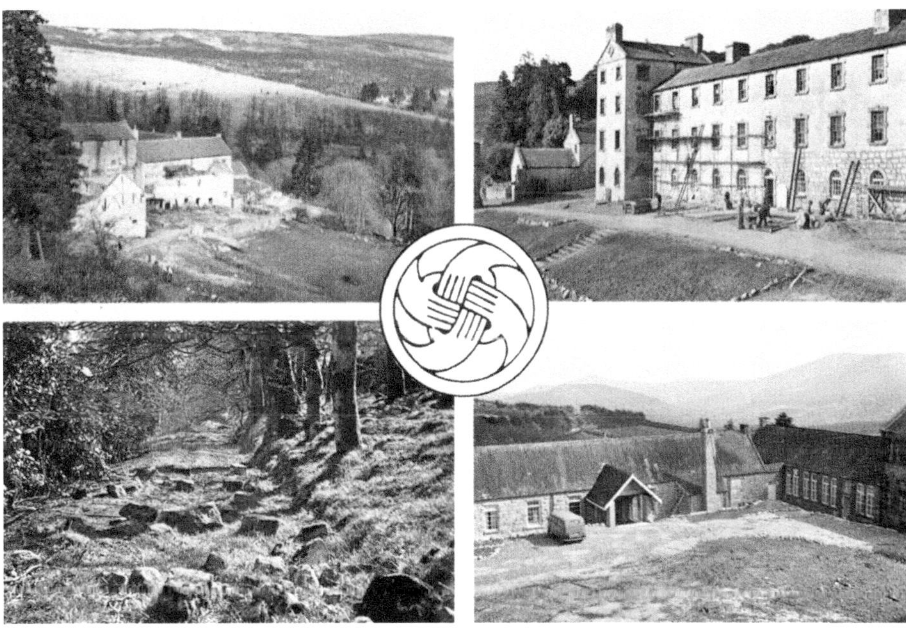

Multiview card showing renovations at the old barracks to found the Glencree Centre for Reconciliation, which opened in 1975 in an effort to improve relations between the Catholic and Protestant communities in Northern Ireland. The interdenominational centre hosts groups and gives training in conflict resolution and peace studies. Young people are involved in many of the projects and the politicians and activists, who come to study at Glencree, enjoy the peace and beauty of the surroundings.

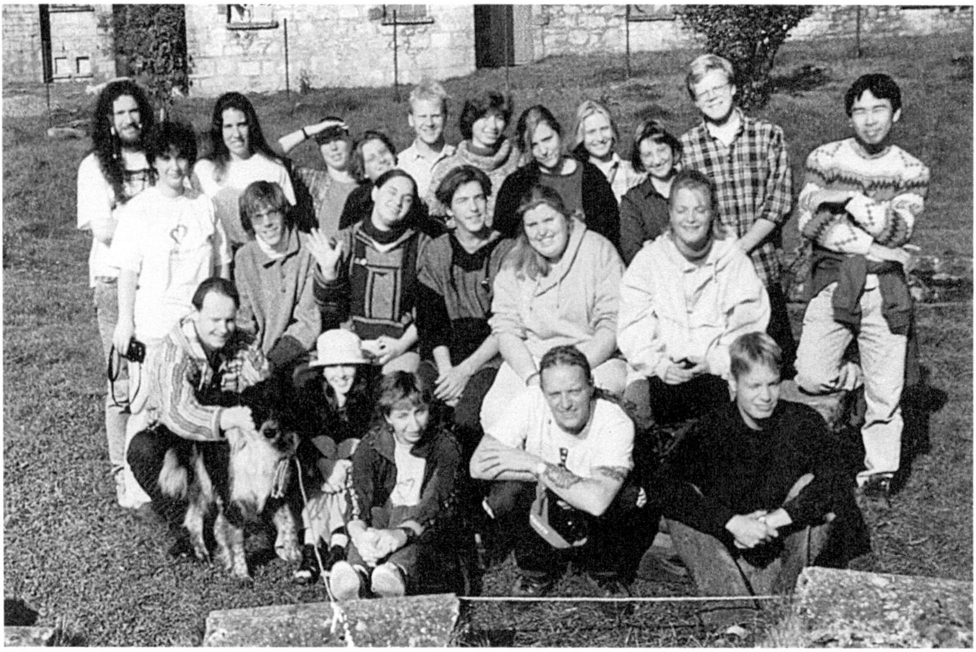

A happy group of young people and workers from different backgrounds enjoying the varied activities including work projects, 'peace training' and 'peace making' at the Glencree Centre in September 1996. The main aims of the centre are to promote understanding, justice and peace in society.

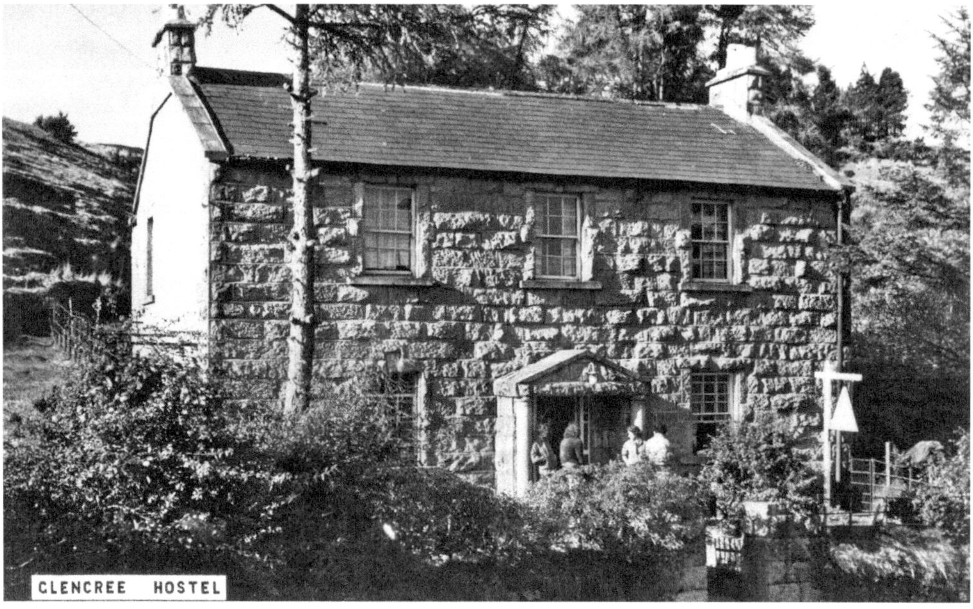

Glencree Youth Hostel, near to the centre, was popular with walkers and climbers and was operated by An Óige from 1950. It was a great place for a holiday close to nature. The building was sold in May 2006.

7

BLESSINGTON, POULAPHOUCA, DUNLAVIN, GLENALMURE & GLEN OF IMAAL

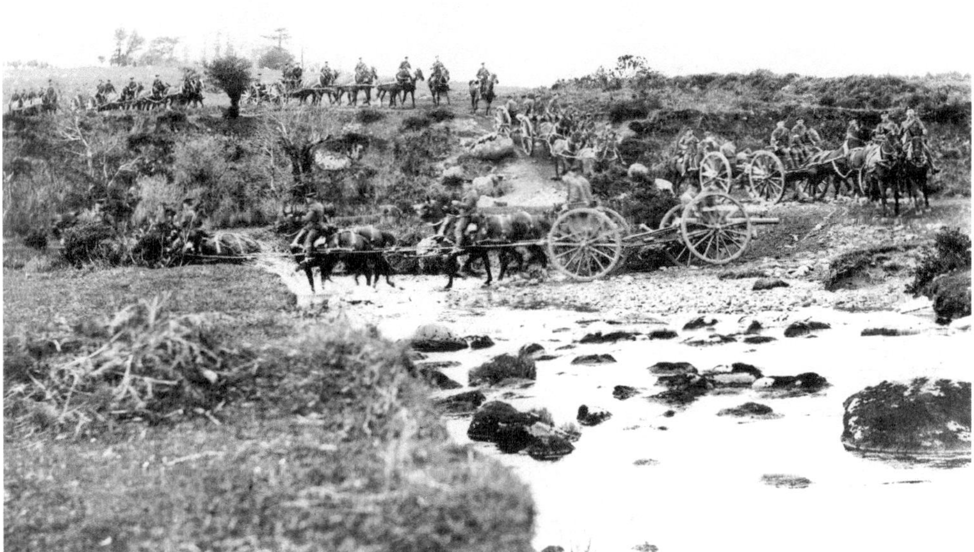

The 137th Battery of the Royal Field Artillery on manoeuvres in the Glen of Imaal in May 1904. The photograph shows troops advancing to action with the horses pulling the guns over water and very rough ground. The area was ideal as a training area and also as an artillery firing range. It is still used by the Irish Army today.

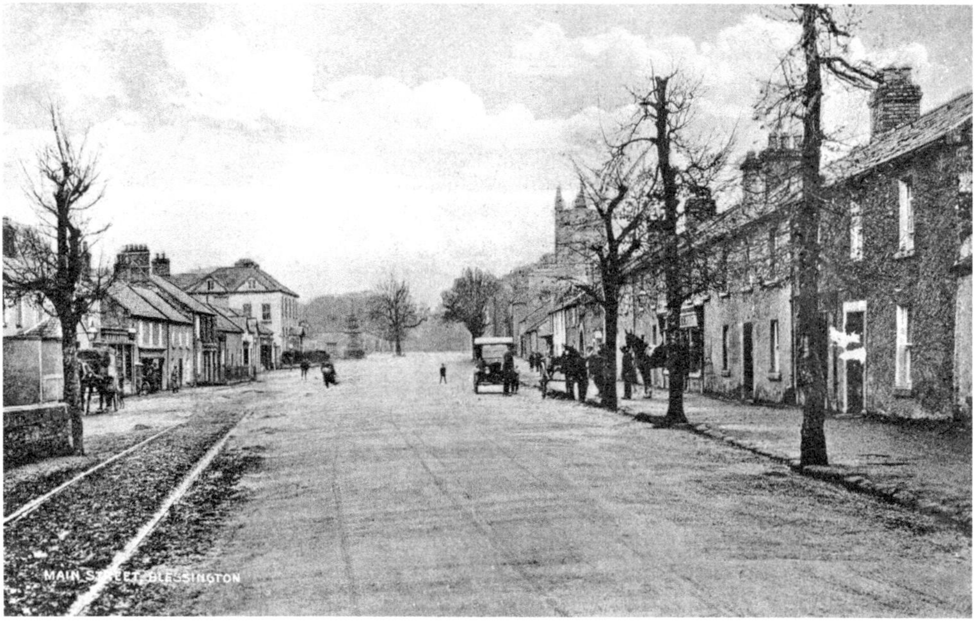

The town of Blessington, showing the south end of the wide tree-lined Main Street from the south-west. The Protestant church is on the right and its tower houses the original church bells, made in 1862. The tower clock is said to be the oldest working turret clock in Ireland.

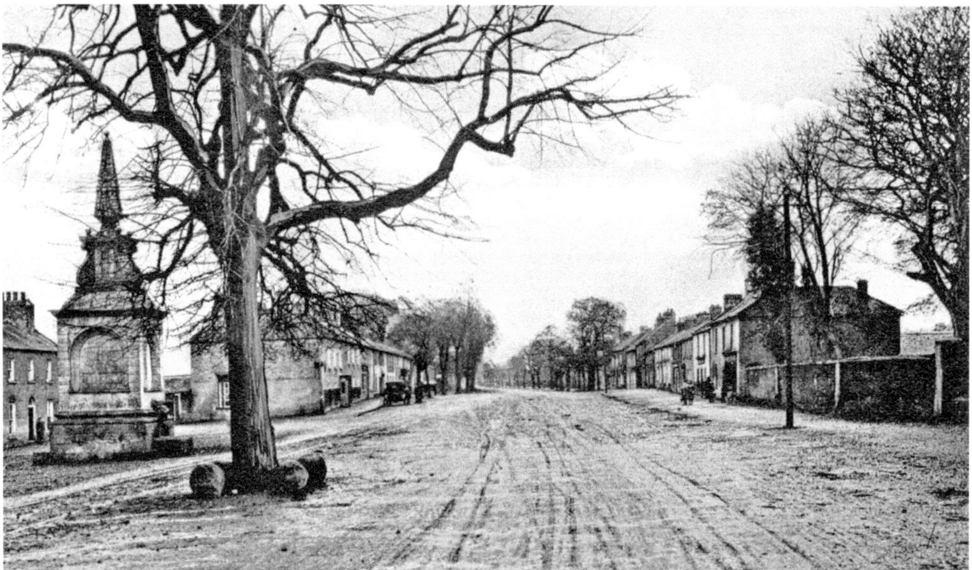

The north end of the Main Street in Blessington. The lime tree surrounded by four granite stones (Four-Stone Tree) stands on the left of centre. The Downshire monument, which commemorates the coming of age of Arthur Hill in 1865, is on the far left. On the death of his father in 1868, Arthur inherited the family estates and became the fifth Marquis of Downshire. However, he died six years later, aged only 29 years.

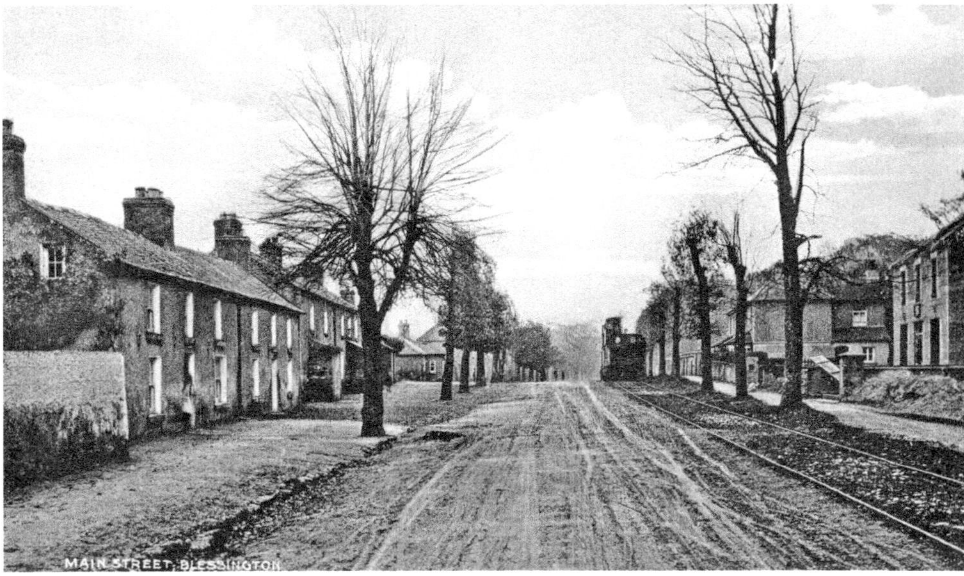

The extreme north end of the town, looking towards Tallaght. The steam tram can be seen in the middle distance.

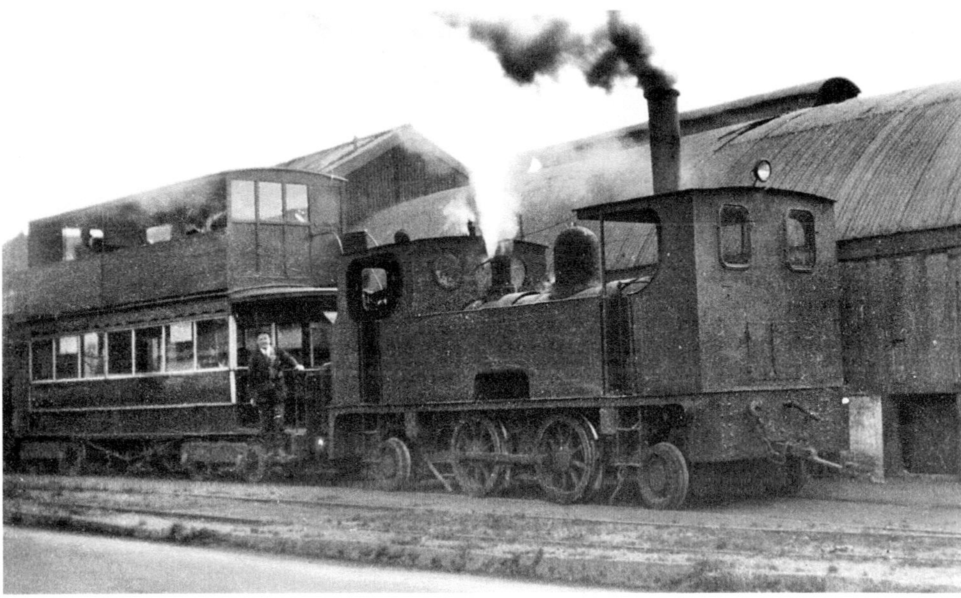

The Dublin and Blessington steam tramway service began in 1888. It ran from Terenure through Tallaght to Blessington and was later extended to Poulaphouca. Its safety record was not great and many pedestrians met a sad end when they were hit by the trams. Crosses were erected at the sites of fatal accidents and the line became known as 'the longest graveyard in the world'. The last town before Blessington was Templeogue and if there were any fatal accidents near there, the dead were taken to the Templeogue Inn for arrangements to be made. This led to the pub being nicknamed 'The Morgue'. The tramway service ended in 1932, when it was no longer commercially viable and it was replaced by a bus service.

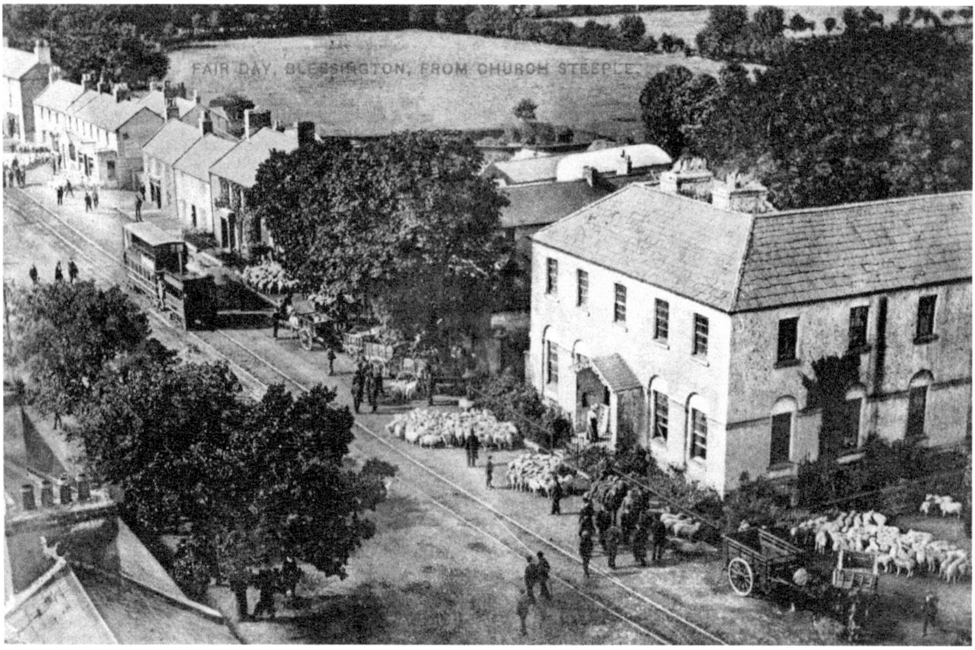

The fair day at Blessington, seen from the church steeple. The steam tram is on the left. The tram could be used to pull wagons transporting cattle and sheep on the day of the fair. The Main Street is very busy and farmers are shown driving herds of sheep to be sold at the fair.

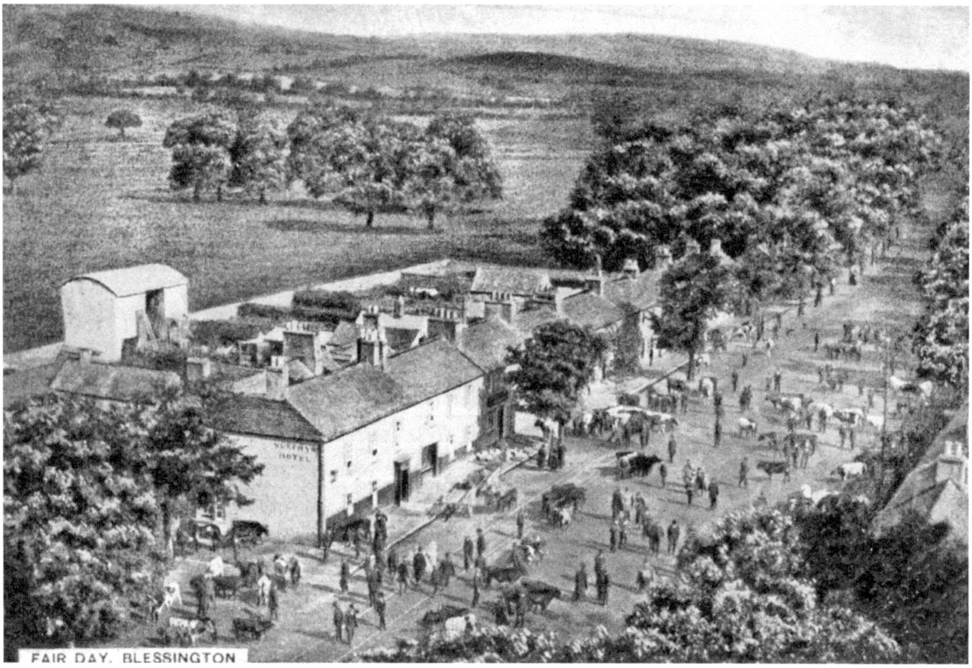

Another view of the fair day at Blessington, showing groups of cattle in the Main Street. On the left, farmers are bartering outside Murphy's Hotel.

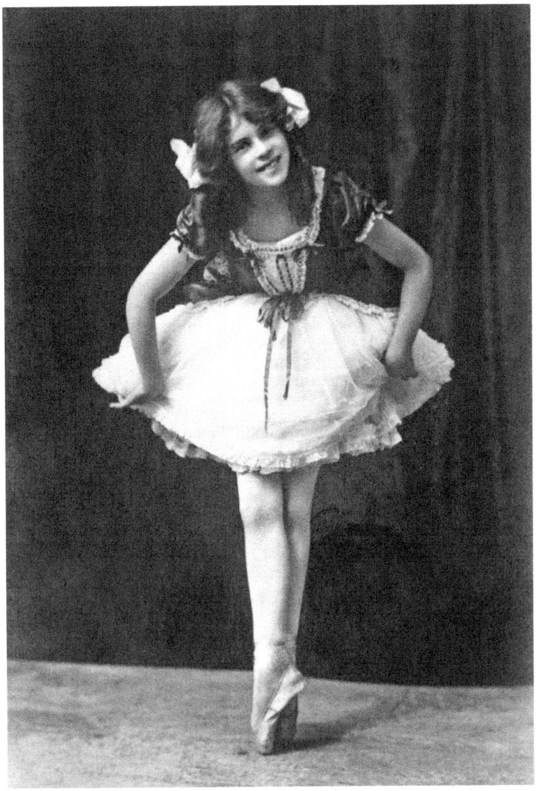

Ninette de Valois, founder of the Royal Ballet, as a young ballerina. She was born Edris Stannus of Anglo-Irish parents in Baltiboys on 6 June 1898. She began dancing at the age of 10 and was soon noted to have an exceptional talent. She moved to London before joining Serge Diaghilev's Ballet Russes Company in 1923 and working with them for three years. She then returned to London convinced that Britain should have its own National Ballet. She became the driving force for British Ballet. Her Sadler's Wells Company was very successful attracting the world's best dancers. In 1956, she achieved her ambition as her company was granted a charter as the Royal Ballet. She was a remarkable leader and she received many awards during her career for her services to ballet.

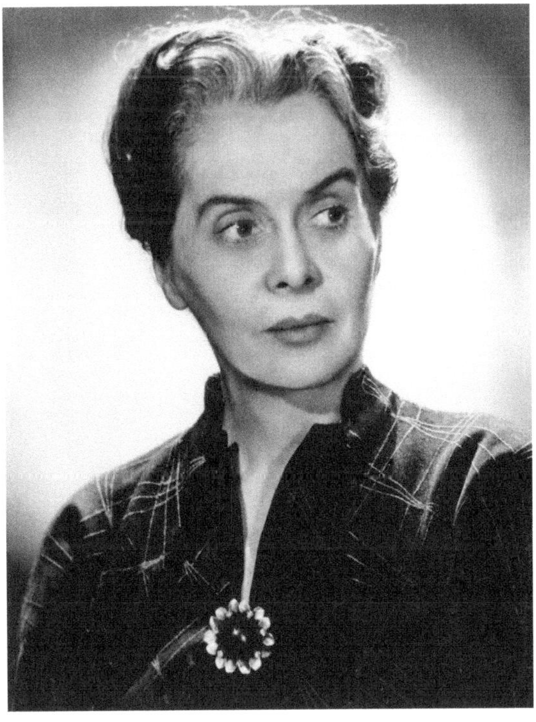

Dame Ninette de Valois in 1958. She gave up dancing herself in 1926 as she discovered she had been suffering for years from polio. However, she was an administrator and teacher of genius and she used her energy to promote ballet throughout Europe. To most people in the world of ballet, she was known simply as 'Madam'. She retired from the Royal Ballet in 1963 but continued to make public appearances until her death on 8 March 2001 at age 102. She had lived in three centuries (1898-2001).

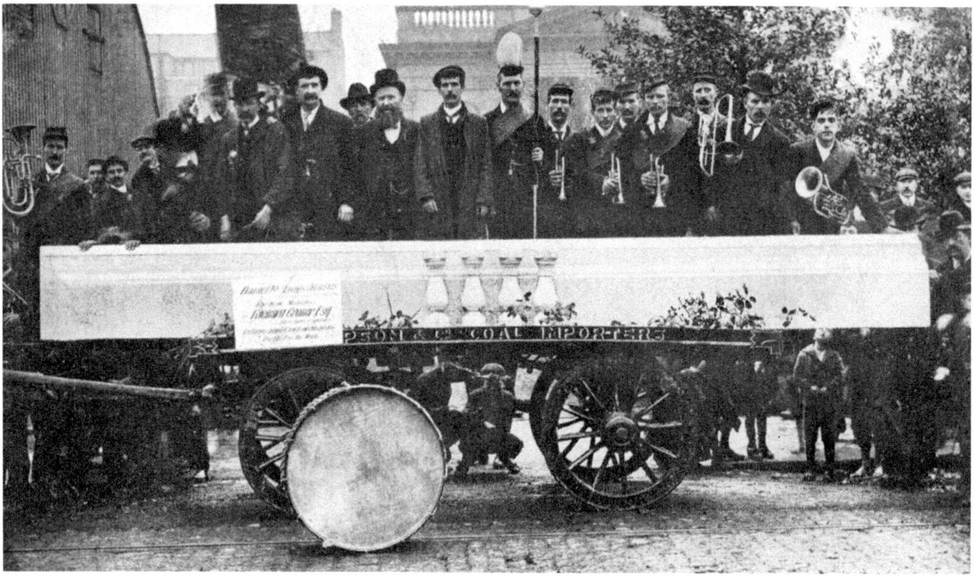

Overlooking Blessington Lake is the small village of Ballyknockan. The white-grey granite in the area is of very high quality and the village is known for quarrying and stonecutting. From the 1820s onward, many fine churches and monuments in Dublin used Ballyknockan granite. Stone from the quarries was used for the Wellington Monument in Phoenix Park. This card, posted on 22 March 1905, shows a giant granite stone 6 metres in length, from Daniel McEvoy's Quarries in Ballyknockan, being taken through the streets of Dublin in a great parade of Irish industries. The stone was to be used for construction at Glencairn in Stillorgan, South Dublin; this was the home of 'Boss' Richard Croker, the former leader of Tammany Hall, New York, who had returned to Ireland a wealthy man.

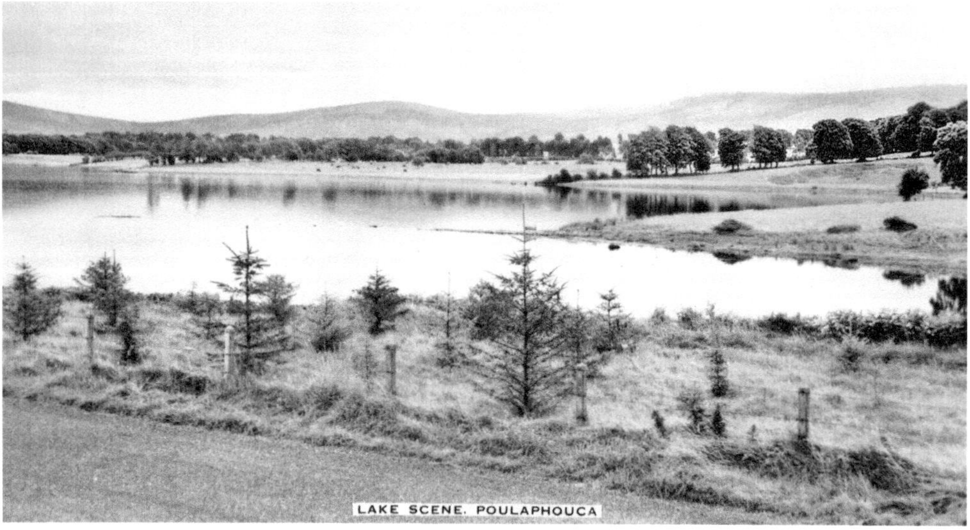

The tranquil lake scene at Poulaphouca, *c.* 1950. The Blessington Lakes were formed when the Liffey valley was flooded in 1940 to create the Poulaphouca reservoir. The Liffey and Kings rivers flow into the lakes and the water is held there by the Poulaphouca dam.

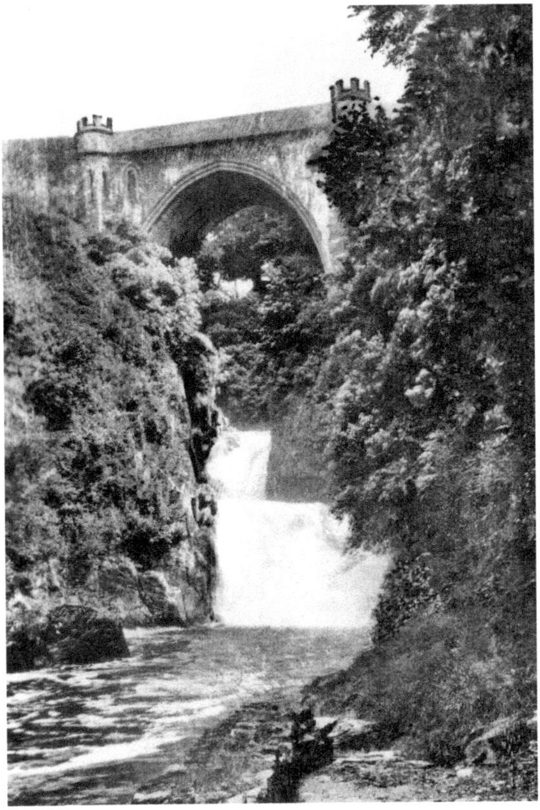

Poulaphouca Bridge across the river Liffey, designed by Alexander Nimmo in Gothic style, was built around 1825. The waterfall, about 47 metres in height, was once one of the best known in Ireland, but the construction of the hydroelectric dam much reduced the flow of water over the falls.

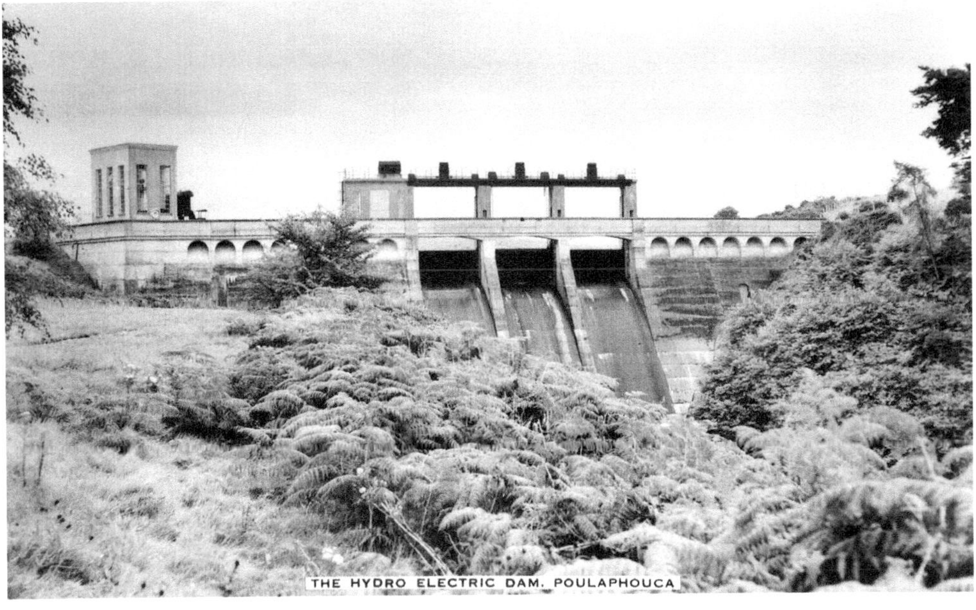

The hydroelectric dam at Poulaphouca, which holds back some 2,000 hectares of water in the reservoir to supply Dublin with fresh, clean water and also to create electricity.

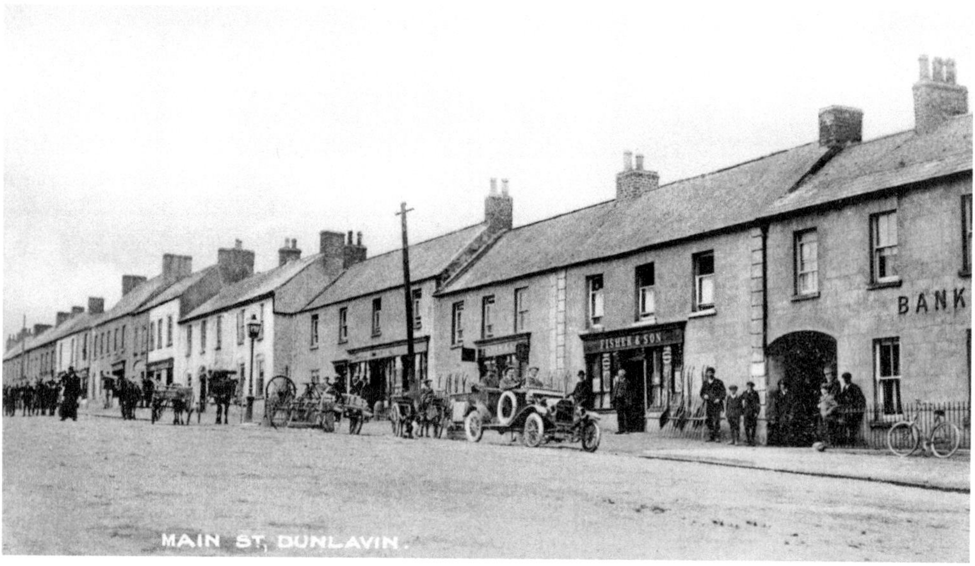

A busy scene in the Main Street, Dunlavin, shown on a card posted on 10 April 1921. The market town had a good range of shops selling groceries, bread, tobacco and hardware. It also had public houses, a post office and an RIC police station. People from Kildare and West Wicklow came to trade at Dunlavin. The picture shows a vintage car parked outside Fisher & Son on the right, which is next to the Bank of Ireland.

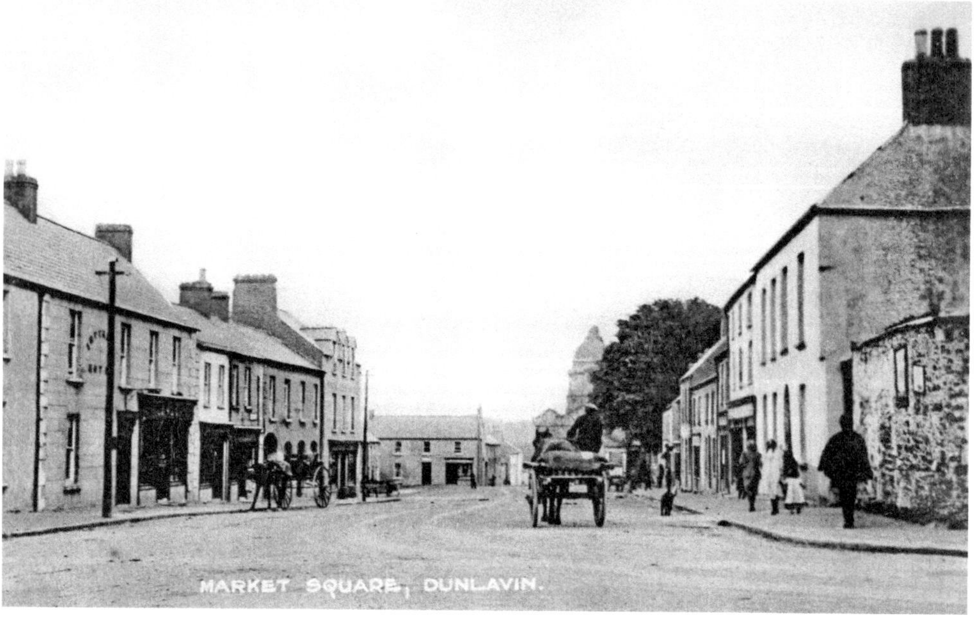

The Market Square, Dunlavin, *c.* 1920. The village was expanded from a small hamlet by Sir Richard Bulkeley at the end of the seventeenth century and soon developed and flourished as a market centre during the eighteenth century. Sir Richard's estate was taken over by the Tynte family, who commissioned the Market House in 1737.

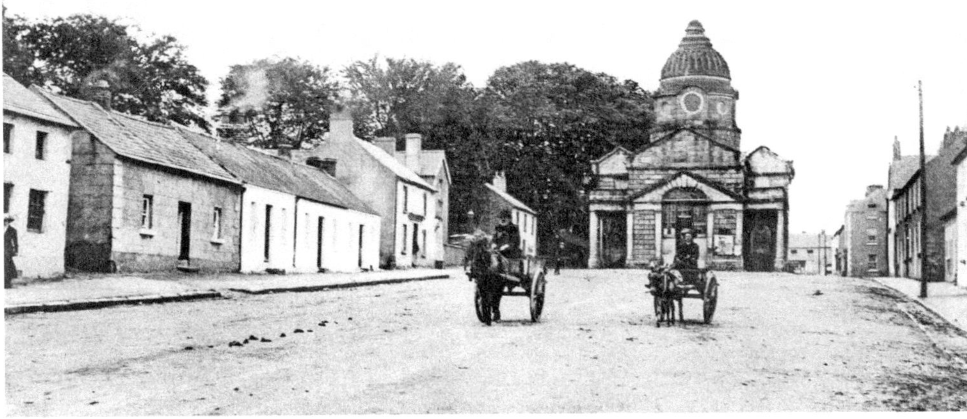

Kilcullen Street, Dunlavin, on a card dated 5 May 1921. The Dunlavin Market House or Courthouse, with its classical architecture and fine dome, was built in 1737 by Robert Tynte from Richard Castle's designs. It was from this building, on 24 May 1798, that thirty-six prisoners were led out to be executed by firing squad on the local green at Dunlavin. This was meant to act as a deterrent to other rebels, but instead the massacre prompted the 1798 Wexford Rising and left a legacy of hatred in the community and continued insurgency in the area for many years.

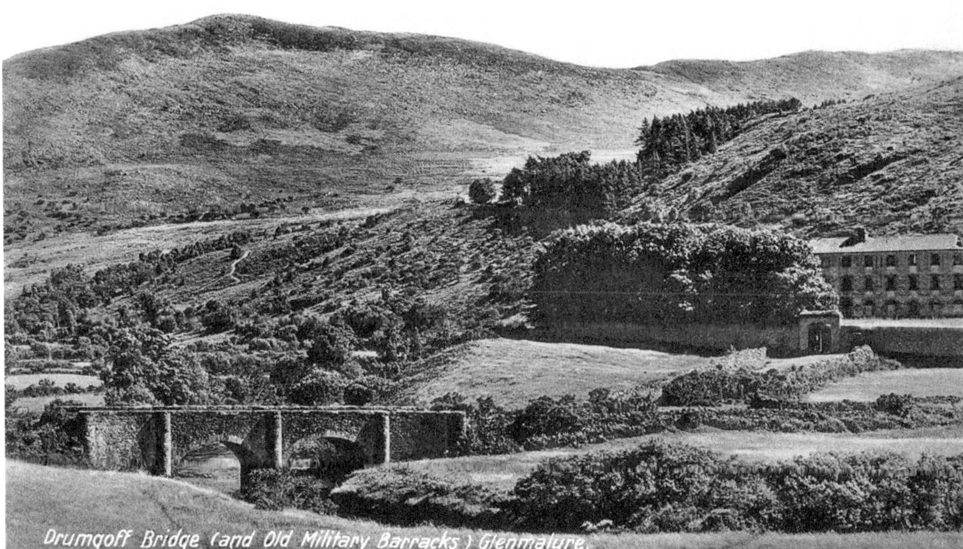

Drumgoff Bridge (and Old Military Barracks), Glenalmure, on a card posted on 2 July 1933. The barracks, which were the second on the military road, are at the entrance to Glenalmure. They were attacked and burned down by Michael Dwyer and his men (see page 126), but were later rebuilt and re-garrisoned.

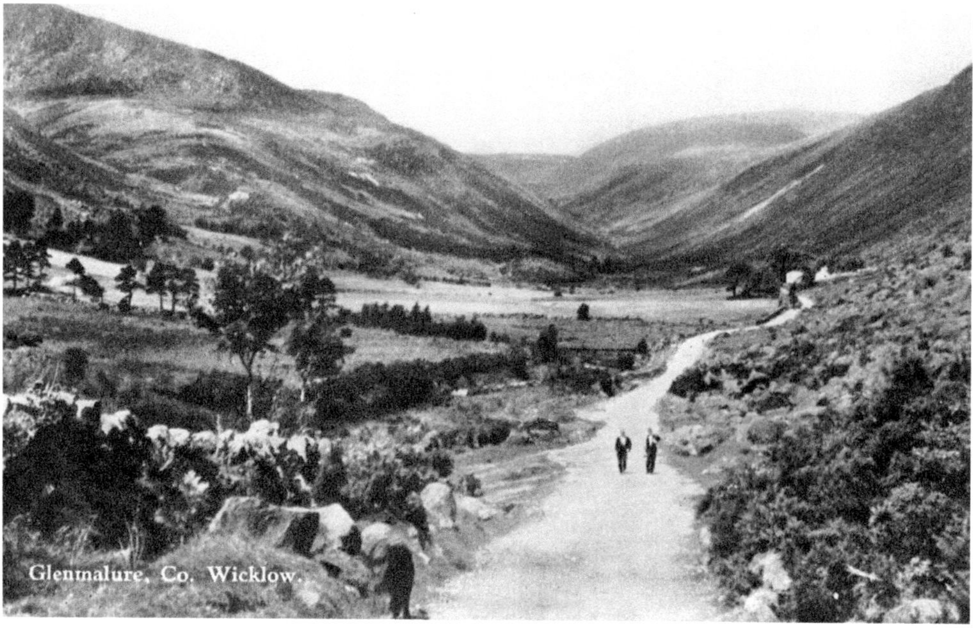

Glenalmure, the 'wild glen', is the longest glacier valley in the UK and Ireland. It was the site of a famous victory by Fiach MacHugh O'Byrne and his men over the English in August 1580. O'Byrne out-manoeuvred the English troops, who found themselves stranded in the valley, where they were routed with the loss of around 1,000 men.

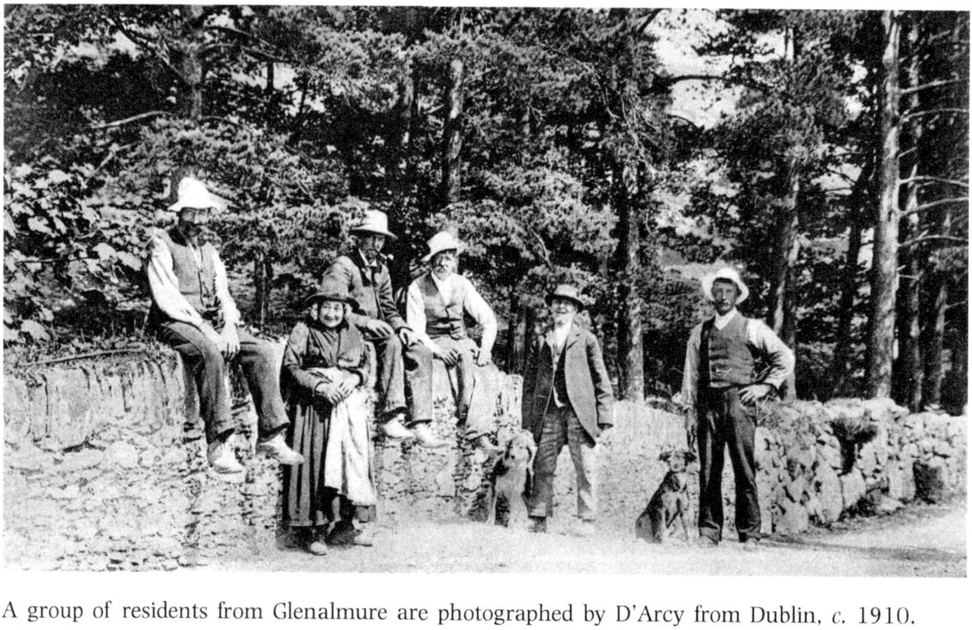

A group of residents from Glenalmure are photographed by D'Arcy from Dublin, *c.* 1910. There were many small farmers with sheep and cattle working in the Glen. However, in the early nineteenth century, there was also a lead mine near Drumgoff, which provided much-needed employment in the area. Workers at the mines stayed at the old Drumgoff Barracks (see page 123).

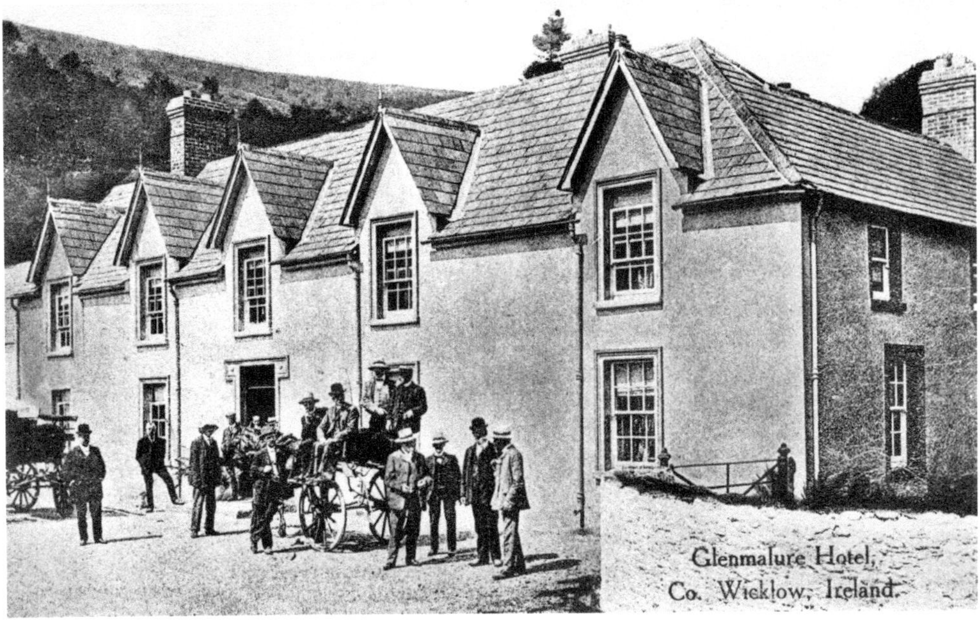

Glenalmure Hotel was originally built as a hunting lodge in 1801 and was known as 'Wiseman's Inn'. It is a popular destination for tourists and walkers. The card shows a group of visitors gathered outside the hotel.

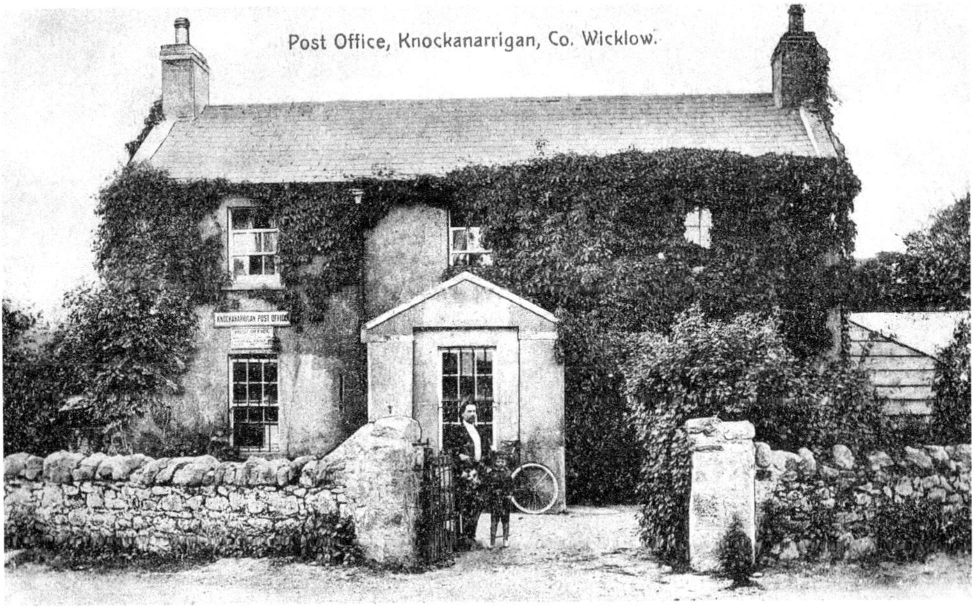

A father and son stand at the gates of the General Store and Post Office at Knockanarrigan. This was a fine building with ivy-covered granite walls and bars on the downstairs windows. It was in the middle of the Glen of Imaal and was the only post office for miles around. The postcard is from a soldier at Coolmoney Camp, Knockanarrigan, to his girlfriend in Worthing, Sussex.

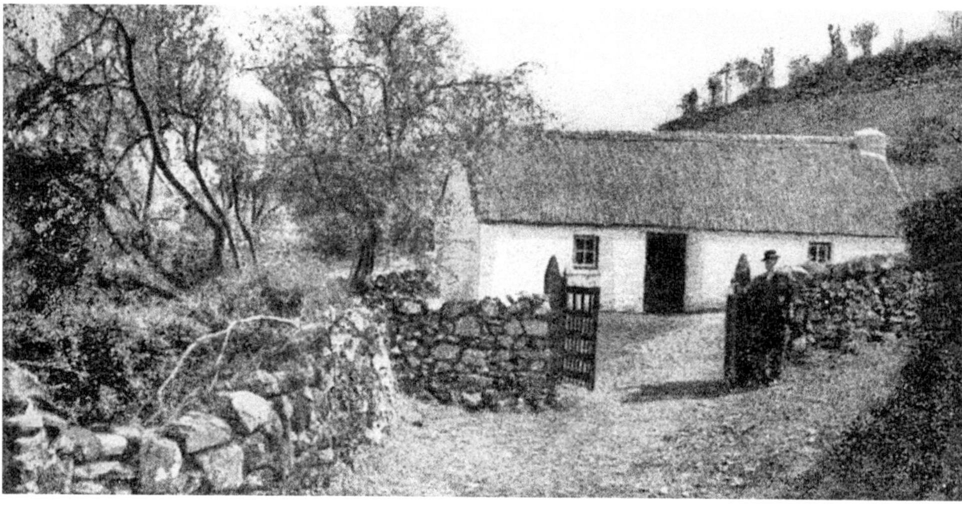

The Dwyer McAllister Memorial and 1798 Period Cottage in the Glen of Imaal. It is a traditional whitewashed thatched cottage built with local stone. Michael Dwyer was the leader of the Society of United Irishmen in the 1798 rebellion, who later fought a guerilla campaign against the British Army in the Wicklow Mountains. However, on 15 February 1799, after being betrayed by an informer, he was trapped with his group of rebels in three cottages in Dernamuck. The cottages were surrounded by over 100 troops and the rebels had little chance. The last cottage to fall was on the memorial site. Sam McAllister, who was wounded, drew the fire and was killed while Dwyer managed to escape over the mountains and spent the next three years on the run.

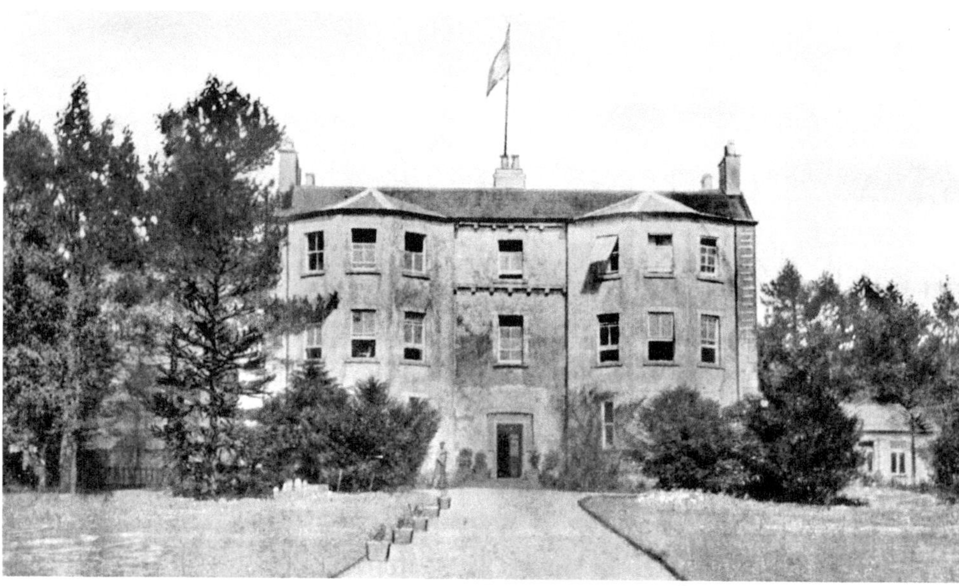

View of the Artillery Barracks, Glen Imaal, on a postcard dated 8 January 1907. The barracks were built in 1803 to guard the mountain road from Glen Imaal to Glendalough and also served to restrict the movements of Michael Dwyer and his group of rebels. At that time, the barracks could provide accommodation for up to 200 men.

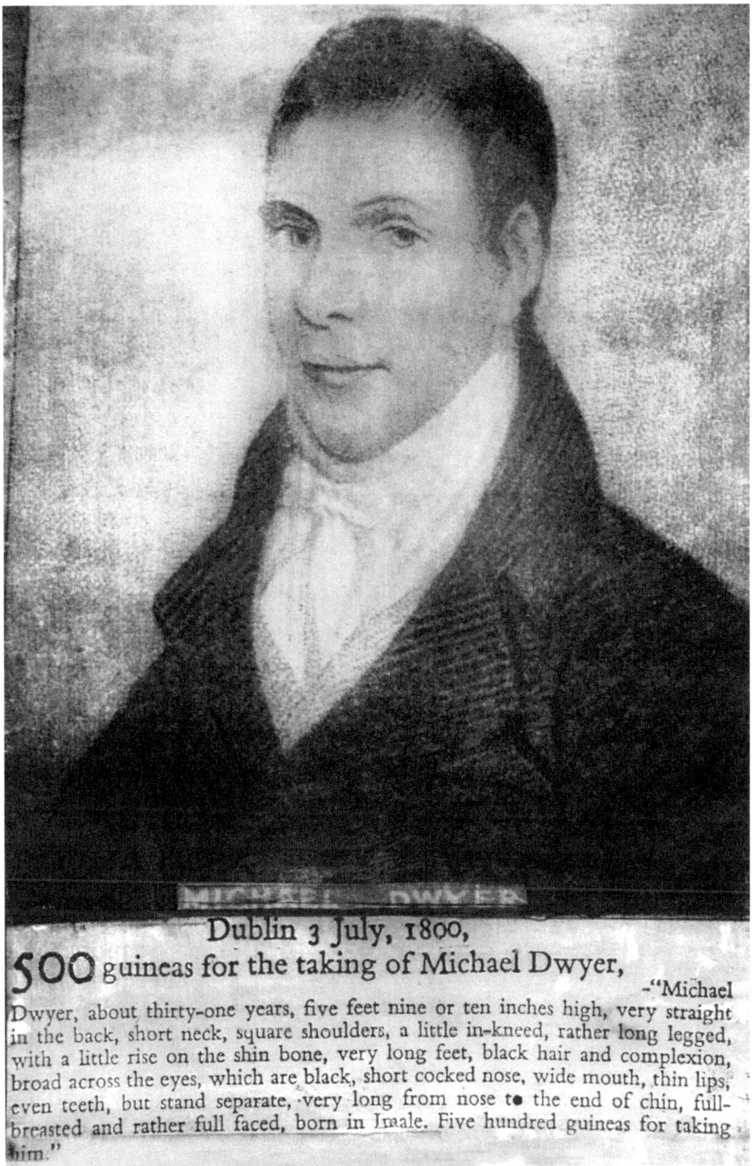

Dublin 3 July, 1800,

500 guineas for the taking of Michael Dwyer,

-"Michael Dwyer, about thirty-one years, five feet nine or ten inches high, very straight in the back, short neck, square shoulders, a little in-kneed, rather long legged, with a little rise on the shin bone, very long feet, black hair and complexion, broad across the eyes, which are black, short cocked nose, wide mouth, thin lips, even teeth, but stand separate, very long from nose to the end of chin, full-breasted and rather full faced, born in Imale. Five hundred guineas for taking him."

A 'wanted' poster for Michael Dwyer, 'The Wicklow Chief'. He was a thorn in the side of the British Army, who desperately wanted to capture him. They threatened severe punishments for those who gave him shelter and offered huge rewards for information leading to his arrest. Thousands of troops were sent to Wicklow and a series of barracks were built at Imaal, Glencree, Laragh, Glenalmure and Aughavannagh, linked by a military road. However, it was not until December 1803 that Dwyer agreed to surrender when he was promised passage with his family to America. Unfortunately the government did not keep to the agreement and he was held in Kilmainham Gaol until August 1805, at which time he was transported with his wife and two children to New South Wales. He died in 1825.